I Wake Up Screening!

And then I wrote . . .

Plays
    Broadway

The Subject Was Roses
That Summer—That Fall
The Only Game in Town
Last Licks

    Off-Broadway

Who'll Save the Plowboy?

    One-acts at the
       Ensemble Studio
       Marathon

Present Tense
The Next Contestant
Dreams of Glory
Real to Reel
Match Point
A Way with Words
Give the Bishop My Faint Regards

Novels

Private
From Noon till Three

Children's Book

Little Ego (written with Ruth Gilroy)

Television Scripts
    "Golden Age"

Omnibus, Playhouse Ninety, Studio One,
U.S. Steel, Kraft Playhouse, etc.

    "Not So Golden"

"Have Gun—Will Travel," "Wanted Dead
or Alive," "The Rifleman," "Burke's Law"
(which I created), etc.

Television Scripts
Written and Directed

"The Turning Point of James Malloy"
    (from the John O'Hara Gibbsville stories)
"The Doorbell Rang" (from the Nero
    Wolfe novel by Rex Stout)

Screenplays

The Fastest Gun Alive (with Russell
    Rouse), starring Glen Ford
The Gallant Hours (with Beirne Lay, Jr.),
    starring James Cagney
The Subject Was Roses, starring Patricia
    Neal, Jack Albertson, and Martin Sheen
The Only Game in Town, starring
    Elizabeth Taylor and Warren Beatty

Screenplay and Direction

Desperate Characters (from the novel by
    Paula Fox), starring Shirley MacLaine
From Noon till Three, starring Charles
    Bronson and Jill Ireland
Once in Paris, starring Wayne Rogers and
    Gayle Hunnicutt
The Gig, starring Wayne Rogers and
    Cleavon Little
The Luckiest Man in the World, starring
    Philip Bosco

I Wake Up ———
——— Screening!

Everything You Need to Know
About Making Independent Films
Including a Thousand Reasons Not To

Frank D. Gilroy

SOUTHERN ILLINOIS UNIVERSITY PRESS
Carbondale and Edwardsville

Library of Congress Cataloging-in-Publication Data

Gilroy, Frank Daniel, 1925–
    I wake up screening! : everything you need to know about making indepen-
dent films including a thousand reasons not to/Frank D. Gilroy.
        p.   cm.
    Includes filmography and index.
    1. Motion pictures—Production and direction.   2. Gilroy, Frank Daniel,
1925– —Diaries.   3. Motion picture producers and directors—United States—
Diaries.   I. Title.
PN1995.9.P7G445   1993
791.43'0232—dc20
ISBN 0-8093-1856-3   92-12038
ISBN 0-8093-1918-7 (pbk.)   CIP

The paper used in this publication meets the minimum requirements of American
National Standard for Information Sciences—Permanence of Paper for Printed Library Materials, ANSI Z39.48-1984. ⊚

For the McLaughlins (*Jim*, *Jean*, and *J. C.*),
who put their money where my mouth was
so frequently and so generously

Contents

—— *Illustrations*

The Gig, following page 242

The boys in the band.

Paradise Manor (Sacks Lodge).

Wayne Rogers. Would you buy a used car from this man?

Warren Vaché, Daniel Nalbach, Jerry Matz, Andrew Duncan, and Cleavon Little.

Warren Vaché entertaining between takes.

Nick Romanac, Herb Forsberg, Jeri Sopanen, and Herr Direktor.

Most of the cast.

The Luckiest Man in the World, following page 334

Philip Bosco and Yamil Borges, looking for the poster shot.

Still looking. . . .

And _still_ looking. . . .

Mrs. Posner (Doris Bellack) and Mr. Posner (Philip Bosco).

Producer Norman Cohen's expression suggests we're on schedule.

Posner (Philip Bosco) rehearsing his proposal to Laura (Joanne Camp), his mistress of many years.

The Posners (Philip Bosco and Doris Bellack) the second time around.

No matter what they tell you, they hate us!
— John Cassavetes on the System

A load is first impossible
When we have put it down —
— Emily Dickinson

The average cost of films is some $25 million, and the cost
to market can be even more.
— *Wall Street Journal*

Nothing happens unless one man or woman pursues a
vision fanatically.
— Me

I Wake Up Screening!

—— *Prologue*

I've written, directed, raised the money for, and opened four independent films without a prearranged distribution deal, presale, or hedge of any kind.

The combined cost of these four pictures is $2 million.

In Leonard Maltin's *TV Movies and Video Guide,* each of the four pictures is accorded *three stars.* Twelve stars divided into $2 million comes to $166,666 per star, which must be a record of some sort.

At a recent luncheon, a young screenwriter confided, "What I really want to do is make independent films the way you do."

"Before you do that, have your wife call me," my wife counseled.

There is a spirit of fraternity among independent filmmakers, engendered by *us* against *them* (the system), that disposes one to share information.

Of late I find myself spending more and more time with new-comers contemplating the leap or stuck in the tunnel: "I'm sitting here with my picture, and no one wants to open it. What do I do?"

Answering such questions, I began to realize what a repository of information about independent filmmaking I'd inadvertently be-come.

To put it immodestly, I'm sure there are many people who know more than I about some particular phase, but I'm equally sure there are few (if any) who, via firsthand experience, know more about the total process from blank page to image on the theater screen and beyond (the netherworld of distribution).

An assiduous journal keeper, I thought about publishing the logs of my independent films.

"Do it," said my wife. "If it stops just one person from following in your footsteps, it will be worthwhile."

PARAMOUNT
PICTURES
presents an
ITC & TDJ
production
SHIRLEY
MacLAINE
in a FRANK D. GILROY film
DESPERATE
CHARACTERS

SHIRLEY MacLAINE
WINNER OF
BEST ACTRESS AWARD
1971 BERLIN FILM FESTIVAL

ALSO STARRING
KENNETH MARS SADA THOMPSON **JACK SOMACK**
AND
GERALD O'LOUGHLIN AS "CHARLIE" FROM THE NOVEL BY **PAULA FOX** CO-PRODUCER **PAUL LEAF**
PRODUCED · WRITTEN DIRECTED BY
FRANK D. GILROY **COLOR by TVC** A PARAMOUNT PICTURE

Desperate Characters

While I was scouting locations for *The Only Game in Town* in 1968 with George Stevens (his final film, from my screenplay), he repeatedly asked me to look through his viewfinder. When I asked why, with matter-of-fact certainty, he said, "You're going to direct someday."

That possibility had not occurred to me, but I didn't tell him he was wrong because many weeks of daily association had given me awed respect for his insights and intuitions.

The Only Game in Town, a Las Vegas story shot in Paris because Elizabeth Taylor refused to be separated from Richard Burton, was a failure of considerable proportions. But that's another story.

Two years after George Stevens's prediction, unhappy with a screenwriter's minimal participation in the moviemaking process and hungering for a wider life, physical challenge, adventure (all the things that success as a writer conspires to deprive you of), I optioned a novel, *Desperate Characters*, by Paula Fox, that I was determined to direct.

Had I the slightest hint where I was going and what I was in for, I would have stopped. But the way unfolded day by day.

1970
Wednesday, June 3, 8:30 A.M.: Home, Upstate New York

Today I launch my quest in earnest for money to make a movie of *Desperate Characters*.

Inertia beckons righteously: "You're a writer. Stay out of these gross areas."

Bullshit! If I don't raise the money and do it, I will be at the mercy of inferior people forever.

I will pick up fifty copies of the screenplay (purple cover) from Studio Duplicating today.

About the budget: I had one done by Kenny Utt[1] a couple of months ago. I told him I was going to direct the picture, so he should keep the budget as low as possible to make the gamble inviting. He came back with a ten-week shooting schedule that totaled $987,000 below the line and told me to add another $500,000 for above, which includes all writing, acting, directing, producing costs. It seemed high, but I took it as gospel and went to California.

Jerry Perenchio[2] did not respond to the script. It's hard to empathize with urban problems when you're in Malibu. I quoted the $1.5 million figure, and that killed it altogether.

John Gay[3] read the script and liked it very much.

Back to New York. I gave it to David Picker at United Artists. He was a few years behind me at Dartmouth, and we've known of each other for years but had never met. I was not in an up mood for our meeting; exuded an air of wanting something I was not entitled to, which he sniffed directly. "I thought you were taller," he began.

I gave Picker the script sans budget. After several weeks he passed, saying it was too depressing. To be exact, he said, "It makes me want to blow my brains out."

I took the script to Bosley Crowther[4] (some sort of adviser to the head of Columbia Pictures), who said he liked it "enormously"

1. A premier production manager then. Now a movie producer.
2. Promoter of the first Ali-Frazier fight, the Bobby Riggs–Billie Jean King tennis match (stepping-stones to a brilliant entrepreneurial career). He was (in 1958) assigned by H. N. Swanson (my agent) to handle me when, broke (TV dead in New York), I came to L.A. to repair my fortune. In two weeks I pitched and sold seven stories to "Have Gun Will Travel," "The Rifleman," "Wanted Dead or Alive," et al. "I don't know what the hell we're doing," Jerry enthused, "but ain't we doing it well!"
3. Screenwriter (Academy Award nominee—*Separate Tables*, *Run Silent Run Deep*, *Sometimes a Great Notion*), TV writer and docudramatist beyond compare (*Fatal Vision*, *Blind Faith*, and on and on). He and his wife, Bobby, are our dearest friends. At Hecht-Hill-Lancaster, where he was a mainstay, they called him "Honest John," a label richly deserved.
4. No movie critic ever wielded more power (more equably) than he during his tenure at the *New York Times*. A close friend of my New York agent, Blanche Gaines (who raised John Gay, Rod Serling, and me, among others, from pups in TV's "Golden Age") he once clinched a deal for me at Sardi's by going out of his way to suggest to the Hollywood producer (Mel Frank), who was debating whether to purchase a story of mine, that he and I were much closer friends than was really the case.

and was forwarding it to Schneider (the president) "with my highest recommendation."

Paula Fox (author of *Desperate Characters*) likes my screenplay; wants only two words changed.

Having kept her posted on rejections, I was pleased to phone with the promising news re Columbia.

There is an ulterior motive to apprising her of every twist and turn: If I need more time (I took a one-year option for $3,500 against $35,000) or a cut in the price, she will be more apt to grant it if she knows where things stand.

I called Gordon Willis[5] (acknowledged to be "the hottest young camera man in town"), who stumbled upon the script on someone's desk and wants to do it.

He came to the house, and we got on fine.

I told him that while I didn't know a thing about cameras and would not pretend to, "I do know what I want, think I can tell you what I want, and will know if you deliver it or something better. Can we work that way?" He said yes.

Thursday, June 4, 9:00 A.M.: Home

Took a cab to Studio Duplicating yesterday and picked up the copies of *Characters*. Cost $159.71 and weighed a ton.

Columbia turned it down. Bosley hinted it was because I was to be the director.

"You mean if I let someone else direct, they'll do it?" I said. "No," he said, hastily adding the budget was too high.

"Yes" is yes. "No" has a hundred ways of being said.

Screw trying to get money from studios. Will raise it on my own. Was previously poised for such a move when John Gay called to say he told John Forman[6] that I had a script ideal for Joanne Woodward, and Forman said he'd like to see it. I took it to Forman. Three days later he called. "Paul likes it. Joanne likes it. And so do I. It's got more to say than anything she's been offered in a long time."

Forman would set up a meeting between me and the Newmans. "I'll call you Sunday night," he said, adding, "we're going to have a good time with this."

5. Has more than fulfilled his early promise as an Academy-Award-winning cinematographer (*Godfather I* and *II*, *All The President's Men*, etc.).

6. The Newmans' agent and producer of *Sometimes a Great Notion*, *Butch Cassidy and the Sundance Kid*, *Prizzi's Honor*.

I went off singing to Washington. Spoke at American University, took part in the antiwar demonstration at the White House from which derived that cartoon I gave to Bill Mauldin[7] ("We can't go on meeting this way"), which he used.

No call from Forman on Sunday. No call Monday.

On Tuesday Forman called from Hollywood. "Bad news. I'm afraid our schedules won't allow us to do it."

John Gay phoned. He had been outside Forman's office when the call was made and filled me in: They, Newman-Forman, had taken the script to two studios (which they had no right to do without my permission) and been turned down, which apparently killed their enthusiasm. Plus they suspected I was difficult, despite John's assurances I'm a pussycat.

Friday, June 5, 10:00 A.M.: Essex House Hotel, New York City

The tiniest bit hungover after a night with Mike McAloney[8] and the *Borstal Boy* troupe.

Jim McLaughlin[9] called. He's interested in the *Characters* deal.

Saw Ingmar Bergman's *The Passion of Anna*. How refreshing to see a movie that doesn't cut, jump, pan, and swerve every other frame. Here was a man with confidence in his material—not afraid to subject it to lingering inspection.

Lately at movies I get a great sense of excitement as I anticipate directing.

Paul Leaf[10] has done a budget for me that totals $351,000. I suspect movie budgets are like accordians: You can play the same tune in one octave, five octaves, or whatever.

Thursday, June 11, 8:30 A.M.: Essex House

Called H. N. Swanson (my agent) yesterday. He said four places turned it down, including Disney. My God, how could he send it there!

I asked Frank Weissberg (my lawyer) about Securities and Exchange Commission (SEC) requirements for raising movie money; expect this will be my next move.

Jim McLaughlin just called: "I don't know if I'm obtuse or what, but I read the script, and I don't get it."

I told him his reaction was not unprecedented.

Friday, June 12, 9:30 A.M.: Home

Ruth (my wife) reread the script last night and said, "Go."

11:50 A.M.

Just spoke to Frank Weissberg[11] about the SEC: Once you go over $300 grand, you must file in Washington, which can take ten weeks.

He said a lawyer's normal fee for handling the filing of the offering and all other legal work connected with it is 1 percent of the budget, a budget of $350,000 making 1 percent insufficient. I gather they'll gamble along in some way.

Did I note running into Sam Friedman[12] last week? We went to Sardi's where he told me about the twice-a-week ordeal of dialysis he'd been undergoing for four months.

I mentioned my movie venture, and he offered me a $1-grand investment on the spot. That's the sort of gesture that raises spirits and endears.

Monday, June 15, 8:25 A.M.: Home

My first thought on waking is that it will take too much out of me to make the movie happen and that it just isn't worth it. So begin most days.

I attribute part of the down feeling to a call from Ulu Grosbard[13] yesterday afternoon. He likes the script very much,

11. The best theatrical lawyer I've encountered. Blessed with a talent for divining what people *really* want, which is often different from what they *say* they want—a skill that doubtless serves him well in his current position as a judge in New York.

12. Press agent (deceased). Last of a colorful breed; worked for the likes of Mike Todd. Flinty, uncompromising, relentless, he handled the national tour of *Roses*. Shepherded me on my first cross-country publicity foray. "Are you a hard worker?" he asked en route to Chicago, our first stop. "Try me," I challenged. Starting with a predawn radio show, we hit every newspaper and TV and radio program that could be useful in twenty-four hours. In like manner, we blanketed the nation.

13. Director of *Roses* on Broadway and in the movies, plus others of my works. We worked so intimately that some of his wondrous skills, gained by osmosis, have served me well.

really likes it, but feels the $350,000 budget for a union picture is unrealistic. He said I could get in serious financial trouble since I would be responsible if I went over.

In closing, he again said how much he liked the script and suggested I see Eric Rohmer's film *My Night at Maud's,* which he said would give me confidence in my concept.

Rose Gregorio[14] got on the phone. She liked it even more than Ulu did and wants to play Claire.

I was elated by their reaction to the script. The budget warnings did not take over till bedtime.

Just came in with the mail. A letter from H. N. Swanson[15]

June 12, 1970

Dear Frank,

We've had turn-downs on *Desperate Characters* from John Calley, Mike Frankovich, Disney and National General. Russ Thatcher of Metro is in New York for a week and won't be able to get to it until his return. I'm waiting to hear from Walter Reade and Mort Briskin of Bing Crosby Productions. Yorkin and Lear heard about the script and wanted to read it but while they assured us it would be o.k. for you to produce it they wouldn't want you to direct it. David Brown has promised me a decision on Monday.

Save me a waltz.

Best,
Swanie

That feeling I used to get apropos numerous rejections of *Plowboy* and *Roses* descends: Who's crazy — me or them?

Tuesday, June 16, 8:00 A.M.: Home.

At 11:30 last night the phone rang. It was Bill Goldman[16] saying he'd just read *Desperate Characters* and loved it. Related it to

14. She and Ulu were married in our living room. Just Ruth, me, and our dog, plus a justice of the peace before a roaring hearth. "My God," said Rose, "it's like one of those thirties movies where the actress and director get married at the playwright's house in Connecticut."

15. My Hollywood agent for over twenty-five years. Swanie, who represented the likes of Faulkner, Fitzgerald, O'Hara, Chandler, died in harness in 1991 at the age of ninety-one. In his memoir (*Sprinkled with Ruby Dust*) he says, "Frank D. Gilroy is a gambler at heart. He always has been."

16. Two-time Academy-Award-winning screenwriter *Butch Cassidy, All the President's Men,* novelist, sports freak. We met when he interviewed me for his classic theatre book *The Season,* which followed the destinies of all Broadway-bound plays in 1968, including *The Only Game in Town.*

Bergman. He picked out one phony line that I already was onto. Needless to say, his estimate buoys me greatly.

Arrived at the Colton, Weissberg office, at 10:30 A.M.

The office number, 711, was cheering.

Frank Weissberg said it felt like 1964 and *Roses* all over again; showed me the long- and short-form offering circulars. The long one, for monies over $300 grand, is a time consuming monster I can't afford.

So how do we get the amount needed down to $300,000? He called Eddie Colton[17] in to hear my recital of the project's history to date (rejections included).

When I mentioned Columbia had passed despite Bosley's recommendation, Eddie said, "Stan Schneider, the president of Columbia is a close friend. When he hears the budget is around four hundred thousand [rather than the million-two I quoted Bosley], he'll go for it."

I told Eddie I doubted this since Swanie had been quoting $460 grand on the coast and been turned down consistently. Eddie would not be deterred—put in a call to Schneider, who was in conference.

The name Rugoff came up as someone who might be interested. They said he owned theaters and had taste. I left two copies of the script and departed.

Home, to find a call from Colton. He'd contacted Schneider, who knew the script through Bosley. Schneider said at $385 grand (Colton's figure), they were interested and that Bosley would call me to learn how a picture quoted at a million-two can now be done for $385,000.

I called Paula Fox. Explained where we were and started to ask her about deferring half her money. She said yes before I could even spell it out. *That's my own style, and I love it when it's reciprocated.*

17. Founder of Colton, Fernbach & Weissberg, currently Colton, Hartnick, Yamin & Sheresky. We met in 1953 when my TV play *The Last Notch*, attracted so much movie interest that my agent turned to Colton for guidance. MGM ultimately did the movie, starring Glen Ford, and retitled *The Fastest Gun Alive* ("MGM's sleeper of the year"—*Variety*), for which I received $9,000 (before taxes and agent's fees) and my first screen credit. Eddie, 86, still going strong. George Abbott, 104, among his clients.

11:20 A.M.

A call from Weissberg. He read the script, loves it: "It haunted me all night." He said he'd called Rugoff—rushed a script to him.

2:15 P.M

Bosley, where are you?

Here is a letter just received on Twentieth Century-Fox stationery:

dated June 15, 1970

Dear Swanie,

I am afraid in *Desperate Characters* Frank Gilroy has taken on a very special type of subject without the mass appeal films so desperately need today.

Notwithstanding the low budget and the extraordinarily good writing, this project, in my estimation, is better financed by private investors and distributed by specialized distribution people than taken on as a major company release.

I wish I could give you better news but I feel the appeal of this subject is not broad enough for us.

Best always,
David Brown,
Executive Vice President
Creative Operations

Friday, June 19, 8:00 A.M.: Home

Bosley Crowther called twice, once to ask how the budget went from a million-two to $385 grand. I explained. The second call was for a script.

Wednesday, June 24, 8:15 A.M.: Home

No movement on *Characters*. All those seeds I planted in the past two weeks, and not one response. The stock market dropping eighteen points yesterday won't help.

I won my Democratic committeemanship yesterday with twenty-six votes. Tomorrow the world.

Thursday, June 25, 8:30 A.M.: Home

Paula Fox called. Enjoy talking to her because she is onto so much without explanation. She is going to approach an eccentric millionaire she knows, made him sound like Huntington Hartford. I said it's a shame that people like that keep falling into the wrong hands. "Instead of ours," she said.

Friday, June 26, 9:30 A.M.: Home

Bill Goodman, Paula Fox's editor at Harcourt Brace, read the *Characters* script and flipped over it. He told me Paula is working on a big book (eighteen months away) and that they'd give me first look at the galleys, which is a reflection of their feeling about the *Characters* script.

I think I'll arbitrarily lower the budget to $300,000 on Monday and seek the SEC clearance.

Eddie Colton just phoned. Rugoff admires the script but feels the final product will not be commercial.

Colton, who was so high on the script before, now has doubts: "There isn't much action, is there?" "It's a character study." "That cat business in the front is supposed to be symbolic about biting the hand that feeds you, but I don't see it in the other characters." And finally: "Don't be discouraged."

10:20 A.M.

Each rejection is like a jab you don't feel till a few moments after it lands. The Rugoff punch just registered. Onward.

Wednesday, July 1, 2:30 P.M.: Wyndham Hotel, New York City

Columbia said no again—a contemporary picture from a middle-aged point of view is just not commercial. (That's a paraphrase of Bosley quoting Schneider.)

No sooner gave Mike McAloney a copy of *Characters* than he said, "We'll fly to Toronto and see my friend who owns the Maple Leafs. We'll do it in Canada which means the government puts up sixty-one percent, et cetera, et cetera." I suggested he read it first.

To the Colton office. Jerry Edelstein, the young lawyer who will be handling *Characters*, said that in order to file with the SEC, I would have to give him a copy of the budget; a copy of my contract with Paula; a signed agreement with Paula confirming her deferral, and four précis summing up my career as screen, TV, stage writer and producer, plus a three-sentence summary of *Desperate Characters*.

Since time was vital, I said I'd assemble these documents and get them to him by 4:30 P.M.

I called Paul Leaf. Yes, he would come right down and do a new budget, revised to $300,000.

I called Paula. Yes, she would agree to the increased deferral and would come to Jerry's office at 4:30 P.M. to sign whatever was necessary.

The next few hours a swirl of documents. Ultimately it was all accomplished. The papers go to the SEC on Tuesday and then a three-week wait.

Wednesday, July 8, 8:30 A.M.: Wyndham Hotel

At lunch, Ruth and I got on our different attitudes about my money-raising. She still feels uneasy about my going to people we know.

At Ulu's suggestion, I went to see his agent, Howard Hausman, spelled out the history of *Character* to date. He said (accurately, I think) that by handling it as I have, I've given it an amateurish feel.

He took my budget (without having read the script) and envisioning disaster upon disaster, elevated it to a million dollars in less than a minute.

"Negative recoupment" means the limited partners have received their investment back. I thought so, but the language in the agreement contradicted this. Edelstein just called to say I'm right and the appropriate change will be made. Another proof that I *must* take the time to study these documents, no matter how tedious.

Thursday, July 9, 10:15 A.M.: Wyndham Hotel

Called Swanie yesterday . He said no one who has read *Characters* has been sufficiently interested to ask for a budget or to meet me. I told Swanie I was filing with the SEC; could feel him bolt the door against solicitations.

Have cut down on booze and am exercising each day, even in hotels. Felt so good after a day of no alcohol that I almost vowed not to have another drink till all the money is raised.

Called Hausman. He read it and liked it but sees why the studios shy away at any price. He said that the most any Bergman picture has grossed in rentals in America is $300,000, which is a fierce argument against financing me.

On the plus side, he asked me to send him two more scripts and he would check some sources that might have been overlooked. Advised me to keep on with my SEC business. Said when I got clearance, he might be able to help me with smaller investors.

I achieved a great calm during the morning. Did Ahab have moments like this?

Would I *really* welcome someone handing me a check for the full $300 grand right now? Isn't it possible I want the adventure of fund-raising more than I know?

Friday, July 10, 9:50 A.M.: Home

Phoned Swanie to request he announce my arrival in L.A. on Monday in the trades. He had a letter from Russ Thatcher at MGM saying (I paraphrase), "No one can handle the plight of the little guy better than Gilroy—witness what he did in *Roses*. But *Roses* did poorly at the box office, which is one of the reasons we must turn *Characters* down."

Saturday, July 11, 9:00 A.M.: Home

I *will* make this movie.
I *will* make this movie.
I *will* make this movie.

Tuesday, July 14, 8:15 A.M.: Beverly Wilshire Hotel, L.A.

I am directly below Warren Beatty's penthouse suite; have his name on my list of "might-sees."

I checked the trades. No announcement of my arrival. I called Swanie. My irritability surfaced. I should have kept my mouth shut since it's in *Variety* today.

Mann Rubin,[18] hearing the recital of my adventure to date, said, "This time when you're looking for investors, don't forget me." He allowed it wouldn't be much, but it means a great deal and is appreciated.

Wednesday, July 15, 8:30 A.M.: Beverly Wilshire Hotel

I have a date this morning with Harry Keller,[19] his business manager, and a potential investor in the hotel drugstore. I will lay out my plan—a dress rehearsal prior to meeting Jerry Perenchio.

---

18. Screenwriter (*First Deadly Sin, An American Dream*) and TV writer. We met at Twentieth Century–Fox in 1958. Clifford Odets was there at the time, and one day Mann and I were about to knock on his door and tell him how much his earlier work meant to us. We had second thoughts, saw what we were about to do as coltish and unprofessional, and to our lasting regret, refrained.

19. Director, producer, and outstanding film editor at the beginning and end of his career (*Stripes, Stir Crazy*). We met at Disney (1958) when he directed several segments of a TV series I wrote. A dear, dear friend whose passing has taken much of the joy out of going to Hollywood.

A photographer at Jerry Lawrence's[20] party said he had a statement from my *Roses* log tacked on his wall: "If friends can't encourage one another's dreams, then what is friendship for?"

It was good to hear that at this time.

Thursday, July 16, 1:00 P.M.: Beverly Wilshire Hotel

I met Harry, Paul Gilbert, and one of his "big investors," a corpulent cloak-and-suiter whose face demanded a cigar.

After a few minutes of general chat, I stopped worrying about what sort of an impression I was making and laid out the deal.

As (loath to give them a script) I summarized the story, the heavy man said, "You know, it reminds me of a picture I saw and liked the other night called *Passion of Anna* by Bergman." I could have kissed him. He went on at length about Bergman. His interest genuine if a bit confused. We had been hitting it off before that (both of us being from the Bronx), but Bergman married us, if only for the moment. I insisted he take the script when we parted. I suspect his business head will ultimately prevail, but the moment was a joy.

Friday, July 17, 8:45 A.M.: Beverly Wilshire Hotel

About my meeting with Perenchio: I laid out all the money rejections and critical praise, and above all my determination to make the picture. He allowed that he still didn't think *Characters* would make a dime (if it did, he'd kiss my ass in any window of my choosing), but he was interested in the future possibilities of our relationship.

What I like about him is that he bubbles with excitement and isn't afraid to show it. Bottom line: He wants to put me in a room with some high rollers ("For Gods sake, don't show them the script or we're dead") who if they like me might "fade the whole shoot" because "they gamble on people."

In parting, Jerry implored, "All your pictures won't be noncommercial like this one, will they?" I assured him my interests were catholic.

20. Playwright, coauthor of *Inherit the Wind*, *Mame*. A fellow member of the Dramatists Guild Council in New York.

Tuesday, July 21, 10:00 A.M.: Salishan Lodge, Glen Eden Beach, Oregon

Ruth and I are visiting John and Bobby Gay. John wrote the screenplay for *Sometimes a Great Notion*, starring Paul Newman and Henry Fonda, which is shooting here.

John Forman, Newman's partner and producer, greeted me warmly, said he still likes *Desperate Characters*. I think he's puzzled as to just what I'm doing here.

Thursday, July 23, 11:15 A.M.: Salishan Lodge

Mike Ludmer called. He's the story editor at Universal. He'd spoken to Harry Keller, learned of my *Characters* project. Turns out he'd read the book and liked it. Harry told him the budget was $300,000. Mike said Universal was sponsoring projects like mine and he would like to read the script.

Saturday, July 25, 9:00 A.M.: Salishan Lodge

Harry called: The potential investor who loved Bergman passed. On the plus side, Harry said Ludmer liked the script very much and has submitted it to their small-projects guy.

Tuesday, July 28, 11:00 A.M.: Salishan Lodge

Jerry Edelstein called to say things look great with the SEC They only want three minor additions in the "risk" area. Instead of being elated, I felt my heart sag a bit. Until I have SEC clearance, I can only talk in general terms, but once I get it, I must get down to cases and ask outright for dough, which scares me.

Chatted with Henry Fonda at Forman's birthday party. He said that the section from *Roses* included in his one-man show is the high point of the night every time. I note that Fonda flies kites, makes ice cream, collects stones, does needlepoint, and remains as aloof as possible from the rest of the company.

It has taken a while, but I think Forman finally realizes that I am in Oregon only to visit the Gays, with no intention of making a pitch for *Characters*.

Wednesday, July 29, 3:00 P.M.: Wyndham Hotel, New York City

Edelstein just called to say I have SEC clearance and the forms will be delivered tomorrow. So here I am without one penny promised and $300 grand to go.

I saw Edgar Lansbury,[21] arranged to use his office as head-quarters.

Opened a bank account at Manufacturers Hanover this morning. Mr. Flynn, a most amiable man, served me.

Who will be the first person I ask for money?

Who will be the last one?

Channel swimmers, mountain climbers, and marathon runners must be subject to the siren voices that beckon me today: "Give up." "Retreat." "Rest." "It isn't worth it."

Thursday, July 30, 10:30 A.M.: Wyndham Hotel

Jim McLaughlin said he'd invest but gave no hint how much. He equated my belief in this project with his insistence (despite contrary opinions) to come out with a pinewood line when he joined a furniture company in Richmond. My confidence reminded him of his own. Incidentally, his judgment about pine proved sound.

Friday, July 31, 8:15 A.M.: Home

To the office, where Edgar gave me a key and we agreed to split the answering-service cost. He said he was still seeking money for me.

Got a call from Warren Lyons[22] about speaking at the Actor's Studio. I mentioned my *Characters* project, and he said he invested in such things. Will call him Monday.

I'm temporarily blinded to the merit in other people's work. I mean, did Ahab care what other ships caught?

Will make more phone calls today. The more I make, the easier they get.

Bob Ellison[23] called from Chicago to say he not only likes the script but thinks it's commercial. I'm flying there on Thursday afternoon and will spend two days seeing some poeple he's lined up.

Sunday, August 2, 9:15 A.M.: Home

I made a half dozen calls, laid out the deal. All invited me to

21. Produced *Roses* and designed the set. Subsequently he produced two other plays of mine. He also produced *Godspell*.

22. Son of Leonard Lyons, the Broadway columnist.

23. A newspaperman in Chicago, met via Sam Friedman, now a freelance writer in Hollywood.

send offering circulars. I look forward to Thursday and Friday in Chicago as a performer might. Have no idea what I'm in for.

Monday, August 3, 8:00 A.M.: Home

Dan Featherston[24] called. He might have an interested party, requiring a trip to Boston.

Called Ulu. He again voiced doubts about my doing the picture for $300,000. I should remind him of the dictum first heard from his lips: "Let the negatives speak for themselves."

Tony (my eldest son) and I drove to Lake Erskine to see a wealthy, childless older couple (my late parents' best friends) about investing in the picture.

The husband's reaction was defensive and suspicious: that previously unseen side of people any mention of money triggers, which I'm getting used to.

In the midst of reminiscing about my parents and all the great times they'd shared, the husband explained why this wasn't a good time for him to invest, recalling my father's line "I'd like to help you, but all my money is tied up in cash."

Reached a well-to-do old army buddy. "Gee, Gil, I'm the unluckiest gambler you ever met. You don't want my money, it would be a jinx."

As long as I think of the whole thing as an adventure (a safari into the deep dark land of money), I'm fine.

Tuesday, August 4, 9:30 A.M.: Wyndham Hotel

Pat Johnston, a treasure of efficiency, brought envelopes on her own. The right size no less. And she brought the stamp: "Desperate Characters Company, TDJ Productions Incorporated, Suite 7-C, 888 Eighth Avenue, New York." We gave her the honor of stamping the first envelope.

Then to work sending letters, offering circulars, and agreements.

Thursday, August 6, 1:00 P.M.: Airport

Waiting to take off for Chicago.

---

24. A classmate at Dartmouth. We worked on the oldest college newspaper (of which I was editor in chief). As undergraduate he acted in my first full-length play, whose cast included John Gambling, Buck Henry, and Mike Heyman, lately the chancellor at Berkeley. Dan's talents now on display as a criminal lawyer in Boston.

Warren Lyons came by. Gave him several circulars and agreements. To see me in the midst of fund-raising contradicts the image of what he wants me to be. Squeamish about raising money for John Guare's play (his current endeavor), he projects his feelings on me.

Saturday, August 8, 9:30 A.M.: The Mediteranean Suite, Ambassador East, Chicago

Bob Ellison booked this suite, which Elizabeth Taylor and Burton recently occupied, at a special rate, said we'd need the space since he invited many more people than I expected to meet. I feared it might look too elegant to potential investors in a low-budget flick.

Some thirty people showed. I outlined plans and answered questions. All pleasant, but I doubt anything will come of it. Best of all was the realization that holding forth to strangers occasioned no anxiety. In truth, I enjoyed it.

Tuesday, August 11, 7:00 A.M.: Beverly Wilshire Hotel, L.A.

Harry just called to say that Mike Ludmer at Universal reported that Ned Tannen has great respect for me, etc., but it's his considered opinion that *Characters* won't make money.

Wednesday, August 12, 10:30 A.M.: Beverly Wilshire Hotel

You will not hear from me for ten days, as my three sons and I embark on a three-hundred-mile raft trip down the Colorado.

The bank account officially open in New York with a $1,000 check from Sam Friedman.

How much will be in it when I resurface?

Sunday, August 23, 9:45 A.M.: Tropicana Hotel, Las Vegas

The river trip memorable, magnificent, and mind-blowing.

I expect a call momentarily, informing how much money has arrived in my absence.

John Gay called from Oregon to report he'd shown the script of *Desperate Character* to Shirley MacLaine (visiting the location), who flipped over it, said she'll get me all the financing I need, providing she plays the part.

I told him to tell her my boat was a day late, said I wanted to learn how much dough I have and needed a day to envision her (I've never met her) as Sophie.

In addition, I needed time to get over culture shock after no radio, no news, no electricity, no contact with the world for ten days.

Thirty minutes later

Just learned we have a grand total of $7,000!!! I am a bit numb. Was it my mistake for not putting a deadline on it? Must I now call everyone again to impress them with the urgency of the thing? Seven grand? How can that be?

What to do? First I must face the MacLaine situation. I just did. I mentally put her through the script, and it just doesn't work. She is *not* Sophie. I am flattered by her interest, but she's not right for the part. Better not to do the picture than to do it wrong. So *that's that*. What next?

Monday, August 24, 7:30 A.M.: Tropicana Hotel

Phoned Dan Featherston in Boston and Bob Ellison in Chicago. No cheering news from either place.

John Gay called. What about Shirley MacLaine? I said I couldn't see her in the part. John, more emphatic than I ever heard him, said, "Look, Frank, do what you want to do. You're always going to do that anyway. But I'm telling you, after watching her here for a week, she can do it."

That was good enough for me. I said I'd fly to L.A. and meet her. He gave me her number, which I called. She was very friendly. We made a date for Tuesday.

My beard, grown on the river trip, prospers. Can I live up to it?

Tuesday, August 25, 9:30 A.M.: Beverly Wilshire, L.A.

Called New York. No money in the mail.

Just called Shirley. She invited me to dinner at her house at eight o'clock.

I must guard against being swayed by the fact that without her or someone of similar magnitude, I am not going to get the money to do the picture.

Wednesday, August 26, 6:45 A.M.: Beverly Wilshire

With a bottle of Dry Sack and a script, I drove to Shirley's place in Encino last night. I calculatedly wore no tie; debated about bringing the sherry. Would it signal I was courting her instead of the other way around?

She greeted me. Just us. Embarrassment on both sides as we tried to connect. To indicate I was a take-charge guy, befitting my new directorial image, I made drinks.

She very, very much wants to do this picture. Had read the novel and feels the screenplay has greater impact. She brought up Joanne Woodward's interest in it. Her opinion of Joanne in this role is low. She also dismissed Lee Remick and Anne Bancroft as candidates.

She tried to impress me with her grasp of the material. I tried to impress her in various ways. Sometimes no one was listening.

She mentioned finance, said Sir Lew Grade, for whom she was going to do a television series in England, was a likely source. I said money talk was premature since I must want her independent of the dough or not at all.

She sprinkled her conversation with expletives that came across like a kid mouthing forbidden words. It was mostly chat—the real appraisal was in the subtext. Occasionally the air died.

Would the audience, so brainwashed with her gamin image, accept her in this part? She was confident they would.

About 11:30 I said I wanted a day to think it over. If she was disappointed that I didn't say yes then and there, she hid it well.

Still no more dough in New York.

Called Paul Leaf. Asked if a star name would disqualify his budget. He said not as long as it was legitimate, i.e., that the star was truly working for scale. He asked who I was talking about. I said Shirley MacLaine. He said that was a great idea.

Noon

Had another brief meeting with Shirley, at the conclusion of which I was still undecided.

"Christ," she said, "it takes you a long fucking time to make up your mind."

Met two potential backers who had no real interest until I mentioned the possibility of MacLaine's involvement. Immediately they were all over me. Wanted me to send back any money raised so far, so that they could handle everything themselves. Said they preferred not to go through the SEC because their sources might be from out of the country—people with "soft money." "That's money you haven't paid taxes on as opposed to money you have paid taxes on," they explained when I looked blank.

They also spoke of of "active" money and "passive" money. The former demands a say in how a venture is run; the latter doesn't.

They suggested I tell Shirley I had all the money and leave the rest to them. Like an eager, well-rehearsed vaudeville team, they completed each other's sentences.

I felt a little knotting in my gut, a vague sense something wasn't kosher.

To avoid any sense of obligation, I picked up the tab for our lunch.

3:00 P.M.

Returned to my room. Told the operator I was taking no calls. Went through the script again with Shirley in mind. Thought long and hard and then called her: "I've never seen you do a part like this," I said. "But if you're willing to take a chance on a first-time director, I'll return the gamble."

She said, "Fine." I'm going to her place tomorrow morning for breakfast at 10:30 to talk in detail.

Thursday, August 27, 8:45 A.M.: Beverly Wilshire

The other night Shirley said she wondered if I was more interested in the adventure of making the movie happen than in the movie itself. An adroit observation.

Key question: If I had $300 grand, would I accept her so readily or search further? Answer: I would search further. But I don't have three hundred. Am still $293 grand short.

Key question: If I felt in my heart of hearts she was wrong for the part, would I take her just to get the picture made? Answer: *No!*

2:15 P.M.

A call just now from that wealthy good friend of my father's, who said he showed the offering circular to the attorney in charge of his estate, who didn't want his money tied up in case he passed away.

As we spoke, I realized he sees his money as some sort of passport to the hereafter. Truly believes, without realizing it, that his wealth will secure advantage beyond the grave.

This on the heels of a three-hour meeting with Shirley, Sander

Vanocur,[25] and (enter the villian) Herman Citron, her agent, is almost more than I can bear.

Sandy, she, and I got on fine until Citron's arrival.

His attitude was "Okay, you took the kid in, but you can't fool me." I repeated my proposal, which Shirley previously agreed to, that she and I split 50-50 down the line.

"I don't like that," he said, and recited a list of pitfalls that could derail the picture. All this in the guise of saving us from ourselves.

In reality, he hates this no-frills concept of picture making: It's okay for the creators, who get their kicks, but an agent gets only money, so there's nothing for him in such a romantic venture.

I tried defusing his hostility, to no avail, as he went on about Shirley's usual salary ($800,000) and how the unions could exert pressure on any star who tried to make a picture for this little.

I expected Shirley to muzzle him. But all she kept saying was "My God, being a star is like having leprosy."

Unable to restrain myself, I congratulated Citron for having "pissed on the flame" so effectively and departed.

> *4:20 P.M.*

Shirley just called.

I expected her to be upset at the way Citron behaved. Wrong. "These business things are necessary," she began. Started on how 25 percent of the profit wasn't enough for either her or me, etc. I told her it was enough for me and she had to choose between doing it for love or money since this picture wouldn't tolerate both.

> *6:00 P.M.*

Shirley called again. Her lawyer (at her house reading my offering circular and partnership agreement) had some questions. Could I come over? I said I'd talk to him on the phone but was too tired to make that drive again. How about tomorrow? Fine, I said.

Friday, August 28, 12:30 P.M.: Beverly Wilshire

Just back from Shirley's.

Only her lawyer, amiable and reasonable, was there. Citron wisely reduced to an off-stage presence.

Bottom line: If Shirley can come up with a sweeter deal (artistic

25. Prominent TV newscaster and Shirley's companion.

controls still mine), I'll cancel present plan and send the money I've raised (all $7 grand) back to my investors (all three of them).

Harmony reigned again but on a different plane than B.C. (before Citron).

Harry Keller just called: His business manager has a guy who will put up the whole $300 grand for Shirley MacLaine. I told Harry to tell him he'd have to get in line.

Saturday, August 29, 8:35 A.M.: Airport (waiting to take off for New York)

I leave L.A. satisfied I did all I could as well as I could.

Sunday, August 30, 10:30 A.M.: Home

Talking to Paula Fox, I recounted the shock of surfacing from the Grand Canyon into Las Vegas. She likened it to "suddenly being confronted with the laundry of the world."

She sees the risk of MacLaine as Sophie but agrees it's worthwhile.

Tuesday, September 1, 9:45 A.M.: Home

No word from Shirley.

Have a slight fear I may have treated her too cavalierly, but if she really wants to do it, nothing will stop her.

Wednesday, September 2, 3:00 P.M.: Home

Shirley just called to announce she has the money!

Sir Lew Grade has guaranteed it sans any creative strings.

She, now burdened with the responsibility of safeguarding his dough, was suddenly anxious: Could I really do it for $300,000, etc.?

Faced with the likelihood that it's going to happen, I too am anxious. Felt us clinging for mutual reassurance on the phone.

I told her I tried her name on a few people who know the script and they were enthusiastic. That cheered her.

Note: In her voice just now I detected a vulnerability I must tap for Sophie.

Saturday, September 5, 10:00 A.M.: Wyndham

Went to the Colton office and met with Frank Weissberg and Jerry Edelstein. Brought them up to date.

When I said Shirley MacLaine, I gained Frank's attention in an unprecedented way. I told him I was meeting her the following morning. Frank said that he would be at his summer place in Westport but if I needed him at the meeting, he would drive in.

Frank, to his credit, suggested I include my investors in the MacLaine deal. I confessed there were only three and the sum was less than $10,000. Given that paltry figure, he said it was better to send the money back rather than embarrass myself by letting Shirley know that's all I'd raised.

Bobby Greenhut, a production manager we'd approached, called to say that Paul's budget seemed much too low on a hasty inspection. What a blow to get just before a crucial meeting with Shirley when I must, above all, radiate confidence about the numbers.

Took a cab to Shirley's fashionable digs on East Fifty-first Street. The elevator man waited and watched till Shirley admitted me as an expected guest.

Good news. No Herman Citron. Just Sandy having breakfast. Friendly vibrations.

Experienced the uneasiness that assails in the presence of people who enjoy greater celebrity than I.

Sandy left. What Shirley and I talked about, as usual, subordinate to what was going on unsaid: It was our last chance to sound each other out before the boat sailed.

We went over motivations in the script, casting, production ideas. There were occasional blanks, but mostly we rolled along enthusiastically.

At one point, Shirley rambling endlessly, I interrupted, said that beneath the pointless chatter I detected a serious concern she was reluctant to express.

Bull's-eye. But before she could tell me what it was, Sandy returned.

We—Shirley, Sandy and I—decided to go see the movie *Joe*, which had been made for a reported cost of $235,000.

Before we left the apartment, Shirley insisted she and I write a joint letter to John Gay, who'd brought us together.

She penned her side, which said I was "fabulous," and gave it to me.

I wrote, "This is another fine mess you've gotten me into. And I do mean fine." She read this and laughed.

In the cab bound for the theater we passed a movie marquee

that advertised *Spend a day with Clint Eastwood*, prompting Shirley to say, "Only with a bottle of baby oil and champagne."

Shirley said she can control being recognized or not by her own frame of mind. When she thinks, "Shirley—star," people spot her. I said that would help us steal shots.

Shirley, Sandy, and I became part of a group that dropped in on James Jones (*From Here to Eternity*) whom I'd never met, at one o'clock in the morning.

That Jones was on the wagon inclined several "friends" to bait him about this and his position on the Vietnam War, which they felt was ambivalent.

The game seemed to be that if they could provoke him to violence, they would win. And so they kept sniping, knowing he was somehow safely leashed.

Liking Jones instinctively, I stomached as much as I could and started to leave which inspired one of the prime baiters (Trzcinski, coauthor of *Stalag 17*) to mark my departure "cowardly" since "crisis is imminent."

I told him the only crisis was a shit crisis of his making.

"He's only putting you on," Jones said to calm me.

Gloria (Jones's wife) showed me to the door, saying she was sorry Jim and I didn't get a chance to talk to each other.

About my novel *Private*, due out shortly, she said, "Send it to Jim. He'll give you a quote. He does it for everybody."

Tuesday, September 8, 10:00 A.M.: Home

Sir Lew Grade just called Weissberg. Here's the deal. We can start drawing on the $300 grand at once. Any bank interest returns to him. He wants worldwide distribution rights. He and Shirley get 80 percent of profit. I get 20 percent. Any points given away come off the top. Frank said he'd get back to him.

Frank feels the split should be two-thirds to them, one-third to me, plus $50,000 deferred until negative recoupment since I'll get nothing in front.

Above all, I reiterated, I *must* have creative control.

Wednesday, September 9, 8:00 A.M.: Home

We appear to have a deal (terms as sought), with one kicker: Shirley will get 10 percent of gross from first dollar, which was never suggested before.

Abe Mandel, who heads a subsidiary (ITC) of Grade's empire in New York, will implement the deal at the direction of Shirley or someone she designates.

Thursday, September 10, 6:30 A.M.: Wyndham

I recall liking the actor James Olsen in *Rachel, Rachel.* Paul will try and get him here.

Incidentally, Paul called a guy connected with *Joe* who said the picture cost $135,000, not $235,000, which is heartening.

Friday, September 11, 9:15 A.M.: Wyndham

Called Paula with a full report. Made a date to see the locale of the story.

A cab to Shirley's with three weighty casting books.

I wondered about involving her, decided the risk was worthwhile. If there are going to be problems, let's face them now. Thought how consistent with the spirit of the project if Shirley's name appeared below the title no bigger than her costars'.

She greeted me cheerfully: "How do you feel?"

I said something intended to convey excitement, nervousness, and confidence.

We went through the casting books for three hours, interspersed with discussion of Sophie's character and other relationships in the script.

Early on, she brought up billing, suggested it might be smart if her name appeared below the title as proof that this was not the same old Shirley.

I said it was spooky to hear her voice a notion that had occurred to me in the cab. But while it was intriguing, I advised she not commit herself too hastily. This in deference to Citron, who, presented with a fait accompli, would not be happy.

The casting game wedded us as nothing else has. We found we were in tune in our estimates of talent.

I mentioned Olsen. She didn't know him. I showed her his picture in the book. She saw the possibilities I'd seen in his face.

As we progressed through the casting books, we recited anecdotes that certain names touched off—laughed a lot.

In discussing Sophie, Shirley shows a tendency to think too much. What she's done in movies until now, and done well, I would guess is done instinctively. I must guard against excessive probing lest she become self-conscious about the big switch she's making, which could undermine her essential vitality.

We sent a script to James Olsen's agent on the coast.

We (Paul and I) interviewed potential secretaries, script supervisors, production managers, etc.

Numerous calls from Jerry Edelstein, who is drawing the contract pursuant to Frank's memo.

Jonas Halpern, from Shirley's publicity office, read me the initial release. It sounded fine. Would I give him a capsule summary of the script?

I said, "It's forty-eight hours in the lives of a couple who have the best New York can offer. In short, a horror story."

Monday, September 14, 8:30 A.M.: Wyndham

Adeline Leonard, hired as production secretary, says the phone company wants a $1,500 deposit because movie companies frequently stiff them.

An experienced hand, she doesn't believe we can do the picture for $300,000. Thinks Paul and I merely quote that figure to keep costs as low as possible.

I sat her down and laid out the history of the project, let her know that $300 grand was *the* figure and there were no reserves.

Apparently I convinced her because by late afternoon she was trying (with evident delight) to save us a nickel here and a dime there.

I must infect all hands with the same spirit.

Going through a casting book, the face of Kenny Mars registered as a possible Otto. I had a script delivered to his agent in Hollywood.

Wednesday, September 16, 8:50 A.M.: Wyndham

Paula, Paul, and I began our Brooklyn Heights tour, seeking something so unique and attractive that it would justify losing an hour of shooting to transport the crew back and forth each day.

L. J. Davis, the novelist, offered himself as tour guide. Took us to three homes. The first two disappointing. The third ideal, as though the novel had been written with it in mind. Plus the street has the desired mix of renovated homes and run down places.

Olsen's agent called to say, "Jim is apeshit over the script."

A potential production manager echoed Adeline's reservations about the budget, assumed we'd get more dough via Shirley. I told him three hundred meant three hundred, period. Don't think I convinced him.

Thursday, September 17, 8:45 A.M.: Wyndham

Norman Cohen hired as production manager.

He sees the budget as a challenge and feels we'll pull it off, given the full cooperation of producer, director, writer, star.

Shirley suggested someone shoot a documentary of us making the movie. I said I didn't want the clutter, plus it would be embarrassing if they had a larger crew than we did.

She asked if she could release the announcement of our venture to the press.

I, interpreting that as her way of signaling she expected no breakdown at today's meeting to finalize the contract, said yes.

Friday, September 18, 8:00 A.M.: Wyndham

Six of us took our places at a round table — Frank Weissberg, Ben Newman (Shirley's attorney), Lawrence Kornblum and Abe Mandel (representing Sir Lew), Paul, and I.

Someone said it looked like we were setting up for a card game. And how true that proved to be.

Mandel sat back like a beneficent father while Kornblum, carrying the ball for ITC, went over the agreement point by point.

Several debatable items surfaced, but the sense that everyone wanted to make the deal prevailed until Shirley's lawyer, with a sudden burst of emotion, insisted Paula Fox's profit points come out of my end exclusively.

"This is fundamental to the contract," he stated categorically. "If we don't get it, we might as well stop talking and tear these papers up."

Silence.

I felt sweat on my palms — experienced a slight urge to reply in kind. But only slight, for I knew what I wanted and felt confident I was reading the hand well.

"Let's put that aside for now and hear the rest of Kornblum's points," I proposed.

Kornblum continued. Harmony for a paragraph or two and then *Boom*: They would consult with me about the final cut, but ultimately the final cut would be theirs!

I kept myself in check, leaking just enough to underline the significance of the matter, and suggested we hold that also in abeyance and move along.

When Kornblum concluded, I huddled with Frank and Paul, told them everything was negotiable except the final cut.

The meeting resumed.

Frank went over the points at issue (arriving at agreement in every case) until only the final cut remained.

All eyes on me, I said, "From the outset, I've let it be known that artistic controls had to be mine. Without final cut, those words are meaningless. The matter is not negotiable."

A long silence . . . and then capitulation.

Paul and I left them to redraft the contract.

"This will be the first three-hundred-thousand-dollar picture with a legal fee of one hundred thousand," Frank quipped.

At 5:00 P.M., Paul and I returned to the Colton office, where Ben, Kornblum, Jerry, and Frank were still going at it.

It was Friday. They were all tired, short-tempered. A time when lawyers and agents, in the absence of principals, have dynamited many a deal out of personal pique and fatigue.

Ultimately all was resolved and at 7:00 P.M. I signed, shook hands, and left.

Saturday, September 19, 10:00 A.M.: Home

Milt Felsen,[26] outlined a course for us to pursue vis-à-vis unions.

First go to the IA (International Alliance of Theatrical Stage Employees)—explain our project and be precise about what concessions we seek. If they say they'll go along, call a fellow named Conrad, representing the city, who will summon all parties concerned to a meeting.

I'm going to the coast next Tuesday to audition James Olsen and Kenny Mars. Must confess I'm leaning to Olsen.

---

26. Former union head and cinematographers' agent.

Tuesday, September 22, 11:20 A.M.: En route to L.A.

Norman drove Paul and me to Paula's house yesterday. Norman tipped me it is de rigeur for the director to ride in the front seat beside the driver.

Walking those streets, one senses a danger I want the actors to experience. To foster it, I will have as little police protection as possible.

The Pierces' brownstone even more appealing for our purpose on second viewing.

Wednesday, September 23, 8:00 A.M.: Beverly Wilshire

As I flew yesterday, I worked on the script—picking angles. Stopped at first hint of fatigue, so it gets only my best energy.

Had drinks with James Olsen. We meet for breakfast tomorrow after I've had a chance to case the competition.

Kenny Mars arrives in twenty minutes. Olsen having made such a favorable impression, I struggle to keep an open mind.

Thursday, September 24, 8:20 A.M.: Beverly Wilshire

So I kept my mind open and met Kenny Mars, who could be excellent.

I confessed my fear of casting two people (Shirley and he) who have done almost nothing but light material. Mars said, "That's *your* problem." I must stop thinking aloud.

Interviewed five other actors. None registered like Olsen and Mars—so different from each other and both so right for the part.

I decided to fly both to New York to meet and, just possibly, read with Shirley.

Front-page announcement in both trades, headed, *MacLaine and Gilroy.*

Jerry O'Loughlin[27] came by for a script. I told him I was interested in him for Charlie but couldn't cast the part till Otto was set.

Called Shirley in London. She'd seen *Five Easy Pieces* and was even more enthusiastic than I: "When I walked out of there," she said, "I made up my mind I was going to forget everything I knew about acting and start over."

---

27. He played the lead in *Who'll Save the Plowboy?* (my first play produced in New York, at the Phoenix Theatre), which won an Obie as "The Best American Play, 1961–1962."

Tuesday, September 29, 8:15 A.M.: Wyndham

Cameramen, actors, script girls, came through the office all day.

Norman thinks the 10:00 A.M. to 7:00 P.M. shooting schedule is not right for us since going past 7:00 P.M. would result in meal penalties, plus it gets dark before 5:00 P.M. toward the end of November. Paul checked the *Farmers Almanac* for sunset times.

Wednesday, September 30, 8:30 A.M.: Wyndham

In an hour, Paul, Norman, and I meet with the union heads.

It is more crucial than I was led to expect; if we don't get the concessions, it could make the whole deal prohibitive.

Thursday, October 1, 9:00 A.M.: Wyndham

The union meeting, chaired by John Hall at the IA, went nicely.

Paul introduced me. I gave a capsule history of the project, stressing how hard it had been to get this far.

Norman then outlined the concessions we'd need.

The heads of the various unions questioned us amiably, but it's clear we won't get all we want.

A disquieting note when we were asked if we had made deals with the Scenic Artists and the Teamsters, who were not present. We said no, which seemed to give pause.

Norman filled me in later: Scenic and Teamsters are very tight with each other and at odds with the IA.

I told Norman to set up appointments with Teamsters and Scenic.

Olsen arrived last night.

Friday, October 2, 8:30 A.M.: Wyndham

Called Shirley. We agreed I would bring Olsen to her place at 3:00 P.M. I told her we'd probably read a bit—sensed a little spurt of fear.

Went to the office, sent back money I'd collected via the SEC offer.

Urs Furrer seems to be the leading candidate for cinematographer.

Olsen arrived to go to Shirley's. While Olsen was in the john, Paul said he looked right for the part.

At the appointed hour, Olsen and I rang Shirley's bell.

While they chatted about how much they liked each other's

work, I noted Shirley's latest experiment with her hair: Simply combed back and long (with the aid of a fall), it gave her a clean, unaffected look just right for Sophie.

The reading commenced.

The first time through the sections I'd designated was deadly.

Here was my initial test as a director. I could do nothing and let Olsen disqualify himself, or I could try to coax something better out of him at the risk of failing.

Shirley out of the room, I talked to Olsen.

The second reading was a shade better, but not significantly.

Something bold was needed immediately, not just for Olsen but for Shirley, who was losing confidence in herself and the project.

I suggested we do it again, but this time I wanted Jim to improvise the prior life of the scene and launch into the script only when he felt ready.

Olsen began, and life surfaced as he described what it had been like at the office that day. Shirley did not participate until he segued into the script.

Back to the beginning. I asked Shirley to improvise with him this time.

Action: Olsen beautiful, always within the context of the character. And little old Shoiley, rising to the occasion, matched him. Life spiraled. They drifted into the script with Olsen still half improvising.

Again from the top. This time I wanted all points in the scene covered but totally improvised. To ensure it, I took Shirley's script away from her. Linus never looked more deprived.

Okay, go. And did they go. The life they generated evoked laughter, which Shirley showed a tendency to suppress. I told her to let it out, said the worst trap would be to think, "I'm doing serious stuff and must therefore reject my natural impulses." We did it once more improvised (as good as before) and then again, adhering strictly to the text.

Afterward we all three sat there, spent and happy, aware no audience could give us what we had just given ourselves.

Shirley like a kid on Christmas who finds a toy that wasn't on her list.

"I've never done that before," she said. "They wouldn't let me."

I told Olsen he'd have our decision Monday after we see Mars, whom he knows about.

After his departure Shirley said, "For the first time, I think I may be able to do this part."

Sunday, October 4, 8:30 A.M.: Home

At 1:00 P.M. Jack Somack (he's in that popular Alka-Seltzer speecy-spicy-meatball commercial) arrived. Sada Thompson, whom I'd long looked forward to working with, appeared moments later. Shirley arrived, dressed in a girlish outfit replete with a bow that made her look like someone trying to pass for years younger. I realized she was trying different clothes and hairdos to help me define the character.

The three of them began to read. One reading with Sada was enough. I let her know how much I liked what she'd done, said I'd call her on Monday. Ditto Jack.

Rose Gregorio read the part of Ruth with Shirley and was right on the nose.

Good feelings all around when I parted with Shirley.

Probably the first movie she's done where no one picked her up or took her home. She even had to pay for her own cab.

"My God," she said, "doesn't this company even spring for lunch?"

Paul reports we've been granted flexible shooting hours plus no wardrobe or makeup except when needed. Still no word from Scenic or Teamsters.

Lunching with Urs Furrer, cinematographer, I confessed the depths of my technical ignorance and the strength of my vision. Neither seemed to disturb him. I told Paul to make the deal.

Tuesday, October 6, 8:45 A.M.: Wyndham

I didn't look forward to Kenny Mars's arrival since I was sure Olsen would get the part.

Mars seemed quite relaxed. I suggested we walk to Shirley's. He asked for a clue about the part. I said we'd go over it a couple of times, preferred to see what he did on his own the first time.

I made up my mind to give him as full and fair a test as I gave Olsen—improvisation, the works.

Shirley and he chatted a bit. I said okay, whenever they were ready.

Mars began so naturally and effortlessly that it took a moment to realize we were under way. The subtext often lost, but whatever was happening between them was *really* happening. He wasn't acting. He was being. And Shirley was right there with him.

I resisted the impression Mars was making. It just couldn't be that the comic Nazi out of *The Producers* was going to get the role.

Hoping to discover a weakness, I moved to tougher sections. Scene after scene, and he was there every time, with Shirley keeping pace.

A bloody miracle was taking place—most inconveniently.

For all his "involuntary humor" (Shirley's phrase and a good one), there is a sadness about Mars that allows him to be as funny as he likes without ever obscuring the deeper purpose of the story.

There was no need to improvise.

We bid him adieu.

Both Olsen and Mars would be fine.

The former seemed a safer choice, a significant factor for a first-time director. The latter hinted at imponderables—a gamble.

"I'd hate to be in your shoes," Shirley said, signaling that in deciding between them, I was strictly on my own.

I walked and thought; ultimately referred the matter to my gut.

Calling Olsen, who had seemed a lock, with the bad news was one of the most difficult calls I've ever made.

Calling Mars was just the opposite.

Wednesday, October 7, 7:45 A.M.: Wyndham

I intend to shoot a roll of film in the location house with available light (natural light) only. This to give myself a standard of comparison before artificial light is added.

Sada Thompson, Jack Somack, Rose Gregorio, and Elena Karam[28] signed. What a fine cast we're assembling.

Norman and Paul disgruntled after a meeting with the head of the Scenic Artists union. He said other people who claimed they wouldn't use a scene designer and were given the go-ahead got nonunion people to do the work.

Despite assurance we'd play fair, concession is in doubt.

28. She was in *That Summer–That Fall* (my updating of the Hippolytus legend), starring Irene Papas (Ulu Grosbard directing), which introduced Tyne Daly, Jon Voight, and Richard Castellano to Broadway. If the writing had matched the casting, the outcome (a two-week run) would have been different.

Thursday, October 8, 7:45 A.M.: Wyndham

Shirley called. She'd just seen Kenny Mars on the Don Knotts show and was shaken by it. Was I sure he'd be all right, etc.? I assured her he'll be fine.

Shirley, voicing qualms about Mars for the record, makes me totally responsible if he fails. Should he succeed, I'm sure my exclusivity will vanish.

Norman, Paul, and I drove to Long Island to inspect locations. Shirley's name no little help in gaining access.

A Mrs. Parsons, hearing us discuss the pros and cons of doing the lovemaking scene in her bedroom, wanted assurance it wasn't a skin flick.

Paul, affecting injury she'd think such a thing, pointed out that I was a Pulitzer Prize winner.

Friday, October 9, 8:30 A.M.: Wyndham

Norman asked what I wanted in an editor. I said, "Someone who can accomplish my own intention better than I can."

Paul and I inspected rehearsal facilities at the YWCA. Got what we wanted for five bucks an hour.

On to Downey's to meet with the Teamsters head, Tommy O'Donnell.

The hostess showed us to a table for six in the center of the room. I said we wanted to talk. She said, "With Mr. O'Donnell?" When I said yes, she pointed to a back table and said, "That's Mr. O'Donnell's table because he shouts a lot."

O'Donnell and an associate arrived. Drinks for all. I felt comfortable—back with the boys of my youth.

After some chitchat, O'Donnell said, "Okay, let's hear it." I outlined our project and limited resources. O'Donnell listened attentively and indicated they would help us a bit on the condition that we live up to what we say.

Business aside, I enjoyed myself. When the check came, I told Paul to pay, but O'Donnell grabbed it, saying, "This one's on the Teamsters because that's the saddest fucking story I ever heard."

Ran to the Regency to meet Shirley and Sir Lew Grade: short, rotund, full of life and hope. We got on fine.

Saturday, October 10, 10:00 A.M.: Home

Auditioned a cat yesterday. An orange cat, not as big or ugly as I wanted but according to the girl who brought it, real savage when cornered. I said I wanted two cats in case one escaped or proved uncooperative. She said to recapture a cat that was out of control, you threw a blanket over it.

I read eight black actors for the part of the guy seeking money for train fare. Realized I'd never read a black actor before.

Met Urs Furrer and his crew. They seemed vigorous and interested.

Urs's natural caution and my impulsiveness should balance nicely.

Wednesday, October 14, 9:00 A.M.: Wyndham

First rehearsal at the YWCA yesterday. Most of the cast present.

I told them I desired no performance; I just wanted to give myself and them a sweep of the story.

After the read-through, I turned everyone loose except Shirley and Kenny.

Sara Cohen (Norman's wife) sat on the script, and it was just we four until 1:00 P.M. Broke till 2:30. Worked again until 4:30.

Shirley, delighted with the process, said it was the first time in her entire movie career that she had rehearsed.

All hands comfortable.

Friday, October 16, 8:30 A.M.: Wyndham

Whenever someone tests the material (probes a point for motivation or clarity), the material stands up to the challenge, which gives the actors confidence.

As we rehearsed, I noticed Kenny and Shirley looking over my shoulder. I turned. A black hand, disembodied in the entryway, seemed to be groping for a light switch. Whatever the hand was doing, it had a vaguely comic effect. And then a thin, angular man with a big smile appeared.

I asked if I could help him. He mumbled something about meeting a girl here. I explained that we were working. The smile unchanged, he said, "You're cold, man. You're the sort who would piss on a drowning man."

A thought hit me: Could this be an actor cleverly auditioning for that black man's role? If so, I had cast the wrong actor because I was feeling just what I wanted Otto to feel at that moment.

As he hung there repeating, "I just want to meet this girl," I, apropos of this being the YWCA, flashed the psycho who killed those seven nurses.

With a curse, he departed.

I asked Kenny if he was afraid. He said yes. Sara also admitted apprehension. Shirley mocked our timidity.

Kenny and Shirley arrived back from lunch in hot debate about the visitor, he trying to make her admit uneasiness at what took place, she adamant in denial. It was a perfect Otto-Sophie confrontation.

Rehearsal barely resumed when I heard the door open behind me. Turning, I found a heavy, short, dungareed girl in a sweatshirt.

"I want to play the piano," she said. I said I was sorry, but we were rehearsing.

"What are you rehearsing?" she asked.

"A movie," I said. "I know a lot about that," she said, approaching aggressively. "What's it called? Let me see the script."

"That scares me more than the man," Shirley whispered, and followed Sara from the room on some pretext.

The girl now poured out a long rambling, disjointed story of her life to Kenny and me. When Shirley and Sara returned, I told the girl we had to get back to work, and she went off demurely.

Kenny and Shirley begin to memorize and probe the script, which I, confident I can always go one layer deeper than they in sounding the "why" of any point or action, encourage.

Hired Bob Lovett as film editor.

Saturday, October 17, 8:30 A.M.: Home

A run-through yesterday that augurs well.

Paul and I to Shirley's to view her wardrobe. Went through the script change by change and had all her "costumes" in an hour and a half.

Told Urs I was not using a viewfinder. Not sure if that relieved him, as was the intention.

Took Shirley and Kenny to the house on Pacific Street to give them a feel of it as we rehearsed.

Wherever the house would not accomodate the script, we went with the life of the house and turned it to advantage. By the end of the day, we had the overall staging.

Some Sturm und Drang when I realized that with a week left before we shoot, we still lacked one major location plus several minor ones and the right car hasn't been found.

Have I been letting things slip, lulled by the fine rehearsals?

Tuesday, October 20, 8:25 A.M.: Wyndham

The Teamster captain drove Paul, Kenny, Shirley, and me to the location on Pacific Street. When I said we would break for lunch at 1:00 P.M., the captain informed me *he* broke at noon.

The crew arrived. Introductions all around.

We (cast and crew) walked through the house scenes to see what problems, if any, staging presented so far.

Looked at another cat. Too sleek and pampered. I asked the owner if he had anything tougher. He said he wasn't in the cat-torturing business, or words to that effect.

To Gage and Tollner's for lunch, where I separated from Ken and Shirley to do an interview for my just-published novel, *Private*.

Interview concluded, I collected them just in the nick of time. Shirley, after an argument, had gone to make a phone call, and Kenny was sure she was phoning her agent to get him fired.

We went back to work, and the moment of crisis was soon forgotten.

Roberta Hodes is our script supervisor.

Is Urs making nice to Shirley? He suggested an angle favoring her and proposed makeup to alter those character creases I love.

At one point I exclaimed, "I'm having a great fucking time." "I know," said Shirley, and seemed glad for me.

Urs shot available light footage, which we'll see tonight.

Danger: A couple of unions show signs of reneging. Paul and Norman meet with them at 10:30 A.M.

Wednesday, October 21, 7:45 A.M.: Wyndham

Started through the script with Urs at my shoulder. A rehearsal for the actors and a chance for Urs to familiarize himself with my intentions and the material.

Paul called with ominous news: The head of the Cinematographers union is taking back the concession previously granted that would let Urs serve as both cinematographer and camera operator.

If we give in, it will falsely signal there's more dough to be had inviting other unions to do the same.

More bad news: The Teamster captain says captains don't pick up talent and drive them to work, contrary to what O'Donnell led us to believe.

Norman and Paul recommended fighting the camera union (the serious threat), which they feel is bluffing.

I told them to set up a 4:00 P.M. meeting with the camera head. Resumed rehearsal, which went so well that I forgot the crisis until Paul and Norman arrived to fetch me.

I decided to go right to John Hall and the IA. Placed calls to him and spoke to Chris Conrad, who looks after movie matters for the city. Said I was afraid to begin the picture without reaffirming original commitments. Said I hated like hell to bring all this to Shirley's attention, but if I didn't get those assurances, I would have to.

Aware of her independent and volatile nature, Conrad urged me not to inform Shirley.

Walter Diehl, head of the IA, met us, with John Hall, in their conference room.

It was obvious they were sympathetic and that the camera head was playing a lonely hand.

Diehl phoned him in our presence and with jovial vigor asked if he had made a deal for a three-man crew, as we contended. I don't know what the other man said, but Diehl said, "It sure sounds like a deal to me."

In conclusion, he told the other man that the rest of the IA intended to keep making movies and did not intend to be stopped by him. Threw in a few "pappys" and "old buddies" to take the hard edge off his message.

When he hung up, he said the man sort of agreed that he'd made a deal, but it hadn't been "consummated." He laughed as he said it, asked me to hold off telling Shirley till the next day when he expected to have final word.

I don't know what transpired in the time it took us to walk to the camera head's office. But as we entered, he said it had all been a misunderstanding; told us to go back to work (conditions as previously agreed) with his blessing.

The available light footage was instructive and encouraging: I didn't know unaided light could do that much, and the house looked fine.

Norman took me to join the Directors Guild; $2-grand initiation fee.

I went to Shirley's to finalize her wardrobe. Found great things, especially the black hat and coat, which smacks of Chekhov and alters her entire personality.

Friday, October 23, 7:50 A.M.: Wyndham

Tempo quickens and confusion escalates at Pacific Street as heavy artillery is unloaded. Full crew on. Sound department had not been there before. While the crew rigged and made blackout screens for the windows, I took the actors through the script for the benefit of Urs and the sound man.

For test-footage purposes, we set up the first table scene.

Norman asked for quiet. Checked that everyone was ready, then said, "Roll."

Ronny Lautore stepped in front of the camera with the sticks: "Take one—scene one." Sound said, "Speed." I said, "Go."

Because it was only a test, I let the scene continue despite numerous flaws.

Urs took me aside and said Shirley seemed upset with him.

Moments later, Shirley confirmed Urs's suspicion by asking me what his credentials for the job were. Her complaint? She thought he was making her look ugly in a mistaken notion of what would please me.

I sensed her growing apprehension as we near the starting line. Felt she missed the familiar supports and reassuring attentions of wardrobe people, makeup people, et al.

A long wait for lunch produced an interesting vignette: Shirley beautifully portraying a spoiled child bawling for food.

We shot a night scene at the table, then shot Shirley in that black coat I love.

I tried to get her to repeat the story about the Masai ritual (drinking a mixture of blood and urine) that made her a blood sister. She couldn't do it in that coat, which locks her into ladylike comportment. It gives me a new respect for what the *right* clothes can do.

Urs drove Norman and me to scout the hospital, which will do nicely. Then to see a bar. I "bought" it and a nearby lunchroom as well.

Urs has three sons (four, five, six), raises flowers in a greenhouse. His first orchid came out yesterday.

Norman and I went over the budget. He is worried about over-ages that are already popping up.

More trouble with the Teamsters. The captain seems to alter his position each day about who he will drive or whether he'll drive at all. No other employees are accorded the solicitude offered the Teamsters. When one of the drivers calls, an ingratiating note enters Paul's and Norman's voices. Mine too.

To avoid overtime on an eight-to-five day, I must pull the plug at 4:30 P.M. so that the crew can travel to the other side of the Brooklyn Bridge by 5:00 P.M.

Went to Bide-a-Wee animal shelter and was shown two cats. The lady in charge said she'd bring them when needed. Told her what we hoped to achieve. The cats have no claws, but we won't tell the actors.

Saturday, October 24, 8:15 A.M.: Home

Viewed rushes of test footage. First impression (mine): Color too blue; angle not right; acting rigid; sound unsatisfactory.

Ran close-up tests and was pleased by their faces sans makeup.

Had a discussion with Shirley and Ken after we ran the tests a second time.

She criticized sound, but her performance was really the culprit. That somber "see the other side of Shirley MacLaine" thing we want to avoid. Her flu wasn't helping.

I spoke separately to the crew. Since I wasn't pleased, I couldn't say otherwise, but I think I could have phrased it better.

I felt Shirley's head—hot. Told her secretary to take her home.

Whenever, or almost whenever, I part from the actors, I feel the lifting of a weight. I now see how much directors have to repress.

Rumbles from the crew that they want fifteen minutes to get to an eating place for lunch and fifteen minutes to get back, plus their hour.

Monday, October 26, 6:30 A.M.: Wyndham

D-Day!

How do I feel? Not sure.

Do I know exactly what I'm going to do in that first scene? No.

Will the crew revolt about lunch? Will the sound work any better? Will the teamsters drive as agreed?

Can I forget all those things and focus on the actors?
We'll see.

Tuesday, October 27, 6:44 A.M.: Wyndham

Paul here at 7:15 A.M. Kenny and the driver arrived. Picked up Shirley, who was sniffly. Everyone studiedly casual.

Shirley gave me two miniature metal cats and a note: "Love. Love. Merde."

Crew setting up when we got there. Ready for the first shot about 9:15 A.M.

I had the comfortable feeling I'd done this before as I stepped to the plate for my first official at-bat.

We did the scene where the cat bites Sophie. Three takes. I, off camera, executed the bite with my fingernails. Drew blood the last time in my zeal to get a good reaction shot. Broke at 1:30 P.M. with the whole day's scheduled shooting done.

Back at 2:30. A confident spirit in all quarters. Maybe too confident. Took a bit long to set up bedroom shot. Light changed. Urs wanted to relight. Okay. He was right. Got two takes. Pulled the plug at 4:40 P.M.

Wednesday, October 28, 7:00 A.M.: Wyndham

Lost what I gained the day before due to intricate stuff in a small room. The rushes were encouraging.

Kenny is beautiful—all that life. Shirley great in the cat bite. But a bit stiff and superficial in the master. Might have to shoot that first scene over if the other takes (not available for viewing last night) aren't better.

Thursday, October 29, 6:30 A.M.: Wyndham

Everyone relaxed on the way to work, reflecting good feelings about the first day's rushes.

Began with the bathroom scene. Shot so many takes of Kenny changing from his underwear to his pajamas that at the end of the day he said he felt funny changing clothes without an audience.

A little tiff with Urs. I wanted a steep up-angle shot of Shirley seated regarding her wounded hand and Kenny standing over her. Urs set the camera at nothing close to the angle I wanted. He said all the overhead rigging would have to come down to get that shot. I still wanted it, so we'll do it after we're through with everything else and the rigging is no longer required.

Friday, October 30, 6:45 A.M.: Wyndham

We set up for a complicated master.

Sure something would go wrong the first time, I didn't shoot the rehearsal, which of course proved to be a beauty.

Fourteen takes later, we got it right again.

I find it hard to recall each day what I shot the day before.

An air of celebration after the rushes.

Things going so well that Paul tried to rewrite his contract.

Saturday, October 31, 7:45 A.M.: Wyndham

The crew threw an apéritif after work.

Rushes fine, the actors left.

Bob Lovett now ran (for Paul, Norman, and me) a rough assemblage of the opening sequence. It didn't work. We ran it a second time to be sure. In shock, I told him to be ready to work with me Monday night after dailies. I must know if a new master is needed before we leave the house.

Monday, November 2, 6:45 A.M.: Wyndham

Flew to Chicago Saturday morning to plug *Private*. The Willie Colon band on the flight cheered me up. They gave me one of their records.

Whiskey flask broke in my suitcase, prompting the cabdriver who took me to my hotel to say, "Boy, you must have had some night."

Did the Kupcinet show plus several interviews.

Flew back yesterday. Worked with Bob Lovett. Will have to reshoot first scene for sound and focus.

Tuesday, November 3, 8:00 A.M.: Wyndham

All sorts of bad vibrations yesterday morning. Kenny sour in the car. A general disgruntlement among the crew. Did no one have a good weekend?

It was almost 10:00 A.M. before they were ready for the first shot.

Again Urs gave me a bland angle when I wanted a steep rake. He said it would take two hours to prepare.

"Do it," I said. Fifteen minutes later it was done.

In the midst of shooting, Shirley said to me, "Do you think with all the natural stuff we're doing that maybe no one will know it's a movie?"

I said, "Now that you've dumped that load on me, you should feel untroubled and be able to devote complete attention to your work."

Got a laugh from all hands, including her.

We worked well in the afternoon. Picked up a great retake (I think) of the opening scene. *Now* they had the easy life I couldn't get because of first-day jitters.

The rushes beautiful. Urs got plaudits. The actors left feeling good.

Crew trouble: Norman wants to fire the grips, who are dissatisfied with the amount of overtime. I said okay, providing it doesn't provoke a landslide.

Wednesday, November 4, 6:40 A.M.: Wyndham

I think I fucked up the black-man scene. Unable to get what I wanted, I felt myself forcing.

Fourteen takes, and not at all sure what I accomplished.

Thursday, November 5, 6:00 A.M.: Wyndham

Enter the cat.

We did the upstairs easy stuff, during which Shirley effectively calmed the cat and got to know it.

Now downstairs for the cat escape, chase, and capture.

Two cameras ready and go.

One abortive take.

Second take went like the cat had read the script.

Broke at 4:30, exhausted.

To rushes in the rain. Ruth (my wife) present, which was probably unwise. I suspect that during shooting actors don't want to know the director has any family but them.

The new master of the first scene excellent, but Shirley, feeling her eyes are too dark, wanted it shot again.

We replayed it. Yes, her eyes are dark, but the damn scene plays. More objectionable to me was her hunching over her food like a voracious peasant, which is most un-Sophie-like.

A power struggle about the reshoot ensued. I finally said okay, which panicked Paul and Norman from the cost point of view.

We parted short of detonation.

Friday, November 6, 9:00 A.M.: Wyndham

Shirley apologized for being disruptive at the dailies.

I said since we were both volatile, a bit of friction was natural.

After two days in which she had very little time in front of the camera, she'd lost the character a bit, had slipped back to the "pathetic little girl." I zeroed in. She corrected it immediately.

Shot seven pages. Crew most cheerful and respectful. My God, the Teamster driver even offered to carry my bag!

My concerns about the black-man scene were unfounded. The improvisations worked excellently.

Then the cat-fight stuff. Great coverage by both cameras, but very, very dark. Urs depressed. We all applauded at the life on-screen, but all he could see was the quality of photography. "Home movies," he snorted.

I called the lab. Turned out that in developing the cat scene, Shirley came out too bright and since she was the star, they had brought everything down to make her look better. My God! All hands, especially Urs, mightily relieved.

Saturday, November 7, 10:00 A.M.: Home

We shot a retake of the chicken-liver scene. Herb Mulligan, the propman who cooks the livers, kept urging the actors to "eat up, eat up."

We broke at 2:00 P.M. Shirley and I lunched at her apartment and then rehearsed with Jerry O'Loughlin.

When rushes of the seven pages shot on Thursday ended, we were ecstatic. Shirley and Kenny were holding hands. Norman said he'd never seen the first two weeks go so well.

Sunday, November 8, 10:00 A.M.: Home

Paul called to report finding two more locations. He quoted Shirley as saying, "This is the best I've ever been."

Woke three times last night, certain I'd dozed off in the middle of a night bedroom shot and everyone was there (invisible in the dark) waiting for me to say "cut."

Monday, November 9, 8:15 A.M.: Home

Woke up again last night feeling I'd dozed off in the middle of shooting that night bedroom scene.

Sat up in bed, hoping the actors would speak and thereby orient me. Called for Norman tentatively. Ruth told me it was the weekend, that I was home. Relieved, I went back to sleep and dreamed that Dean Martin died, prompting fears about our schedule if Shirley attended his funeral.

Tuesday, November 10, 11:20 A.M.: Wyndham

Shot till 5:00 A.M. this morning—seven pages. Jerry O'Loughlin's first day. He wasn't giving me what I wanted and had been so confident he'd deliver that I'd never read him for the part.

His concept subdued, as though trying to prove he could have played Otto.

After several attempts, unsuccessful, to get him to adjust (Shirley whispering, "That's not how you told me he'd be"), I, seeing no profit in forcing him, gambled on the intense credibility he brings to everything.

The rushes won approval from all hands. Shirley brought her secretary, our first visitor, who laughed several times. The first indication of the buried humor I know is there.

This afternoon I meet with the head of the Scenic union, who threatens to strike if we don't put on a costume designer.

Wednesday, November 11, 11:45 A.M.: Wyndham

Worked till 4:00 A.M. this morning.

Think I disappointed Norman and Paul by compromising with the Scenic union, but a strike would kill us since the Teamsters won't cross their picket line.

A drizzle and mist. Great (I'm told) for color effect.

Jerry is fine. Shirley started to knock him early in the evening, but by morning his *life* (achieved with such apparent ease) had won her too.

Thursday, November 12, 9:00 A.M.: Wyndham

We shot from 6:00 P.M. till after 1:00 A.M.

Intermittent rain a hindrance, and we drew a crowd, necessitating extra cops.

The location a tiny luncheonette. Crowding, fatigue, and delay led to minor frictions. A grip argued with an electrician; Shirley felt someone in the crowd was mimicking her laugh; an assistant director threatened to quit because he feels he can't be himself around Shirley; Jerry O'Loughlin, who was in good spirits all night, suddenly flared up over nothing.

And so it goes at 2:00 A.M. when you've been shooting for several nights.

Friday, November 13, 6:45 A.M.: **Wyndham**

We were in the bar all day shooting day-for-night.

Shirley, with little to do for most of the morning, bore out the adage about "idle hands."

The last two shots (with her prominent) were good, and everyone knew it.

We saw three days' rushes. Praise the Lord, they were fine. I was a hero again.

Saturday, November 14, 11:15 A.M.: **Home**

The work goes beautifully, but Shirley becomes burdensome.

I suspect something's wrong in her private life and we're getting the shock waves. Thank God the schedule is only six weeks and we're halfway home.

Norman called the head of the Grips union and got an okay to fire the two men in question. Personally, they didn't bother me, but I had to back him in this.

The IA called to say they were ready to back us if the Scenic union struck. And if the Teamsters pulled out in support of Scenic, they, the IA, would drive the trucks.

No thanks—let them get another film to wage that battle over; told them that we'd made a deal with Scenic we can live with, so there will be no strike.

We finished shooting at 5:30 P.M. Took an hour and twenty minutes to drive to rushes. Got there too late to see more than the last two bar scenes, which looked fine.

When we dropped Jerry at his motel, (he was flying back to L.A. that night), Shirley, by way of adieu, called, "We'll have to postpone that hump till another time."

We parted on a happy Friday note.

Sunday, November 15, Noon: Home

I'm prepared for the hospital scene tomorrow. Five pages to shoot with numerous people. Have been careful not to over-prepare as I did in the bar, which tends to preclude life you might stumble on.

A vignette from Friday recalled:

SHIRLEY
(to soundman extracting a radio mike from her sweater)
You got all the hair off my chest that time.
The next time you'll be after my balls.
(then to me in an aside)
And you know I've got a lot of balls.

Monday, November 16, 7:00 A.M.: Wyndham

Norman said the head of the Grips union would be on the set today to make sure the firings were justified.

I said I wanted no big trouble over such a small item: If the union insists they stay on the job, they stay.

Tuesday, November 17, 7:30 A.M.: Wyndham

We shot in the hospital till 7:00 P.M. Most of the day in the emergency room while regular hospital work went on.

We wild-tracked a woman six months pregnant, epileptic, who had taken an overdose of heroin.

Unable to bear her screams, everyone, including the sound man, who showed me how to turn the recorder off when I had enough, left me there. Curious how directing a movie blunts normal sensibilities.

Wednesday, November 18, 7:30 A.M.: Wyndham

We have to keep the grips.

My relationship to Shirley like a scattered cloudy day: intermittently sunny.

We broke about 3:00 P.M. Used the rest of the day for miscellaneous casting.

To rushes: Almost sure I'll kill the pull-back shot in the bowling alley. The move is just too strong. Again I learn just how potent an instrument the camera is and how delicately it must be maneuvered.

Drank a bit determinedly last night, but not too bad. Needed a respite.

Thursday, November 19, 6:45 A.M.: Wyndham

It's raining, and we leave for the country location at 7:00. The first day the weather has really turned against us. Shot in the sculpture garden in the Museum of Modern Art all yesterday morning.

I'd written the scene to be shot inside the museum, but the cost was prohibitive. They offered us the sculpture garden for a lesser price. I put my writing hat on and made the scene (utilizing the garden) much more effective than it would have been inside. A strong argument for having the writer with you at all times.

Rose Gregorio worked beautifully with Shirley.

To rushes: Wally Rooney[29] was great in his subway moment. So fine that Paul hugged me from behind.

Bob Lovett ran a reel for Paul, Norman, and me. I have some minor criticisms, but he's cut that first bedroom scene skillfully.

I said, "Gentlemen, I think we've got ourselves a movie."

Friday, November 20, 6:00 A.M.: Wyndham

Rained all morning, so we went right into the bedroom love-making scene.

Trying to stay loose, I spilled over into being unprepared—created a vacuum resulting in confusion compounded by Shirley's notion that this is the scene where she must erupt wildly.

Urs and Shirley exchange winks as he slips her an extra light, as though I had no idea what they were doing. They're like fellow technicians.

To avoid a repetition of yesterday, I've been preparing since 4:45.

Saturday, November 21, 9:30 A.M.: Home

The Teamster picked me up at 7:00 A.M. I should note that they have never arrived a minute late.

Urs set up for the nude love scene.

29. He understudied Jack Albertson in *Roses* in New York and on the road. In a recent letter, recounted Jack's convenient illness, allowing him to go on when members of his family were in the audience.

While we awaited the actors, Mike Healy, the DGA trainee, recounted his experience working on a porno flick: "She's stripped and tied spread-eagle on the bed. Various types rape her. We leave her like that while we grab a quick sandwich. After lunch, we shoot the Mexican midget pervert scene, et cetera."

Shirley and Kenny arrive with the artificial casualness of people approaching a duel.

With only Urs, Ronny, and me in the room (the mike planted there), we went to work: Bathrobes off. Roll. Speed. Action.

They thrash about, roll over toward the camera, then back. Something provokes laughter. Genuine mutual laughter. I almost say "cut" but hold back. Doesn't laughter betoken release better than a faked orgasm?

At "cut," Kenny considerately covers Shirley. I return their robes. Then we shoot MOS (without sound) with the hand-held camera.

Taking a clue from Mike Healy's porno director, I cue them: "You've made it . . . Welcome home . . . He's your baby now . . ."

Between takes, good humor abounds. For the moment we all love each other.

Urs asks for one more. "Okay, this one's for Urs," I say.

We do another in slow motion.

We have it.

Joy and relief throughout the house.

I told Norman I was thinking of a shot from under a piece of glass, looking past a dead bird at Otto and Sophie as though the bird were floating in a half-full tub of water into which they peered.

Norman's pain at the prospect of setting this up was too evident for me to continue the gag.

A compliment from Urs, prefaced with "This isn't a compliment." He said this job was going the quickest of any he's ever done.

So the fourth week has ended.

Shirley's press agents (Rogers and Cowan) are now officially on the picture. As long as it isn't a production cost, I don't care.

Sunday, November 22, 11:45 A.M.: Home

Awoke during the night asking what scene we were setting up for. Ruth said it was the weekend. I went back to sleep.

Just finished preparing tomorrow's work.

Tuesday, November 24, 6:30 A.M.: Wyndham

L. J. Davis (his first acting role) was on the nose.

Pat McVey struck me as much more like my father than when he played in *Roses*.

The nude-love-scene rushes last night were excellent. Some applause.

Mike Healy said, "You observed the cardinal porno rule: No pickle, no beaver."

Wednesday, November 25, 5:45 A.M.: Wyndham

Shirley was "up all night" worrying about the damaged-house scene. She fears it wasn't damaged enough. I assured her if the rushes bore that out, we would reshoot.

When we saw the scene at dailies last night, I did wish the damage had read a bit larger.

Hearing Shirley's foot tap around the second take, I cleared the room of everyone but her, Urs, Paul, Norman, and me.

She declared she hated the scene, had reread the book, etc. etc. I said that essentially I bought the scene, but if she felt that strongly, I would re-shoot rather than jeopardize goodwill.

Shirley, the whole thing settled so easily, called me a genius.

Saturday, November 28, 11:15 A.M.: Wyndham

Shirley invited the producer and director of her next film to the set to see how we operate. They seemed dragooned rather than present voluntarily.

The sound man upset because Shirley told him we'd have to loop almost everything. I assured him his work was fine.

Tuesday, December 1, 7:00 A.M.: Wyndham

As we worked on the Claire-Leon scene, it gradually dawned on Shirley that despite Sada Thompson and Jack Somack having most of the dialogue, her reactions are critical.

"And I thought this was going to be my easy week," she said, feigning displeasure.

Rushes fine. My stock up again.

Wednesday, December 2, 6:00 A.M.: Wyndham

A deep fatigue hit me late yesterday afternoon.

The Claire-Leon scene is going well, but I'm losing time.

I scouted locations during lunch hour. Felt myself at odds with Paul and Urs about one site.

Went to rushes and for the first time (or second time) didn't particularly like them.

Flared up needlessly with Norman, Paul, and Lovett.

Thursday, December 3, 6:30 A.M.: Wyndham

A fresh surge of energy carried me through the day.

Did eight pages.

Sada was great. Take after take—all excellent. Shirley seemed mesmerized by Sada's consistency and concentration.

At one point I told Sada how much I liked what she was doing, and Shirley squealed, "He never says anything like that to me." I told her that if she ever did anything good, I would. All this in good spirits.

Norman has been doubtful about the rosy budget picture Paul paints, so I sent him to the accountant's office to go over our records carefully.

While he was away, Shirley confided that Lew Grade, "who watches after every penny," reported we are in good financial shape, which makes her look good in his eyes.

Norman returned all smiles. We *are* in good shape.

Tuesday, December 8, 6:30 A.M.: Wyndham

We shot the party scene on Friday. Mike McAloney pleaded for direction before doing his monologue. I told him every take would cost him a drink. He was letter-perfect.

C. D. B. Bryan, a freelance writer, covered us all day, hopefully for the *Times*. I let him come to rushes, which played well.

Must run to do traveling car shots.

Wednesday, December 9, 6:00 A.M.: Wyndham

Yesterday was almost a total botch. Very cold. Why oh why did we wait until now to do traveling shots? A close call when Kenny, driving, vision obscured by a hood rig, was surprised by a car coming in the other direction. His involuntary exclamation could end up in the film.

It took forever to rig the next shot. Another near mishap in the

Rover when a plug dangling by my head (I was squeezed on the floor in the backseat) burst into flame. No damage.

The sun set sooner than we expected.

We found no traffic jam.

The sound was screwed up.

Norman began to rush. Shirley began to carp.

Rushes were okay, nothing heavy.

Urs, Norman, Paul, and I stayed behind to plan so the same thing doesn't happen today.

Turned out (when I pressed) that a lot of things went wrong they hadn't told me about — like the grips forgetting to bring a vital piece of equipment, etc.

Tired, nerves short, I'm determined to finish the driving shots today. Inspired by Norman saying it can't be done.

> *10:20 P.M.*

All through with sound after a most productive day with the car today.

Kenny wrapped as of this evening.

Shirley will be finished tomorrow after the nude scene with her former lover.

Urs, Norman, and I will pick up a few passing shots on Friday, and the shooting is over.

Melancholy sets in as we near the end.

Thursday, December 10, 4:30 P.M.: Wyndham

We arrived at Abbott Van Nostrand's office (he owns Samuel French) at 8:00 A.M. to shoot the nude memory scene (Michael Higgins and Shirley) in Abbott's office.

Since it was a silent shot, I told Abbott we'd only be using his place for a couple of hours. But one thing after another went wrong (per usual when an easy day is anticipated), and we didn't start shooting till noon.

I told Shirley and Michael that since we had so inconvenienced Abbott, the least we could do was let him watch. They agreed. So bathrobes off and action.

The shot begins with a pan across Abbott's cluttered desk on which a William Saroyan book by chance was prominent. Between takes, I mentioned to Abbott that Saroyan had been an early influence on me.

Abbott returned from a break to inform that Saroyan was outside and took me to meet him.

Saroyan seemed solitary, dispirited—very old and very young simultaneously.

I asked him to verify what I'd heard about his writing *The Time of Your Life* in seven days. "Wrong," he said. "I did it in six, and on the seventh I rested."

I invited him to meet the company.

Shirley said they'd never met, but Saroyan contradicted her.

He thanked the cast and crew for not saying "Who's he?" and left.

The slow-motion camera broke down, so we had to postpone completion of the scene until after lunch.

I ran to Sardi's to speak to Blanche Gaines's Woman Pays Club. Told them their annual Christmas party last year was responsible for my making a movie of *Desperate Characters* because when I'd escorted Blanche the previous year, I'd spotted the Paula Fox novel on her desk and optioned it the next morning.

Raced from Sardi's back to the Samuel French office. I thought Abbott would be sick of all that flesh, but he never missed a take.

Then up to Fifty-sixth Street and Sixth Avenue to get the final shots: Shirley sauntering in traffic, making a phone call, window-shopping. All accomplished in thirty minutes without anyone recognizing her.

On to the wrap party and a few days off before the next phase: postproduction.

Tuesday, December 15, 6:15 A.M.: Wyndham

Viewed sixty minutes of the assemblage.

Despite warnings that assemblages can be traumatizing, I was unnerved.

Paul and Norman equally depressed.

I can't, *can't* believe all those fine scenes add up to so little.

Thursday, December 17, 9:00 A.M.: Wyndham

Bob asked if I wanted to edit roughly.

I hadn't thought about it, but instinct dictated I approach editing the same way I (for the most part) write: polishing each step before taking the next one.

We went through the opening and the cat fight, and were working on the bedroom when we quit at 6:00 P.M.

Given the few takes I printed, it is easy to review all material for a scene before taking a crack at it.

A fine day's work.

Tuesday, December 24, 7:45 A.M.: Wyndham

Working on the bedroom scene, we stumbled on a dividend in a take we'd rejected earlier. A silent beat, ripe with life, occasioned by Shirly omitting the last two words of a speech; Michael, not hearing his cue, uncertain what to do.

Result: a moment of genuine tension that is now in the picture.

At 5:00 P.M. to a viewing room to examine work so far on a larger screen.

A minor flaw here or there, but baby, it's *there*.

Ran it again, and the verdict stood.

Of course, it's only the first fifteen minutes of the picture.

Tuesday, December 29, 9:15 A.M.: Wyndham

We moved slowly yesterday—the material resistant.

Thursday, December 31, 9:15 A.M.: Wyndham

Bob and I in perfect tandem.

Came back from lunch to find him trying to improve a scene I was satisfied with. He worked hard at it. When we viewed it, he conceded it didn't work. Later I was wrong about something. A nice give-and-take.

Bob confessed he loathes Otto, feels Sophie deserves all sympathy and he is the villain.

1971
Friday, January 8, 8:45 A.M.: Wyndham

Wrestled all day with the first bowling-alley scene.

As Bob tried various approaches without success, it occurred to me it wasn't as a director I had failed but as a writer, by introducing a red herring—the first false note in the picture. We eliminated the scene.

Jonas Halpern, Shirley's press agent, is concerned her billing will be too big. This voiced magnanimously, but I suspect Shirley is preparing a lifeboat.

Monday, January 11, 8:45 P.M.: Wyndham

We had three reels ready at 5:00 P.M. today—went to the screening room.

My overall reaction is a good gut feeling that can't be counterfeited.

Feeling cocky and confident, I asked the editors what they thought, invited complete candor. The invitation no sooner expressed than the assistant said he had no idea at any time where the picture was going, had no interest in it, etc. In summary—a total washout. I thanked him. He said it was his pleasure, which I believe.

I cling to my own gut reaction, and that reaction was thumpsup. I mean *thumbs-up*! Ponder *that* slip.

Tuesday, January 12, 8:00 A.M.: Wyndham

Like all addicts, I seem to be letting everything else slide (relationships, correspondence, beard) as I concentrate on the movie.

Thursday, January 14, 8:45 A.M.: Wyndham

Two rather distinguished-looking men in their sixties rented the cutting room next to ours for a day. Beautiful classical music poured from their room. I jokingly suggested it was a cover for a porno movie.

Bull's-eye: One of the equipment guys spliced some of the bits in their trash can.

Two girls, a guy, and a vibrator, in various combinations.

Friday, January 15, 9:30 A.M.: Wyndham

I did not leave the cutting room in a sanguine mood yesterday.

Saturday, January 16, 8:45 A.M.: Wyndham

Fifty pages of script—thirty-one minutes of film.

We begin to work Saturdays today.

Why didn't I make Claire's apartment the sloppy eyesore the script calls for?

Again I learn: For disarray to register fully, you must exaggerate it since the camera tends to mute and beautify.

Tuesday, January 19, 9:30 A.M.: Wyndham

Worked Saturday till 7:00 P.M.

The elevator man thought Rick Shaine, the apprentice editor, was my son. Now I know how Dick Powell felt when that stewardess asked if he was my father on that flight to Cuba to scout locations in 1958.

Wednesday, January 20, 8:00 A.M.: Wyndham

Bob strongly opposed to several cuts I suggested. I invited him to make better ones. He did. We ended the day on an up note.

Thursday, January 21, 8:45 A.M.: Wyndham

We seem to be notching many fine moments.

Worked from 10:00 A.M. till 8:30 yesterday.

Usually one of us (Bob or I) is cooking.

When I sense he has a hot hand, I defer, and vice versa.

Sunday, January 24, 10:00 A.M.: Home

Heard Lee Konitz (stellar altoist) at the Village Gate on Friday. Came away feeling I'd like his reaction to the picture. His classic modern sound a likely candidate for music needs.

Thursday, January 28, 9:15 A.M.: Wyndham

This afternoon at five we screen the first five reels (fifty minutes) for Paul, Ruth, and the sound cutter.

Met the critic Judith Crist in the elevator. She likes *Private*. Said she was looking forward to the day when I make a movie of *Who'll Save the Plowboy?*

Friday, January 29, 4:45 A.M.: Wyndham

How could the screening turn into such a nightmarish disappointment?

I'd seen the first three reels and the last two at separate screenings and loved them.

Yesterday they didn't jell.

The screening not helped by the assistant editor sighing conspicuously to communicate his boredom.

"What is it, 'us' against 'them'?" Paul asked.

Bob present, I told his assistant that while I could abide his dislike of the picture, I couldn't tolerate his behavior at the screening, which amounted to sabotage.

He offered neither apology nor denial, so I fired him.

Bob said he would have done the same.

We put air back into the picture: two minutes of pauses and reactions that in our zeal for pace we'd deleted.

A call from Jonas Halpern saying a man influential in selecting the Cannes Film Festival entries would be in town from this Sunday to Wednesday. Did I care to show him anything?

I did a lightning calculation, said that while I could show only six reels, I was willing to take the chance. He said he'd get back to me.

Abe Mandel (ITC) called about screening for the Cannes guy. He questioned the wisdom of showing unfinished work.

I agreed it was risky but said if he and Shirley felt the possible gain was worth it, I was willing.

Seeking to hedge, he asked if they could see it before the Frenchman. I said no on the pretext that it would disrupt my schedule. I am not about to expose myself to double jeopardy.

Think how I'd feel if they viewed it and deemed it unworthy for the Frenchman's eyes.

Paul reports that Shirley fired the sound man on her new picture for telling her to think of him as her gynecologist when he had occasion to place his lavolier mike in some intimate place. And who did she replace him with? The sound man (John Bolz) from *Desperate Characters* she'd distressed by telling him every line in the picture would have to be looped.

Have just returned from a screening of the first five and two-thirds reels, which went most encouragingly. Fuck the understatement—it went so well that Paul started to breathe again.

This despite the day's not dawning auspiciously. Mornings after a night with McAloney rarely do.

My head cleared as the day progressed, and an hour or so before screening I was in good spirits and relaxed.

Went to the ninth-floor screening room at 4:30. At 4:45 Lee Konitz arrived with his wife, Tavia. Lee seemed shy and apprehensive outside his own world. We rolled, and I was caught up at once. Heard Lee and Tavia laugh. My interest sagged a bit around the party scene but came back almost instantly.

Overall reaction was up. Paul's relief was palpable. Lee and Tavia really liked it. Lee spoke of the suspense, an ingredient I felt was there when I wrote it but due to familiarity had completely forgotten till he mentioned it. I told them theirs were the first eyes to view what we had without any prior knowledge of the script, and of course that is the key test. Lee is getting a script. I'll invite him back to view the whole in two weeks, and then we'll talk.

Rick said, "It's getting there." Bob looked bemused. He is pleased by the reactions, but I doubt he will ever really like the picture.

The best demonstration of Paul's renewed confidence is that he bought Bob and me a bottle of booze each and stayed for a drink that became a little party.

Oh yes—we've spent $280,000 to date.

Tuesday, February 9, 8:30 A.M.: Wyndham

At 8:30 tonight, I show the first six reels to Favre Lebret (who runs the Cannes Film Festival), Shirley, Mandel, and a couple of other ITC executives.

Shirley called in a flap last night, as though the risk of displaying unfinished work had just occurred to her. I said I felt the possibility of being invited to Cannes was worth it.

"Can I bring Jonas and Margaret?" she asked. "Yes," I said. "You *are* a gambler," she observed.

Wednesday, February 10, 10:20 A.M.: Wyndham

Paul called to pass word from Jonas that Favre Lebret couldn't view the picture till 10:00 P.M.

I had the screening time changed.

Shirley, informed of the time switch, said, "Screw Lebret and the festival."

Much back-and-forth on this all day. The outcome: Shirley,

Paul, the ITC team, and I dined together prior to the screening.

At 9:30 P.M., I excused myself to precede them and make sure all was ready.

Arrived at the screening room to find one of the generators had broken down and the screening in doubt.

Enter Jonas and Margaret Anderson with a cadaverous-looking man (Favre Lebret) who, exuding weariness, made it plain he was putting himself out to accommodate us.

Taking me aside, Jonas said in deference to Lebret's fatigue we should screen at once despite it wasn't 10:00 P.M.

I told him to call the restaurant and goose the others.

Now Margaret came out to say that Lebret said that if we didn't start right away, he would depart. "And he will," she appended.

I told her to remain in the foyer as though she were looking for me.

To add to the confusion, Bob Lovett, not realizing who Lebret was, had started running the picture to test the projector. Ran a minute or two by the time I stopped him.

Miss Anderson said she would sit beside Lebret to translate. Not the ideal way to see a film that relies so heavily on dialogue, and the sound track uncorrected.

Minutes dragged, and still no sign of the others.

With a parting sally ("If you start the picture before Shirley gets here, she'll explode"), Jonas went downstairs to await them at the entrance.

Margaret ducked inside to see how Lebret was doing and returned like a shot to say if the picture didn't start at once, he'd be gone.

Weighing the alternatives (it was 10:10) I signaled Bob to begin.

Several minutes into the picture, I heard doors open and Shirley and party scurrying.

Despite all this, I got caught up in the picture intermittently.

When the sixth reel ended, I was almost surprised to find Lebret still there.

Awkward silence reigned.

I shook hands with Lebret, who was squired out by Jonas and Margaret, like orderlies. As they departed, Jonas said he liked it, with enthusiasm.

Shirley said, "Wow, what a strange picture."

Abe Mandel said, "Some of the tracks could be cleaner" and "Think about music."

I suspect that despite the script making clear it would be unlike any other Shirley MacLaine picture, the ITC people still expected Irma La Douce.

We scattered as quickly and as oppositely as possible, like a gang after an unsuccessful heist.

I was disappointed but not discouraged. I guess my own basic estimate of the work has settled in.

Thursday, February 11, 9:20 A.M.: Wyndham

Shirley called. She, Paul, and I have an 8:30 date tonight. She said nothing about the picture, but her tone implied respect tinged with uncertainty.

George Bowers, an editor working next door, stopped in very depressed. They had screened their film *Slave Ship* (Imamu Amiri Baraka, then LeRoi Jones) for Lebret at 9:30 yesterday morning. "Sent a limousine for him, even had croissants, and with five minutes to go he starts to leave," George recounted. George told him there was only five minutes more, but he left anyway.

George said Lebret asked his interpreter what "shit" meant, which makes me suspect his no-English bit is a cover. I mean, can you imagine any movie critic in New York, even the dimmest of them, requiring a translation of *merde*?

Jonas reports Lebret "was not put off by our picture."

Geraldine Fabricant is our new assistant editor.

Friday, February 12, 9:30 A.M.: Wyndham

Well, she's delighted with herself. That is the essence of our meeting with Shirley last night. So delighted that she wants to see more and more of Sophie. "I don't know how you got such a performance out of me," she said, "but I want to thank you for it."

I praised Kenny Mars, or tried to, but she, while allowing he was brilliant while shooting, now thought everyone paled beside Sophie on the screen.

It was a happy and relaxed meal since we all three have delivered exactly what we set out to do: Paul in terms of the budget, which so many people questioned; Shirley in changing her image completely and effectively; and I in delivering the film I saw in the novel.

A quote from Bob Lovett apropos the Los Angeles quake and why people are so profoundly disturbed by such upheavals: "It's because one of our fundamental assumptions about life is that the ground beneath our feet has integrity."

Saturday, February 13, 7:15 A.M.: Wyndham

I dreamed of a rave review of the film, only they had the title wrong. Called it *Hollywood Blue*.

Thursday, February 18, 8:15 A.M.: Wyndham

Shirley wants 100 percent billing above the title and no other actor's name as big as hers, which I take as a vote of confidence.

Paul spoke to Kornblum because we need more money.

Kornblum gave him the $5 grand requested and, commenting on the six reels he'd seen, said, "This is no *Cat Balou*. It's a serious picture."

Incidentally, this $5 grand brings total expenditure to date to $295,000.

Tuesday, February 23, 9:30 A.M.: Wyndham

Reel seven polished, we worked on the opening credit sequence.

When you find yourself saying "it doesn't matter what's behind the titles" and "music will help," you know you're settling for something less than good.

A better opening occurred to me, but it will necessitate a re-shoot, which we have scheduled for next Saturday afternoon, weather permitting.

Saturday, February 27, 9:15 A.M.: Wyndham

Cannes doesn't want us, Jonas reports. But we've had an inquiry from the Berlin Festival.

Tuesday, March 2, 9:15 A.M.: Wyndham

On Saturday we cut till 2:00 P.M. Then Paul picked Rick Shaine and me up and drove to good old Pacific Street where Urs awaited us.

For ten bucks, we gained access to a roof that looked promising.

I found an angle that offered the street, a pull-back, a pan to "our" house—a hold—and then a slow zoom (all in one), which I hope will be our title shot.

The Pierces never introduced Paul and me to their guests arriving for a party as we, sweaty and dirty (replacing storm windows removed for matching purposes), finished up.

Paul's theory is that the Pierces had bragged about the Shirley MacLaine movie shot in their home and feared introducing us as producer and director would have deglamorized the tale.

Wednesday, March 3, 8:00 A.M.: Wyndham

As we reviewed the nude lovemaking material, Jerry Fabricant winced at the first sight of Shirley and Kenny in the buff. Would she have reacted similarly if the actress were unknown to her? She wasn't sure.

By 6:00 P.M., I'd gone dead on the sequence. Too much flesh.

The title stuff shot on Saturday looks great.

Reeves Sound Studio called to confirm that we have an April 1 mix date.

When Bob declared it would be impossible to make the early mix date, Paul said, "Bob, this whole picture was impossible." Bob said he would need three extra people working weekends as well as daily overtime to save us from our "recklessness."

Despite that, this gets us close to $330,000—the figure at which I begin to trade points for cash—I acceded to his request.

Saturday, March 6, 9:00 A.M.: Wyndham

A new pulse in the cutting room. The earlier mixing date and consequent pressure has added a spice I suspect is secretly enjoyed.

At 2:00 P.M. we assembled at the Reeves Studio to screen for Dick Vorisek, the acknowledged mixmaster of the world.

An amiable man radiating quiet competence, he found our sound tracks not nearly so poor as Bob anticipated. We will have to loop, but minimally.

As we walked back to the cutting room, Bob allowed there might be some humor in the picture because Dick and Sandy (the additional sound editor) laughed repeatedly—this conceded with a slight air of incredulity.

Tuesday, March 9, 7:15 A.M.: Wyndham

Only a few hours until the 5:00 P.M. screening, and we were still on reel six.

We jettisoned all the slow-motion lyrical lovemaking stuff. Back to the script, which depicts it as hungry and loveless.

One hour left to do the drive-back sequence. Bob cut it in—bang, bang, bang. And done. And a great improvement.

At 5:00 P.M. we gathered in the screening room. Blanche, Paula, the Ehrenbards,[30] Lee Konitz, Jim Hall (eminent guitarist) Dick Katz (pianist), Ruth, Tony.

Despite numerous technical flaws, the picture registered overall. Paula had a solid affirmative response.

Wednesday, March 10, 6:45 P.M.: Wyndham

I am about to leave for an 8:00 P.M. screening for some fifty people—our first major test.

Lila Ehrenbard asked if she could see it again.

Paula is coming back with five or six friends.

Repeat business already. Can you blame me for feeling bullish?

Thursday, March 11, 1:55 A.M.: Wyndham

They loved it!!! More later. I sleep the sleep of the innocent—whatever the hell that means.

10:45 A.M.

There were fifty–sixty people present last night.

Herself (Shirley) appropriately late (fifteen minutes). The sight of all those people stunned her momentarily. "Who are they?" she asked. "I don't know most of them," I said—only a slight exaggeration. "My God, it's a legitimate audience," she exclaimed.

I dispensed with the customary apologia about it being a work print, and away we went.

I felt it take hold at the top and continue with but a momentary flagging of interest here and there.

We surfaced to applause, not tumultuous but genuine.

When a screening is sour, everyone flees. These people lingered.

Bill Goldman was ecstatic. It would be immodest to quote him.

30. Lila and Bob. Longtime friends and backers of most of my plays and movies. Bob (a senior partner at Kelley, Drye & Warren) represented me when I sued Paramount, ABC, Four Star, and Dell Books for illegal use of the character Amos Burke that I created for the TV series "Burke's Law." It took thirteen years and two trials, but we won.

Friday, March 12, 9:10 A.M.: Wyndham

Bob had everything nicely prepared for looping (at Manhattan Studio) at 2:30 P.M.

Shirley there when I arrived. We hugged in mutual congratulation.

She is a wizard looper, has the lightning reflexes of a premier gunfighter.

Looping over in two and a half hours. Paul, Shirley, and I went to a bar where she, ever so timidly, suggested we redo the fuck scene with Kenny—to make it more savage.

I said I was happy with what we had but if she felt strongly and would see we were not penalized for the added expense, then fine.

My quick okay jerked her up short. "What will we do there?" she asked, as if the reshoot were my idea.

Tuesday, March 16, 8:45 A.M.: Wyndham

Kenny and I picked Shirley up at her place. The air of a return grudge bout beneath the amenities.

The crew glad to see each other.

I shot Kenny bare-ass and with a sweater. Invited them to go at it to their heart's content.

Finished by lunch. I lifted a few, more in relief than celebration.

Wednesday, March 17, 9:30 A.M.: Wyndham

Looped Kenny in two hours.

Paul met Adeline Leonard, who said, "I hear the picture's great." Paul asked the source. She said her chiropractor is Bill Goldman's chiropractor.

Set recording date with Lee Konitz for Friday. He's using guitar and bass instead of piano, which sounds right for the spare, unobtrusive sound I feel is needed—if anything is needed.

Screened the reshot love scenes. I guess we improved a bit. Worth $5 grand? I'm not sure.

No word from Kenny. I wondered if the screening I arranged for him disappointed some fantasy that it was *his* picture.

Friday, March 19, 9:30 A.M.: Wyndham

"Got your passport ready?" Paul asked by way of announcing a royal summons from Shirley to screen for Sir Lew before mixing. I told Paul that it couldn't be done without lousing up our schedule.

Paul relayed this to Shirley, who said she didn't give a damn about schedule or cost, wanted the picture in London on Monday, period. I told Paul to tell her no way, which is where it stands.

Sunday, March 21, 11:00 A.M.: Home

Arrived at the music recording studio at 3:30 P.M.

Jim Hall there. Konitz arrived. And then Ron Carter, on bass.

When set pieces didn't work, I suggested they improvise as the picture ran.

They leaped at the opportunity. Ron Carter especially adept, often starting to play just when I felt the need.

Some lovely stuff resulted, but I have a disturbing intuition that as fine as the music is in its own right, it will not enhance the picture.

We'll see how the screening goes tomorrow without music, then test music and picture for ourselves. I hate to disappoint Konitz.

Tuesday, March 23, 9:10 A.M.: Wyndham

We screened, without music, for forty people.

Despite projector breakdown and some weird noises, reaction was favorable.

Mandel and the ITC-ATV boys much higher on it than at the six-reel screening.

Thursday, March 25, 5:45 A.M.: Wyndham

We screened, for ourselves, with music yesterday.

Today I sit here agonizing (no exaggeration) whether there should be any music at all.

It works fine in places. But even limited to those places I fear an interruption of the overall mood.

I'm tired of watching the picture, which makes the decision more difficult; the bored mind welcomes any diversion, and music, being a new ingredient, fills that role.

Some intuition sent me to see *Ma Nuit Chez Maude* (Eric Rohmer) yesterday afternoon. It is brilliant. In black-and-white *and* no music.

I left the theater feeling strenghtened in my vision and judgment.

Will there be music?

Still no definitive word from my intestines.

Wednesday, March 31, 9:15 A.M.: Wyndham

Arrived at Reeves at 10:00 A.M. to check reels prior to mix.

It went smoothly because our sound requirements are minimal.

Again and again we discarded added sound effects and went back to the production track. The rule of thumb seems to be if it distracts from the dialogue, it's wrong.

Oh yes—there's some magnetization on the first reel, so it must be retransferred. If I knew what magnetization was, I'd explain it.

We came to the initial music cues.

Seen and heard on a good sound system and big screen, I knew unequivocally, that music was wrong for this film.

My decision no sooner made than Dick Vorisek volunteered, "For what it's worth, I don't think either of those music cues work."

"You're my man," I said, happy to have my own decision (not yet announced) seconded.

I reluctantly called Lee Konitz, who accepted my decison most gracefully.

Friday, April 2, 8:10 A.M.: Wyndham

We worked all day on reel one.

By 6:00 P.M., when we reviewed it, I'd lost all perspective and judgment.

Feeling rotten, I went to the doctor, who, finding me run down, prescribed something to get me through the next few days.

Handing me the capsules to be taken twice a day, the druggist said, "Boy, are you going to have a good time."

Saturday, April 3, 8:10 A.M.: Wyndham

I arrived at the mix feeling like myself. Reviewed the first reel and deciding I had settled for less than I wanted, did it over again.

I'd underestimated what was required of the director in the mixing process. Envisioned it as a vacation in that cozy room while the mixer did nice things to the picture.

Wrong. I have to make decisions constantly, can't tune out for a second.

On to reel two.

My energy began to wane about 4:00 P.M. when I was due to take the second capsule. But the capsule was gone from my pocket.

Dragging by 6:00 P.M., I okayed reel two tentatively, pending review on Monday.

Tuesday, April 6, 8:30 A.M.: Wyndham

We did a reel and one-third yesterday. After mixing, we went back to the cutting room and worked on sounds to come.

Wednesday, April 7, 8:30 A.M.: Wyndham

Finished two reels yesterday.

Thursday, April 8, 7:30 A.M.: Wyndham

Mixed reels six and seven yesterday.

Paul called with a thought from the boys at ITC-ATV: Why didn't we appeal our *R* rating and try and get an *X*! A disturbing thought because it suggests how they might intend to sell the picture.

Saturday, April 10, 9:00 A.M.: Wyndham

We concluded mixing at 6:00 P.M. yesterday.

We've spent about $322,000 so far.

I told Paul that *his* area, the business side, is the only area I have delegated completely to someone else and not ultimately regretted it.

Friday, April 16, 10:00 A.M.: The Churchill, London

Paul and I got a 9:30 A.M. TWA flight to London. We had the eighteen reels (nine sight, nine sound) in three containers. We flew first class to ensure we will not be separated from the film. The thought of its being treated as ordinary luggage offends. First class not full, so the film had two seats all to itself. We checked it occasionally. No problem. Like traveling with well-behaved children.

We arrived in London about 10:30 P.M. Film boxes in hand, we disembarked like two Rover Boys.

A chauffeured car met us. Took us to the Churchill. We had a two-bedroom suite. Paul got the noisier room. That, plus his carrying two boxes of film to my one, distinguishes him as coproducer.

Monday, April 19, 9:00 A.M.: London

A car picked us up at 7:00 P.M. and drove us to Shirley's house in Windsor Forest. Shirley and Pete Hamill[31] looked settled and

31. Journalist, novelist, screenwriter.

domestic. Shirley said Sir Lew has been getting offers from major studios to buy the distribution rights sight unseen. I said I feared giving the picture to someone who might try to sell it like any other MacLaine movie.

Tuesday, April 20, 8:15 A.M.: London

The big screening scheduled for 8:00 P.M. Shirley had invited some fifty people. Paul asked a few. I asked only Jim Goldman[32] to have one stabilizing presence in the room.

At 11:00 A.M. Paul and I went to the screening room at 3 Audley Square. The projectionist most accomodating. We tested a reel. Jolly good we did! Some problem with sound that could have sunk the evening if not caught.

At 7:30 P.M. Paul and I had a drink in our suite. He danced to a Latin beat from the radio and, regarding himself in a mirror, toasted "The New Leaf." His pleasure and expectation were child-like and endearing.

He went on ahead to greet the people while I used the time alone to prepare myself.

When I arrived, almost all seats were filled. Shirley listening to Sir Lew like some wise coach or parent.

I made my little speech. "It's a work print, which means all scratches have been preserved and no sounds or colors corrected. Beyond that, everything is perfect."

With me at the fader (sound control switch) and Sir Lew beside me, the lights dimmed, and we were off. I sensed fair sailing as several people responded to the off-stage voices in the title se-quence. A little chuckle signaling they picked up the comic over-tones in Kenny's irascibility. After some fifteen or twenty minutes, Sir Lew nudges me in the ribs and whispers, "It looks like money so far."

At the end, a silent moment. Have we failed? Then the dam gives way, and praise is everywhere. Well, not everywhere, but in sufficient abundance to mark the night a winner. Sir Lew takes bows for a half hour. As always after a successful screening, peo-ple linger. Jim Goldman agrees with brother Bill that it's the best

---

32. Playwright (*Lion in Winter*), long-term fellow member of the Dramatists Guild Council, brother of William Goldman, and like him, an Academy-Award-winning screenwriter.

thing he's seen in quite a while. Volunteers it's one of the few things he and Bill agree on.

Following the screening, Shirley hosted a large party at L'Ambassadeur.

Pete Hamill said the picture acutely captured the city as "a casualty of the war."

Margaret Gardner (publicist, Rogers and Cowan's London branch) said it was a shame Lebret couldn't have seen the entire picture, felt sure he would have grabbed it for Cannes if he had.

A bit of dialogue overheard between two members of our party, apparently close friends at one time, who hadn't seen each other since a bitter falling-out:

> FIRST MAN
> That was a terrible, terrible
> thing you did to me.
> SECOND MAN
> Yes, but you still love me. I can
> see it in your eyes.

Thursday, April 22, 8:30: A.M.: London

A car picked Paul, Margaret Gardner, and me up at 7:00 P.M. and then to Shirley's home where Lew Grade, Bernie Kingham, his right-hand man, and Abe Mandel awaited.

Sir Lew confessed that he attended the screening expecting to be bored and was most pleasantly surprised.

"My success is based on the fact that I am the common man and what I like makes money," he said. Marveled at what we got on the screen for only $300,000 plus. "I expected two people fighting in a room and then going to the next room and fighting some more. How did you do that, outside and all, for so little?"

Sir Lew encourages you to speak honestly. He also listens. No mean feat, either one. After discussion, the plan is that Paul and I go to New York to correct colors (timing), make minor sound adjustments, and return to London with an answer print to show to a representative of the Berlin Film Festival on May 6.

Margaret Gardner had contacted Dr. Bauer, head of the festival, who said his man would be empowered (after the screening) to say whether we would or would not win "Best Actress" or "Best Picture" award. If we "win," we will then enter the festival, which Shirley will attend, a crucial factor in the illicit equation.

Thus the world turns, and so much for art. Most interesting were our reactions to this contemplated larceny. No one, including me, objected.

What would Pete Hamill say if privy to a similar fix in the world of sports?

My own rationalizations: (1) It's all a meaningless crock. (2) We deserve to win in any case. (3) Maybe we won't win. (4) Maybe I'll reject the prize at the most public moment, a la those Gary Cooper pictures.

Saturday, April 24, 9:00 A.M.: Home

We got a 9:30 A.M. flight from London.

Arrived in New York to find we had goofed by not registering our film when we took it out of the country. Now we had no proof that it wasn't a foreign-made flick being smuggled in. The Customs man who stopped us was pleasant, but his superior was a dyspeptic sort. We were polite, confessed to ignorance and guilt as charged. They impounded the film. Since it was Saturday, we could reach no one who might help. I asked how we should proceed to regain the film. The superior sneered that was my problem.

Monday, April 26, 8:15 A.M.: Home

Paul called. The film has been sprung by ITC's Customs broker.

Thursday, April 30, 7:45 A.M.: Wyndham

We screened the first answer print at 6:00 P.M.

The picture too warm—too yellow. All agreed we should go cooler in the next print. Bob said it was the best first-answer print he'd ever seen.

Monday, May 3, 3:30 P.M.: Wyndham

A call from England. Margaret Gardner wanting to know if I wished to stack the house with friendly folks for the Berlin Festival test screening. I said absolutely not. One "helpful" laugh could sink us.

Wednesday, May 5, 7:00 A.M.: London

Paul and I flew BOAC to London yesterday at 10:00 P.M. One drink, a nibble, then a Seconal (Paul's first), and we slept like babes, five solid hours. Awoke to sunshine, breakfast, and London, due in forty-five minutes.

Still didn't have the right documents, so English Customs detained us.

While we waited for Grade's Customs broker to settle matters, Paul called attention to a wall notice prohibiting the dumping in England of "moving dolls' eyes."

After the broker ransomed us, we entered our waiting car and off to the Dorchester.

Margaret Gardner hinted that the representative of the Berlin Festival may not be empowered to ensure us any prize, which seemed to make her anxious but I found relieving.

Had dinner with Paul, Peter Katz,[33] and an actor named Ty Hardin who had starred in that TV series "Cheyenne." Told about my picture, Hardin said it was just the sort of subject matter he hated. I invited him to the screening to keep a balance in the room.

Thursday, May 6, 7:50 A.M.: London

Paul took the film to the screening room and played two reels to make sure all was in order.

At 2:00 P.M. we met with Grade's people. Everyone agreed the picture would require special handling—limited release, etc.

The screening preceded by cocktails. Among those present were Dimitri Tiomkin (composer), the duke and duchess of Bedford, David Rayfiel (writer), Ty Hardin in a black velvet suit and open green shirt, plus two people from the Berlin Festival.

Margaret nagged me to chat with the festival representative until I finally went to him and said, "If you think I'm avoiding you, you're right. In a few minutes you'll be seeing a picture which must speak for itself. Afterwards you and I can talk."

Early in the screening I realized there would be few laughs. But overall, the picture held stronger than before.

No applause, but no rush to exit at the end. Everyone just sat a moment.

First to his feet and up the aisle was the writer David Rayfiel.

33. An American living in London who would subsequently be the producer of the television movie I wrote and directed (*Gibbsville*), based on John O'Hara's stories, in 1975.

He waved glancingly at Paul as he hurried out, which registered as negative.

I kept an eye on the Berlin representative during the screening. Noted him leaning forward intently during most of the film. More significant, his English associate, who had forewarned he could only stay for thirty minutes, remained throughout.

Dimitri Tiomkin most enthusiastic in his praise.

Paul shook my hand in congratulation. I didn't understand. He said the German man had already made up his mind, wanted us to come to the festival. And Tiomkin was going to try and get us to Moscow.

We dined at the White Elephant. Tiomkin, seated elsewhere, sent drinks. The glad tidings phoned to Shirley in Hong Kong.

To cap the evening, I won a tidy sum shooting craps at the Playboy Casino, tidy enough so they invited me back as a guest the next night.

To cap it further, we arrived back at the hotel to find a note from David Rayfiel expressing admiration for our achievement.

Friday, May 7, 8:00 A.M.: London

Paul and I lunched in Sir Lew's private dining room with him, the German and English representives of the Berlin Film Festival, Margaret Gardner, and Bernie Kingham.

Before the meeting, Margaret informed us that not only was the German representative not empowered to ensure that we would win a prize, but Dr. Bauer could not present us with any such guarantee. I told her, and meant it, that I preferred the competition to be legitimate.

At lunch Sir Lew dazzled the German with mentions of millions and empire, couched in personal anecdote. He told of his last time in Berlin, New Year's of 1929, when he was a dancer. He mentioned owning Northern Music, which means all the Beatles songs. He spoke of a bank trying to force another ten million pounds on him for a project. All of this done artfully and entertainingly, and with an occasional German phrase thrown in.

Sir Lew not only saw us out but personally hailed cabs in the rain. I told him I was game for Berlin and a true competition. If Shirley and he agreed, I would proceed with the German subtitles, which were a prerequisite.

Tuesday, May 11, 7:30 A.M.: Wyndham

Abe Mandel called. The Berlin invitation had officially reached London and been accepted.

Wednesday, May 12, 8:30 A.M.: Wyndham

Met with the man who runs the titling service. Made arrangements to screen the picture and meet the person who would do the translation.

Thursday, May 13, 8:00 A.M.: Wyndham

Screened the picture for Monica Metzmer, a reporter for German newspapers who had never done anything like this before.

Friday, May 14, 8:00 A.M.: Wyndham

Monica will have the translation for me Monday. Jon Swann, a poet whose German is fluent, will check it over, and we'll proceed from there.

Thursday, May 20, 10:00 A.M.: Wyndham

Screened the picture on Tuesday at 11:00 A.M. for Jon Swann and Monica.

I gave Jon Monica's translation of the first reel. He had minor quibbles but felt she could do the job.

In the absence of a German equivalent for *Desperate Characters*, we'll call it *Sophie and Otto*.

Wednesday, May 26, 8:45 A.M.: Wyndham

At a Dramatists Guild cocktail party, I sensed an actress of some reputation being unprecedentedly cordial, which puzzled me. Then a light: I am a director now.

The man who spots the subtitles laid out the places where they go and listed the number of words the audience can absorb at each point. It looks like we'll be straining the limit.

Friday, May 29, 7:15 A.M.: Wyndham

Instead of making a new print to include the subtitles, we are "burning" them in on an existing print. This process will not give us the quality of the other, but it's faster, which is a prime consideration if we are to meet the festival date.

I think I've found an ideal formula for subtitling: Have a native of the country who speaks English work in tandem with an American fluent in the foreign tongue.

What the first one translates the second reads back to me in English, ensuring nothing lost along the way.

Friday, June 4, 9:30 A.M.: Wyndham

Margaret phoned about proposed posters for the Berlin Festival, which sound dreadful. One of them says something like *These two people have one thing in common: They're sick.*

I'll call the man responsible tomorrow and offer my critique as politely as possible.

Tuesday, June 9, 9:30 A.M.: Wyndham

I told the man in London I would have the poster I envisioned prepared in rough form and rashly promised to have it in his hands this morning, twenty-four hours later.

I drove to the city where Paul had the photograph blowup in the works. He suggested the Blaine Thompson Agency might do the rough. I called Matty Serino, who had worked on my play ads at Blaine Thompson. He agreed most generously. I went to his office, showed him what we wanted.

Then to TVC (the lab) at 2:00 P.M. where the new print intended for Berlin was about to be sent to the subtitling place.

I was tempted to let it go sight unseen. But the hard-learned rule "The improbability you don't guard against is the one that always occurs" stopped me.

A few minutes into the print revealed it a mess. Something had shifted. No time to wait for a new print, so I'll have the titles burned in on the one we have.

Back to Blaine Thompson. They'd done a very nice lettering job. I told Ingram Ashe[34] to bill us, but he wouldn't hear of it.

Now how to get the material to London and delivered by morning?

---

34. Head of Blaine Thompson (now deceased), who sat with innumerable playwrights on opening night in the small room above Sardi's when the first TV reviews came in. He was a kind, empathetic man. I'm sure the nights that resulted in heartbreak didn't lengthen his lifespan.

We tried both air terminals in an effort to find someone who would do this for a fee. No luck. Learned it's against the law to deliver mail by hand.

We took a cab to Kennedy, to the BOAC cargo office. There, for $25, we dispatched the envelope to London.

Sunday, July 4, 1:45 P.M.: Hotel Kempinsky, Berlin

Two weeks ago Paul called London to get approval for our travel expenses to Berlin. Sir Lew said okay for Paul and his wife (Nydia) and Ruth and me, but not for Kenny Mars.

Kenny's contribution too great to be slighted, I picked up his tab. About to leave for a tour of East Berlin.

Our crucial screenings take place today at 3:00, 6:00, and 9:00 P.M. in a huge barn of a theater appropriately called the Zoo Palast.

Wednesday, July 7, 1:00 P.M.: Berlin

We won two Silver Bears: Shirley as Best Actress (tied with Simone Signoret) and me for script.

The Golden Bear, Best Picture of the festival award, went to the De Sica film *Garden of the Finzi Contini*, which Rex Reed, one of the judges, said beat us by a single vote (5–4).

He also said I had seemed hands down to get the First-Time Director's award when the Danish man who was jury head (and pressing to get the award for a Dane) said that he had documentation that proved I had directed four other pictures.

Rex stewed about this till the vote had almost gone to the Dane, then announced it was possible he had been fooled and I *had* directed other pictures *but* he was going to call the American Screen Directors Guild, and if they confirmed I had not directed before, he was going to expose what was taking place and create a scandal. The Danish judge now denied saying I had directed before.

Outcome of all this: They eliminated the First-Time Director category entirely.

Berlin Memories:

Jacques Tati accepting for Signoret and upstaging Shirley, who then upstaged him by imitating his walk when she arrived on stage.

As we entered East Berlin (a sudden draining of color), I was taken off the tour bus in East Berlin and had to pay a fine because my passport photo was beardless.

Margaret Gardner skulking hither and yon in search of festival gossip and a clue to our fortunes.

Kenny Mars hugging me the night we screened and took our bows. "That's a great picture," he kept saying in sharp contradiction to his opinion the first time he saw it in New York.

Sir Lew gave the biggest party at the festival on the shrewd premise that the smallest picture was obligated to do so.

A grand festival party at the Schloss. I gave Liza Minelli (in Berlin shooting *Cabaret*) a lift to the party. Photographers snapped our picture as we exited the limousine, giving rise to rumor of romantic liaison in the next morning's paper.

A million less people in Berlin than before the war. Not enough people to fill those wide streets. Gives a haunted feel.

Friday, July 9, 11:30 A.M.: Hotel Alexandre, Paris

Ruth and I, as usual, flew here in separate planes.

I was seated across the aisle from Stanley Kauffman, once drama reviewer for the *New York Time* and now movie critic for the *New Republic*, who'd been at the Berlin Festival.

I had a momentary impulse to introduce myself but afraid it would be misinterpreted, refrained.

Sunday, July 11, 11:00 A.M.: Deauville

Called home. Learned the *New York Times* and *Variety* had stories about the Berlin Festival mistakenly reporting that I'd won an award for Best Director and Writer. We will not seek a correction.

Friday, July 16, 9:30 A.M.: Dublin

A sensible appraisal of *Desperate Characters* by Godfrey Fitzsimmons in this morning's *Irish Times*.

Saturday, July 17, 9:15 A.M.: Dublin

Ruth said something the Irish tourist bureau would love: "We've been here a week and have yet to meet one rude person."

Yesterday we went to Dun Laoghaire to see the Martello Tower, where Joyce once dwelled. Asked a trio of men if they could direct us to it. They seemed ignorant of its location until one of them said, "Oh, you mean that place where the writer lived?"

Thursday, July 22, 8:25 A.M.: London

Paul reports Rugoff saw the picture on Sunday and felt it would be a hard sell, though he liked it. Subsequently he had a woman whose opinion is important to him see it. She apparently liked it a great deal more than he did. Other people in the Rugoff organization are seeing it today.

Margaret called to read Rex Reed's Sunday piece in the *Daily News*, titled "Berlin a Dud." He reveals all the intrigue in the jury room, in which I figure prominently. Margaret fears she'll never be able to go back to Berlin.

Saturday, July 31, 8:45 A.M.: Home

Julian Schlossberg (the Reade organization) likes the picture and offers us the Baronet on Third Avenue or the Festival on Fifty-seventh, which rents for less. It was Schlossberg's opinion that the picture stood a much better chance on Fifty-seventh, away from the youth-oriented milieu of Third Avenue. I agree with him.

Paula Fox called to inform that Stanley Kauffman had a paragraph about us in this week's *New Republic*: "The pleasant surprise is an American film, the first directed by the playwright, Frank D. Gilroy, called *Desperate Characters*. The same theme as Feiffer's *Little Murders* handled differently. I'll save extended comment for its U.S. opening but its quality gave the Berlin Festival a nice lift when it was sagging."

I learned, via Mandel, that Schlossberg saw the picture not once but twice and really flipped, took Mandel over to look at the Festival Theatre.

Shirley thinks the Festival is the sort of theater that Otto and Sophie would go to.

Mandel checked with Lew Grade about the Festival Theatre. Lew's attitude was that he knew nothing about the general situation here. If that was what we all wanted, it was okay with him. Having cleared it with Shirley, Mandel was now asking my opinion. I said, "Lock it up."

So we open at the Festival on September 29.

We will pay Reade $6,500 a week and can stay as long as we do so. We pay for our own advertising. In addition, Reade gets 10 percent of the gross above $6,500. This arrangement is called "four-walling."

In talking to Paula Fox, I said that many of the people I liked most in the world will be immune to the virtues of this picture, which saddened me. She said she experienced a similar alienation as she proceeded further and further along her own way.

Saturday, August 7, 9:00 A.M.: **Home**

We settled on a screening room for the critics—the Park Avenue. It seats about forty-two. We booked it for the dates Jonas laid out.

Story in the *Hollywood Reporter* says we were warmly received in Moscow, had to have a second showing for turnaways.

Tuesday, August 10, 10:00 A.M.: **Home**

A note from Margaret with what really happened in Moscow: They showed it in a big place with a Russian woman playing all the parts over the original sound track. She said that while the heads of some of the delegations liked it, many of the general audience walked out. Margaret's conclusion: "We indeed *do* have a rare bird."

I met Julian Schlossberg. Liked him. His enthusiasm for the picture seems genuine. He showed us the spacious lounge at the Festival. Painted a picture of us still there at Christmas and people warming themselves waiting for the next show.

Thursday, August 26, 10:00 A.M.: **Wyndham**

Monday, August 23, was a year to the day from coming off the Colorado River and getting a call from John Gay saying he had shown the script to Shirley.

Jonas showed us Liz Smith's rave in *Cosmopolitan*.

Paul and I checked the Park Avenue screening-room projector, found a defect that was corrected. Have we ever checked anything and *not* found a defect?

Paul saw the beginning and end of the 6:00 P.M. press screening. He said the audience didn't stay for the final credits, which upset him.

He caught the end of the 8:30 P.M. screening. Said the audience remained through the credits and Pauline Kael smiled at him enigmatically as she exited.

Friday, August 27, 9:00 A.M.: Wyndham

The projectionist at the Park Avenue is unhappy with the changeover marks. Why is he telling us now, after five critics' screenings?

We've decided against having a trailer because no two minutes of a picture that stands or falls on cumulative effect can do justice to either the picture or Shirley's performance.

We went to ITC to check the new artwork. It's fine. Then to the Festival Theatre to plan the "front of house" displays.

Went inside and found that the full screen was not being exploited. Turned out the projectionist had been using the wrong mat for who knows how long.

Wednesday, September 1, 8:30 A.M.: Wyndham

Paul and I to Rogers, Cowan to check the guest list for last night's screening at Lincoln Center.

The *New York Times* called at 4:30 P.M. to say that Vincent Canby would attend.

Met Paul at Lincoln Center.

First impression of the theater: not a movie house but a converted high school audutorium. The projectionist checked the changeovers. At least six different marks of varied hue and design, to which he now added his own distinctive stamp.

We tried a reel. An awful hiss from the speakers. It's almost eight o'clock. They get new jacks and fiddle while I weigh canceling the screening. People arrive. The hiss abates to a tolerable degree.

Up to the booth while the audience files in below. I checked the boxes the two prints (one a backup) arrived in. It's 8:20 (ten minutes to post time) when we realize the reels have been mislettered.

It's 8:30. Canby hasn't arrived. We've roped off seats for him. The hall almost full. Three cops arrive in the booth to view the picture. They wish me luck.

At 8:40, the place is filled. No Canby. What to do?

Spotted Kauffman going in. Flattered he was seeing it a second time. At 8:45, sans Canby, I said, "Go."

Canby never did show up.

Thursday, September 2, 8:30 A.M.: Home

A call from ITC to report that Penelope Gilliatt (the *New Yorker*), who was at the Lincoln Center screening, liked the picture. Wants to see it again, wants a script, wants more bio material on me.

Friday, September 3, 10:00 A.M.: Home

Paul just called to report he inadvertently learned that Pauline Kael loathes the picture. Let's hope Penelope Gilliatt reviews for the *New Yorker*.

Judith Crist's office called. She'd like to see the picture at 3:00 P.M., Tuesday—alone. We are scrambling to set it up.

Thursday, September 9, 10:00 A.M.: Home

A call from Jonas: "*Newsweek* will be a rave, and they might do a cover story on Shirley."

Friday, September 10, 9:00 A.M.: Home

More requests for solo critics' screenings.

Monday, September 13, 8:00 A.M.: Home

The first ad in the *Times* yesterday. I like it. Penelope Gilliatt called. We had a nice chat. Answered some background questions.

Tuesday, September 14, 7:45 A.M.: Wyndham

All reviews we have advance word on are favorable. Does this mean those not leaked are bad?

A call from Jonas to meet Wanda Hale of the *Daily News* in a Chinese restaurant.

An elderly woman nearing retirement, she knew nothing of the picture. I learned infinitely more about her than she did about me in the course of the interview.

Vincent Canby has switched yet again. Instead of Thursday at 8:30, he will see it alone on Monday at 2:30 P.M.

Getting in a cab at Fifty-seventh and Sixth, I found a woman's handbag and informed the driver, who said it probably belonged to a woman he just dropped at the Festival Theatre.

My theatre. What an omen! He wanted to go right back. I said okay.

As we pulled up to the Festival, the girl and her escort were just running out, having discovered the loss. She thanked the driver profusely while her escort gave him sixty cents. The driver took less exception to the paltry reward than I did.

I told the driver I had a movie opening at the Festival next week. The driver said, "That Shirley MacLaine is great. I liked her in *Bloody Mama*." I said that was Shelley Winters. He said, "I always get them mixed up," and asked for my autograph. We rode the rest of the way in happy duet. He insisted on turning off the meter. I overtipped outrageously.

Thursday, September 16, 10:00 A.M.: Wyndham

To Jonas's office to pick up a copy of Stanley Kauffman's *New Republic* review.

Besides viewing the picture twice, he's read the book; sees all that's there, plus a thing or two I never intended but will be glad to take credit for.

Went to ITC. Tried to impress upon them that Kauffman and Gilliatt go to the heart of the audience this picture was intended for. They nod, but do they really understand?

A call from a Miss Harris at the *New Yorker* to say that Miss Gilliatt was reviewing my picture and loved it, and would I supply a few more facts? The review comes out next week. Eat your heart out, Pauline.

I read Bernard Drew's reported rave and found it considerably less than that. Why do press agents feel obligated to exaggerate?

The projectionist at the Festival said he'd heard I was a perfectionist, so he warned of a defect in the sound system, which they are having fixed.

Called Lee Konitz. Invited him to pick any of his own records that he might like played between shows at the theatre. "We'll come down and play live," he offered. I explained why that wasn't feasible.

Jonas reports a "rave" from WINS radio. I'll wait till I read it.

Cue, in a fall film preview, lists word-of-mouth on us as good.

Monday, September 20, 8:30 A.M.: Wyndham

Canby sees the picture at 2:30 this afternoon. Because it's a

Jewish holiday, someone must make a special trip (the office is closed) to attend him. How goy can you be?

The *Times* ad looks good.

Tuesday, September 21, 8:15 A.M.: Wyndham

Time and *Newsweek* will be out today, today, today.

Wednesday, September 22, 9:00 A.M.: Wyndham

Newsweek, touted by Jonas as a rave, is good overall, but qualified. I again asked Jonas not to exaggerate. Just the facts, man.

Len Harris of CBS called for a film clip to use on the six-o'clock news. Would he do that if he was going to kill me?

11:20 A.M.

Picked up *Village Voice* just now. A bad review—bad and extensive. Be still, my heart.

1:00 P.M.

Just back from the theater. Abe Mandel and other ITC people clustered outside. They said there were quite a few people at the first show.

An elderly woman came to the cashier and asked if it was a tragedy. The cashier forwarded the question to me. I said it was a drama. The woman said she liked to see Shirley in happy things.

I picked up *New York* magazine and the *New Yorker*. A devastating pan from Judith Crist, which seemed aimed with a vengeance at Shirley. The *New Yorker* a scholarly rave, which means you can't sum it in a few quotes, must digest its considerable entirety to get the full thrust.

So how do I feel?

So not so bad.

It is the number of people in the theater that cheers me the most. Did I really believe no one would show up?

5:00 P.M.

A pulse, a pulse—by God, there is a pulse!

A great notice from Bill Wolfe in *Cue*.

Stuart Klein of Channel 5 wants a film clip. He is seeing the picture at this moment and will review it at 10:00 P.M.

In addition to Gilliatt's fine review, the capsule at the front of the *New Yorker* is great. Is that Gilliatt too? Can Kael change it when she takes over next month?

We just received word that we'll get three and a half stars in the *Daily News*.

To the theater. Peeked inside. A goodly group. The picture looks at home up there.

Still no banner. I told Irving that Abe said if the banner didn't get there soon, he, Irving, would have to stand in front of the theatre with a megaphone. His face drained. "I'm kidding," I said. He said Abe was capable of that.

Canby called Jonas for photos. Is he making a dart board?

Thursday, September 23, 8:25 A.M.: Wyndham

Canby didn't like us much, but it hardly hurts at all.

Let me recap how we come to this happy state.

Len Harris (CBS), the most important of all the radio and TV reviewers, with our logo behind him, began, "Frank Gilroy wrote the Pulitzer Prize winning play, *The Subject Was Roses*, and then never did anything quite as good till now. And now he's done something even better." In short, a rave.

We stopped at the theater en route to dinner. Business great.

We made selections for the half-page quote ad we're running in tomorrow's *Times*, with Sir Lew's blessing and money.

> *11:00 A.M.*

The phone isn't ringing like it did yesterday. That's the effect of the *Times*. Friends who read nothing else will think we are lost till they see tomorrow's ad.

> *3:10 P.M.*

Would you believe, business up some 40 percent over what we did the first two shows yesterday.

More good notices, *Womens Wear Daily*, *Newsday*, Stuart Klein on Channel 5, and CBS radio.

> *7:30 P.M.*

Just checked, and at 7:00 P.M. we dipped under yesterday for the first time.

I'd like to blame the weather, but its only gray. My heart dips accordingly.

Friday, September 24, 9:30 A.M.: Wyndham

Business down last night. We have much riding on the big ad in today's *Times*.

The *Times*, the *Times*, the *Times*. The more they kill you, the more money they make.

> *5:00 P.M.*

Business appears to be *very*, *very* good. The 4:20 show, with a steady line of twenty people, must put us well ahead of yesterday.

Audiences come out looking glazed, assaulted, numb. Not your usual Shirley MacLaine experience.

The A-frame with this morning's ad went up at 4:00 P.M., and people flocked to read it. Some read it on the way out, as though to discover what it is they've just experienced.

Saturday, September 25, 9:00 A.M.: Home

Last night I went back to the theater for a final check before going home. Are you sitting down? There was a line all the way to Fifth Avenue—and people still buying tickets. They finally announced a sellout and turned the others away. That was the 9:30 P.M. show, and still one show to go. While I watched, Paula Fox hailed me from across the street. She and her husband, Martin, had driven over to see what the theater looked like. So we experienced the first long line together. And we both felt guilty, undeserving and uncomfortable. A slight line, fine—but this was too much. Surely the gods would smite us.

Paul just called: We did $5,500 yesterday!

Sunday, September 26, 10:00 A.M.: Home

Abe Mandel brought two couples from Mamaroneck to see the 9:30 P.M. show last night and was delighted that he could not get in.

A note from Paul: At 10:00 P.M. the theater manager was predicting $8,500 for the day.

Paul said last night's line went to Fifth Avenue and around the corner. Oh, to reach Doubleday's!

Monday, September 27, 8:00 A.M.: Home

We did $8,700 on Saturday. Abe called to say that at 6:00 P.M. Sunday we were ahead of Saturday. He said, "When these figures get out, I'll have to fight my way past distributors into my office."

I told him the rule of thumb I feel we should follow wherever we go: "The smallest theater in the most sophisticated part of town."

I phoned Shirley in London. She, like me, is happy, but surprised to the point of suspicion. What makes us so is that the grosses can only go down, where we had looked forward to a slow start and gradually modest build. She put Warren (Beatty) on the phone. He said, "Eight thousand in one night sounds great to me." In the background I heard Shirley squeal "*Eight thousand seven hundred!*"

Tuesday, September 28, 10:00 A.M.: Wyndham

We broke the Festival Theatre's all-time weekend record, $22,117. In addition, our Saturday figure was the biggest one-day figure ever recorded there, and our Sunday figure was the biggest Sunday ever recorded.

Joy, Joy, but still that uneasy feeling I used to get in punting days when my horse was too far in front too soon.

Wednesday, September 29, 10:45 A.M.: Wyndham

Abe was asked by Frank Yablons, head of Paramount, to let them take over distribution of the picture. Abe said he offered a $350,000 advance. I opposed the deal. I told Abe I feared they would not give the picture the special handling it required and thereby kill the goose.

Thank God I have that clause in the contract saying any sub-distribution deal for the United States and Canada is subject to my written approval.

Saturday, October 2, 10:00 A.M.: Home

My education continues.

Found Abe with a Mr. Roth who runs an outfit that checks against larceny at the box office or by the exhibitor or distributor.

Theater checks are done either "blind" (secretly) or "open" (a person stationed in the cashier's booth, counting). The people Roth employs for these checks are graduate students. Abe asked how he could be sure *they* were honest. Roth said he had checkers who checked the checkers. He said it's no wonder there's stealing, considering the cash first flows through the hands of low-paid cashiers and theater managers. Higher-echelon thievery is done with bookkeeping. He said two sets of books was not uncommon: one with low figures for public consumption; the other with true

I suggest. . . .

Shirley reacts. . . .

We consider. . . .

Shirley, between takes.
The bandage marks
the cat bite.

Otto (Kenneth Mars) and Sophie (Shirley MacLaine) find their
summer place vandalized.

Left to right—myself, Kenneth Mars, and Paul Leaf, on a day when things must have been going well.

Jacques Tati (*left*) presents Silver Bears, Berlin's version of the Oscar, to Shirley and me.

figures for the government because they fear the Internal Revenue Service.

"But that's about all they fear," Roth said. "Even when they're caught red-handed, they are rarely prosecuted or sued."

A good review in the *Hollywood Reporter*, which, refreshingly, says I'm a better director than a writer.

A late call from Abe. Sir Lew had the following offer from Paramount: a $500,000 advance against 50 percent of every dollar they get for film rental up to $2 million; a sliding scale in their favor thereafter. Sir Lew wanted my immediate answer. I said I wanted time to think and that before I would even consider the proposition, I would have to be guaranteed all deferments ($25 grand to Paula, $60 grand to me, of which Paul gets $10 grand) would come out of that advance.

11:25 A.M.

Sir Lew called. He will guarantee the deferments. Weissberg calls him in an hour for particulars.

Sunday, October 3, 9:30 A.M.: Home

Sir Lew insists we take this deal at once. Seasoned his pitch with a dash of fear: "Our grosses are dropping—we must act before the news gets out."

I told him I felt an obligation to the actors and other people who'd been given profit pieces of the picture. He said that since the Paramount offer (for domestic-theater release only) almost brings us even, they will surely get some money. Contrary to what he promised Shirley and me, he hasn't any intention of distributing this picture himself. So there's no alternative.

Frank Weissberg called: "We've got a deal subject to a meeting with Frank Yablons, head of Paramount."

Tuesday, October 5, 9:00 A.M.: Wyndham

Abe, Frank Weissberg, and I to Paramount to meet Frank Yablons.

He had six people with clipboards taking notes as he launched into the specifics of release. I interrupted him to say that I would like to review the terms of the deal. "Review?" he said. "I thought we had a deal. If we don't, say so. I might change my mind. You dropped from eight thousand to six thousand four hundred yesterday." And on and on.

When he concluded and it was still plain I wanted to review the terms, he told the clipboard people to vanish. "But stand by, while we talk money."

The terms are as outlined previously. "I should have gotten TV," Yablons complained. Remarked on our falling grosses again and what a fool he probably was to make this deal. As he talked, I got the distinct impression that he hasn't seen the picture.

The terms agreed on, Yablons summoned the clipboard brigade. "I want a Cinema One campaign around the country. The best under-six-hundred-seat house in all the major cities. If there's a thousand seat that's good and a small one that's shit, take the thousand."

Despite his repeated promise that the picture would receive boutique treatment, I envisioned it passing into a meat grinder.

Apropos Abe's attire, Yablons said, "I never trust a man with jade cufflinks and a monogrammed tie."

On which note we departed.

P.S.

As anticipated, Paramount opened *Characters* wider than promised, with predictable results.

Despite Sir Lew's assurance that the $500,000 he got from Paramount, for American theatrical rights only, would just about recoup his production cost, the statement I received from ITC, in 1981, claimed they were still $160,000 out of pocket despite having grossed $836,320.23 on a film made for $369,445.92. One of the more intriguing charges was "INTEREST—$147,031.83," which smacks of usury to my uninitiated ear, but I'm sure Art Buchwald (patron saint of all "profits-if-any" participants) understands.

On the plus and more important side, I knew that in directing *Characters* I had found the perfect and replenishing complement to writing and would do it again. How George Stevens divined that before I was aware of it remains a puzzlement.

Late Bulletin

Gil Karson (lawyer), who now handles my affairs at the Colton office, just received (at his request) a financial statement from ITC that reveals as of June 30, 1991, *Desperate Characters*, which has grossed $1,213,523.00, is in *profit* to the tune of $27,161.96.

That it has taken over twenty years for *Desperate Characters* to join the exclusive (many would say mythical) ranks of movies acknowledged to be in the black, however modestly, doesn't diminish my sense of wondrous achievement.

I think I owe Buchwald a drink.

Late Late Bulletin

More profits.

I tracked down the seventeen actors and crew members (profit participants) that ITC was unable to locate.

Modest sums but the surprise and delight of the recipients made it a most rewarding chore.

MITCH LEIGH & THE McLAUGHLINS   present a Frank D. Gilroy film

once in paris...

starring

**WAYNE ROGERS
GAYLE HUNNICUTT**

introducing

Jack Lenoir

composer/conductor Mitch Leigh
co-producers Manny Fuchs/Gérard Croce
producer/writer/director Frank D. Gilroy

68th St. Playhouse
3rd Ave. at 68th St.   RE 4-0302

Once in Paris

Arriving in Paris in 1968 to work on the script of *The Only Game in Town*, I was given a car and a driver.

The driver, Jack Teboul, an Algerian who as a youth attached himself to an American army unit that he accompanied to Paris, was a sometime bit player and effects man whom (by his account) John Wayne had nicknamed "Black Jack" during the making of *The Longest Day*.

Black Jack's English, gleaned from GIs, was fluent and colloquial, with almost no hint of accent. He was a large, handsome man of boundless energy and appetite for whatever engaged his interest, and we hit it off from the first day, which began with his (apropos of nothing) informing me he was Jewish. Asked why he volunteered this, he said sometimes people made anti-Semitic remarks without realizing they were giving offense.

I informed him I'd grown up in the Bronx and was an authentic *shabbas goy* (one who performs functions, like turning on lights, which Jews are forbidden to do on the Sabbath).

The same age (like Jack, at nineteen I'd been in Paris, a GI), we formed a relationship beyond work hours. Played *pétanque*; bet the tierce; consumed many a bottle of champion wine, courtesy of Twentieth Century–Fox.

Some years later it occurred to me that the relationship between an American screenwriter whose French was minimal and a colorful French driver contained the seeds of a movie.

I wrote it and unable to interest the studios, decided to raise the money and direct it myself.

Seeking the money involved me briefly with (among others) shadowy silver traders and an Indian chief (Push-Ma-Ta-Ha is as close as I can get) who tracked me to the pool of the Beverly Hills Hotel where on a scorching day, the chief, a huge man in full Indian leather, perched at the edge of my chaise gulping double bourbons and making deals in the air or on a cocktail napkin that bore figures of a huge deal made at some bar shortly before descending on me.

"How much do you need?" he asked.

"Half a million," I said.

"Is that all?" he said, affronted by the paltriness. "Well, you've got that. Now what else can we talk about?"

(See Laura Cunningham and Bruce Jay Friedman, wide-eyed witnesses to this encounter, for corroboration.)

I also sought financing from traditional sources, including Walter Mirisch (a prominent producer), who said he loved the script but wouldn't do it because it was too small.

"Suppose there was a magic button that guaranteed the return of your investment plus twenty-five percent profit in a year?" I said. "Would you do it then?"

"No," he said. And as the implication sank in, appended, "My God, I'm just like the rest of them."

At that moment it hit me how at odds I was with a system whose primary goal was making killings, while mine was making pictures.

I came close to doing the picture with Zev Braun (producer), who endorsed my choice of Alan Alda and authorized me to make an offer to Alda, who'd read the script and wanted to do it.

"Sounds fine," Alda enthused on hearing the terms. "Call my agent to finalize it."

That call began an unraveling that saw not only Alda lost but Braun as well.

Wayne Rogers crossed my path. We knew each other casually, but I'd never considered him for the part until that day when for some reason not remembered he began to talk about business, an area I'd heard he was expert in.

As he talked, something shrewder, more calculated, and focused supplanted his normally boyish demeanor.

Later, reflecting on the conversation, it occurred to me that given those new facets to draw on, Wayne could play the writer.

By that night, he'd read the script and said he wanted to do it: from Hawkeye to Trapper John.

Now all I needed was a budget, the money, and a French actor who could speak English in the unstereotyped way (sans Chevalier lispings) that Black Jack had accustomed me to.

When I told Wayne that in the event I was unable to find an established actor who was suitable I might read the man who'd actually been my chauffeur, Wayne had misgivings about me and what lay ahead.

1977
Wednesday, June 1, 8:00 P.M.: Home, Upstate New York

I leave for Paris tonight to begin my quest in behalf of *Once in Paris*. I go to secure a French actor to play the chauffeur. Will start by reading Black Jack Lenoir (Teboul), who was my driver in 1968 when I did *The Only Game in Town* and is the prototype for the role.

I will also try to get the true budget picture.

Thursday, June 9, 7:30 P.M.: Hotel Mont Blanc, Paris

Have been in Paris since June 2. Stayed at a dump of a hotel on boulevard Raspail (sans bath or toilet) the first two days because all Paris crowded due to air show.

Black Jack got me into a hotel that seemed an improvement until last night when it proved to be literally a fleabag.

Unable to find a French actor who talks like Jack and detecting promise in Jack's readings, I've decided to gamble on him.

Friends of Jack produced a budget that says the picture can be made for $300,000.

I phoned Wayne Rogers to inform him of these developments. His response was one of cautious enthusiasm—emphasis on *cautious*.

Monday, June 13, 8:00 A.M.: Home

The long pull (getting the money) has begun.

I contacted John Doe (so named for reasons which will become obvious), who said he'd get back to me.

Tuesday, June 14, 8:00 A.M.: Home

Began rewriting the script. Will meet Dennis Smith[1] this morn-

---

1. Author of *Engine Company 84*, an account of his life as a fireman in New York's busiest fire house, which launched him as a novelist and entrepreneur who founded *Firehouse* magazine.

ing. Gabe Katzka[2] expressed interest via Swanie.

Thursday, June 16, 8:00 A.M.: Wyndham Hotel, New York City

Lunched with John Doe on Tuesday. He wants a good many points for any money he raises. Despite outstanding credentials, there is something slippery about him I can't define.

Now to work on the script and then study French.

Wednesday, June 22, 8:30 A.M.: Wyndham

Lunched with Eddie Colton, who said I should have adequate insurance since an accident could take all I have in the world.

Wayne called. I brought him up to date. There is still something short of total commitment in his voice.

Saturday, June 25, 8:00 A.M.: Home

I worked on the script and my French. A call from Swanie last night to say Katzka loves *Paris* and has given it to his money man.

Wednesday, June 29, 8:00 A.M.: Wyndham

Marsha Brooks, who seems efficient and enthusiastic, is riding herd on this project at the Colton, Weissberg office. She wanted to Xerox the budget I brought back from Paris (my only copy), but I was hurrying to get to the theater.

Ruth and I, after seeing *Sly Fox*, walked two blocks before I realized I'd left my briefcase, with the budget, in the theater. I sprinted back. The stage-door man admitted me reluctantly. An actor guided me through the dark backstage area. I tripped, fell, bruised my left leg, and landed on my hand. What an irony if I had broken my leg in that theater (the Broadhurst), where *Only Game* broke my heart in '68.

I did not find my briefcase. The actor trying to show me out via the front of the house succeeded in getting us locked between the street doors and the house doors. We had to knock on the glass to get a passerby to fetch the stage-door man, who rescued us. I suffered hives on the ride home.

2. Movie and play producer (now deceased) whom I picture most clearly at the drugstore in the Beverly Wilshire Hotel years ago where we occasionally breakfasted together, exchanging the gossip of the day.

Monday, July 18, 7:30 A.M.: Home

I've cut twenty-two pages out of the script.

After endless meetings with John Doe, there was a showdown in Frank Weissberg's office.

John Doe said he could guarantee most of the money.

To amplify the "go" spirit that prevailed, I invested what I'm to receive for writing and directing. That made it $230,000. John Doe, apparently moved by that gesture, said he'd raise even more.

I lunched with John Doe and one of his "heavy hitters." There was some talk of John Doe's wife for the woman's role, which I nipped in its cradle.

The picture is going to happen!

I called Paris. Notified Black Jack I'd arrive in a couple of weeks. He was to scout crew and an apartment. I called Manny Fuchs[3], who would also scout.

Swanson called me with two big offers, from Paramount and Warner. The latter via Shirley MacLaine. I told him no because my Paris project was on.

Wayne and I have been meeting about the script. He had a valid criticism which I said I'd fix. Our meetings so far strengthen his feel for the part and bind us.

Monday, August 15, 7:45 a.m.: Wyndham

I arrived at Sardi's at 1:00 P.M. for a lunch with Bob Lovett (film editor) and Dan Sandburg (TVC Lab) to make sure I understood all that had to be done when we brought the film back from Paris. I included John Doe so he would feel involved and could take care of things back here in my absence. He was uncharacteristically subdued.

After lunch, when the others left, he said, "I've got a problem that doesn't concern you." Right away I knew one thing for sure—*it concerned me.*

He claimed it just occurred to him that his investors all did business with his company, where he was in a position to give them multimillion-dollar orders, and feared it might look as though he were using his position to feather his private nest.

3. Recently resigned from our local paper (*Middletown Times Herald Record*) where he was chief photographer, he was working with his brother Leo, a movie producer, in Paris. Married to a Frenchwoman (Michelle) and fluent in the language, he volunteered assistance that was to prove invaluable.

"Therefore," he said, "I'm not going to sign any papers with you. I trust you and know you'll give me all we've agreed on."

I told him that if one of his investors subsequently yelled foul, I would end up on a witness stand.

He said his investors were aware that he was getting points for their investment. I said, "Fine. Then just inform your company, and you're beyond suspicion." When he said he couldn't do that, I called Frank Weissberg, who, apprised of the problem and sounding less than sanguine, suggested we all meet tomorrow.

On that gloomy note we parted.

The need for a sympathetic ear led me to Gene Wolsk's[4] office. On hearing my situation, Gene invited Mitch Leigh (with whom he is doing a revival of *La Mancha*) to hear my sad tale. Mitch, who has an interest in movies, asked for a script, which I left with him.

Tuesday, August 16, 8:15 A.M.: Wyndham

John Doe showed up with one of his investors for our meeting.

Frank Weissberg read the criminal statute that plainly states that a deal such as John Doe's must be disclosed not only to his investors but to his employer as well. Doe's investor's response was "I am a very wealthy man. Even if we're caught, the penalty is minor."

I said, "My name, headlining such a story in *Variety*, would not be minor."

So there it was. I insisted he disclose. He wouldn't. Three months suddenly come to naught. *Finito*.

I canceled reservations to Paris, put Black Jack on hold, made SOS phone calls to other potential money sources.

Mitch Leigh loved the script and is in for $100,000. That's the only bright spot.

Wednesday, August 17, 7:45 A.M.: Wyndham

I met Jim McLaughlin at the Oak Room. I gave him a script and papers, and he'll call by the weekend.

Right now I have $160,000 pledged. If I don't reach $300,000 by this weekend, I will have to abandon the quest.

---

4. Theater producer and old friend who volunteered cash without strings to support *Roses* in the dark days after opening.

Thursday, August 18, 8:15 A.M.: Wyndham

Jack Albertson[5] called to say he checked with his accountant and there was no money available—no cash, that is.

"I want to hang on to my stocks and other things," he said, adding he was sure I'd understand.

Friday, August 19, 8:15 A.M.: Wyndham

Mitch Leigh phoned—our first contact since he pledged $100,000. *La Mancha*, for which he wrote the music, opened big in Washington. He is now gung ho for my project. Asked where things stood, I told him that besides his $100,000, I had $70,000. He was indignant that "an established artist [me] should have difficulty raising such a paltry sum."

He said that his money will come in the form of a personal note, not a letter of credit. How and when we translate the note into dollars wasn't mentioned. He asked for the additional points that I was going to give John Doe, which I agreed to.

Wayne called. Gave me a pep talk apropos of my sounding a bit down, referred enthusiastically to that rewritten scene I'd sent him.

Jim McLaughlin called. Said he and Jean (his wife) were investing $100,000. I was pleasantly surprised and said so.

Wednesday, August 24, 7:30 A.M.: Wyndham

On Monday to Jim's office—McLaughlin, Piven, Vogel, Inc., 30 Wall Street—where he gave me two checks from him and Jean. Milt Kurtz, another Dartmouth alumnus, is in for $30,000.

Called Mitch Leigh, who will give us a promissory note for his $100,000, payable on October 15. I phoned Wayne to say it looked like we were on again.

Yesterday I spoke to the insurance man, Bob Boyar, who gave me a clear, concise lesson in insurance needs and costs.

I spoke to a man who is going to see what in the script might be traded for dollars via discreet advertisements, which I understand is normal movie procedure.

I study French intensely.

5. He starred in *The Subject Was Roses* on stage, winning a Tony. In the movie version, both he and Patricia Neal were nominated for Academy Awards. Jack won. He later starred in the hit TV series "Chico and the Man."

Tuesday, September 6, 9:00 A.M.: Home

I fly via TWA Flight 800 at 7:30 P.M. to Paris with François Moulin, who will be production manager and first assistant director. I hope his knowledge of Paris and fluency in French will compensate for my lacks.

I've arranged for insurance, accounting, and brokers to get the film through Customs.

A last-minute hitch almost derailed everything when Mitch Leigh introduced a new condition: He wanted a guarantee that I'd finish shooting before his dough was used. Faced with the alternative of calling off the project, I overrode Frank Weissberg's objections and agreed to underwrite Leigh's $100,000 if I abandoned the film before completion of principal photography. In essence, this means I have put my home on the line.

David Harmon[6] and John Gay invested the final money needed.

Wayne Rogers suddenly a bit skittish as the reality of doing it looms.

I feel like Lindbergh setting forth in a crate bound with rubber bands and adhesive tape. And like him, I feel certain that somehow I'll succeed.

Friday, September 9, 8:15 A.M.: Hotel Regina, Paris

Black Jack met us at De Gaulle Airport. We dropped François at his brother's home where he'll be staying. After checking in at the hotel, we went to the Manufacturers branch bank where I introduced myself to Denise Bouchet, who outlined procedures for transferring money here.

Jack took me to the home of Gerard Croce, an actor who is interested in movie production and had been working on the budget and schedule for my film. He speaks little English. I liked him instinctively. Saw at once that he could be a fine aide for François.

As Jack drove me about, he practiced his lines—played a cassette of himself rehearsing a scene from the script. My impression of the reading was that it was lifeless. The trick will be to make him as vibrant as he is in life on film.

I fell asleep at midnight after some thirty-six hours with only two hours' rest.

6. Movie and screenwriter (founding member of the Hi-be-lo-be poker game). I met him at Disney in 1958 where we worked on the TV series "Texas John Slaughter." "If we make good here, we can get back into show business" was his initial greeting, the first of many laughs (and kindnesses) he's provided over the years.

Yesterday Jack and I tried to find me an apartment. While waiting in a real estate office, I noted he was dispirited. When I probed, it turned out the source of his dissatisfaction was a line in the script wherein a woman, after sleeping with his character, says, "It wasn't any fun." Jack incensed because he took it as a personal indictment that he wasn't any good in bed. I made him happy by altering the line so the woman says "It wasn't any fun for him or for me."

It alerted me I must treat him guardedly and be prepared for anything.

I took an apartment for 8,250 francs per month plus a 6,000-franc fee (robbery) for the agent. Four bedrooms—very nice.

I left a script with Jean-Louis Levi,[7] who will give me advice on casting the Englishwoman.

I gave a script to the director of the Hotel Regina where I am staying, with an eye to shooting here.

Saturday, September 10, 8:00 A.M.: Paris

François, Jack, Gerard, and I went to the bank where Madame Bouchet exuded a new air of full and friendly confidence, doubtless attributable to my banker in New York having confirmed that I was a person of substance. There is now $50,000 at my disposal.

I had to give two month's rent in advance for security on the apartment—plus the first month's rent, plus the agent's fee of 6,000, which is a gyp because that is their commission on a year's rental. Incidentally, the rate of exchange is about 4.80.

We scouted locations and labs.

I met the actress that Orson Welles, via Wayne, pressed me to audition. I will read her, but it's a long shot.

Manny Fuchs increasingly helpful.

The Regina wants $3,250 for four days' shooting. I said I'd get back to them.

Sunday, September 11, 7:45 A.M.: Paris

I am settled in at 72 bis rue de la Tour. I'll use the master bedroom till Wayne arrives and then give it to him. This will allow

---

7. Agent and (then) husband of Tanya Lopert, who costarred with Claude Brasseur in the Paris theater production of *The Only Game in Town* (*Le Joue de la nuit*, 1975), which was a huge success, triggering a number of foreign productions of the play.

considerable separation from the other bedrooms, where Bob Lovett and I will be.

You can walk to the Étoile in about twenty-five minutes. I did it to get some soft toilet paper. You know how we Americans are.

My French improves, but it is a constant strain to be grasping for meaning.

I went to see Gerard Croce acting in *Irma La Douce* at the Theatre Fontaine where *The Only Game in Town* was so successful.

Sady Rebbot, who acted in *The Only Game* was in the audience and introduced himself.

Gerard and I went to eat at the Cloche D'Or, where he insisted on paying. His generosity is appealing. The other day, having met me only hours before, he was ready to advance the apartment money if my own funds didn't arrive. He is Corsican and Indian (Venezuelan). I realize that almost all the people I like in Paris are not French.

A brisk walk this morning to the Trocadero for *croissant et café au lait,* with the Eiffel Tower in the background, has improved my mood considerably.

Monday, September 12, 10:00 A.M.: Paris

An excellent budget session with Gerard and François yesterday. We worked until after 2:00 P.M. It will be tight, but we can make it. In the extreme emergency, I'll do it in four weeks instead of five. Gerard has Paul Leaf's passion for production figures and economy. The challenge of the latter arouses him. François is nothing for figures, so they combine excellently.

My comprehension of written French gains tremendously. Verbally, I go much slower. The French edition of *Playboy* a great teaching aid.

Just chatted with the tenant upstairs, who speaks no English, about a defective pipe in her rear bathroom, which requires that I not use ours while the plumbers work for two days. At least I think that's what she said.

Tuesday, September 13, 9:30 A.M.: Paris

Walked to the Trocadero for breakfast. Learned you can order *one* croissant. I thought two was obligatory.

Gerard and François arrived at 10:30 A.M. They use the dining room as an office, which violates the lease. The owner was expected, so every time the doorbell rang, they scooped their para-phernalia from the table like a bookie joint in a police raid.

Black Jack arrived. He's been bugging Gerard about his ward-robe. I told him it would be attended to but more important items now required attention. I rehearsed the script with him for several hours in the living room. He's going to be fine. He has a tendency to indicate, but when I point it out, he adjusts at once.

I accompanied Jack to get his annual medical exam, required of all people in the movie business.

We looked at other hotels, but the Regina is by far the best for our purpose. I will call this afternoon and attempt to lower the price.

Gerard took a script to Peugeot, seeking a car deal. François is in contact with Air France.

I must write a five-page summary of the script to submit for government authorization to shoot.

I called Wayne. Told him I was sitting in "our" living room. He will arrive next Monday or Tuesday. He said Merv Griffin[8] volun-teered financial help if we run short at the end.

Wednesday, September 14, 8:45 P.M.: Paris

Worked with Jack, who gets increasingly comfortable with the script.

Thursday, September 15, 8:30 A.M.: Paris

I met with the director of the Regina. He wanted $3,250 for four days of shooting in the hotel. I offered $1,600. He said he couldn't do it for less than $2,000. I said okay. We shook hands.

We have a handsome price from GCT Lab. Saw two cine-matographers. Both agreeable, both with much better English (a prerequisite) than those seen previously.

---

8. Early in 1965, having exhausted any and all credit sources in our effort to keep *Roses* going till the prizes (Tony, Drama Critics, Pulitzer) were awarded, we were about to give up and vacate The Little Theatre (next to Sardi's) when Merv Griffin, unaware of our predicament, offered us money to quit the theater, which he wanted for his talk show. Edgar Lansbury and Joe Beruh, general manager, conducted negotiations with me (as heavy) offstage till we got the price up to $40,000. With that money we moved to the Helen Hayes and hung on, barely, till the prizes were given. We won them all (the triple crown), and business zoomed. Merv Griffin, whom I've never met, tells the story differently, making it sound as though he came to our rescue voluntarily. In any case, I thank him.

The apartment makes a most attractive office. Peugeot seems certain for a couple of free cars.

A clothing house will spring for a few needed garments.

François pessimistic about our doing the picture in five weeks.

Friday, September 16, 9:30 A.M.: Aboard Flight 001, BEA

En route to London to see actresses (arranged by Jean-Louis Levi).

I worked with Jack all day yesterday. It went excellently. I tailored certain speeches to make him comfortable.

Jack and François seem to have an instinctive dislike for each other.

Gerard is a godsend. Without him, we'd be in trouble. He's off seeing people all day while François ponders his production board.

Gerard, François, and I went to see the work of a prospective cinematographer on rue Lauriston, the notorious street where Gestapo headquarters was located.

Saturday, September 17, 9:00 A.M.: Blake's Hotel, London

Because of the flight controllers' strike in London, I arrived an hour later than scheduled. Took a cab to 194 Old Brompton where Patricia McNaughton, an agent Jean-Louis Levi had contacted on my behalf, has her office.

At Gerard's repeated suggestion, I had asked to meet Gayle Hunnicutt. It turned out that she, while not a client of the McNaughton Agency, lived close by. She came over. A Texan, she's lived here long enough to seem genuinely British. She made a fine impression. Attractive, sophisticated, natural, with a sense of humor. I gave her a script to read.

Interviewed other actresses, who made no particular impression. Gayle Hunnicutt phoned. She loves the script and the part.

I tried halfheartedly to get into the Playboy Club Casino without a membership. Didn't succeed and was relieved. Gambling of that sort has little appeal beside the enormous risk of this enterprise.

Sunday, September 18, 8:20 A.M.: Paris

Back at good old 72 bis.

If you want to make yourself feel at home quickly in an alien abode, take a side trip to a still newer place, and on your return to the former, it will smack of home.

Due to the strike, the London departure terminal, with flights backed up five and six hours, was packed. The mixture of Africans, Poles, Spaniards, Italians, Japanese, et al. gave the feeling of a World War II movie, and we all trying to escape from a soon-to-be-overrun zone.

Very cold when I awoke this morning. The weather looms as a threat to the film.

Monday, September 19, 7:30 A.M.: Paris

I walked to the Relais at the Plaza Athénée. Silently toasted George Stevens and Freddy Kolmar, director and producer of *The Only Game* (both deceased), who introduced me to that place.

I asked the concierge about heat this morning. She said the law forbids turning it on till next month.

Tuesday, September 20, 8:15 A.M.: Paris

Wayne due this morning. Jack and I will meet him. I'm going to see if we can make a *Michael Moore* sign for Jack to hold at the airport, as he does for the screenwriter the first time they meet in the movie: Life duplicating art duplicating life since that's how Jack and I met.

Interviewed several more actresses yesterday.

Gerard went to see a man about use of Longchamps racetrack. The man, elderly, took moral exception, in the script, to betting on *pétanque*, the chauffeur's prison record, and most of all to a chauffeur sleeping with the woman of his boss. Told Gerard he should be ashamed of himself for promoting such a bad image of France.

The boys now have us budgeted to spend $214,000 in France. That's still $14,000 too much since we can't touch Mitch Leigh's money till we get back to the States.

Wednesday, September 21, 9:45 A.M.: Paris

Jack and I met Wayne with the *Michael Moore* sign. They sparked to each other immediately.

Wayne impressed by the apartment. Told me he brought a $10,000 letter of credit in case we run short. I told him of the condition Mitch Leigh imposed, which made it crucial to get out of France for $200,000. I sensed he likes the challenge. By

3:00 P.M., Wayne was working. Read with an actress who wasn't right. But despite jet lag, he had several live moments.

Jack, Wayne, and I dined at a bistro near Sacré Coeur. Jack recounted the story of his complicated romantic life to Wayne. He was performing a bit, and quite effectively. Wayne will have to fight for his life on screen and senses the difficulty since his role is essentially passive.

There was a guitar on the wall that Wayne played—displayed a pretty good ear as he accompanied Jack singing some Spanish song. Madame so-and-so came by. She said that while Jack and she are no longer active lovers, she has this absolutely certain feeling that they will eventually wind up together. Her certainty drives Jack up the wall.

I sat in the back of the car (and will always do so from now on) to observe Jack and Wayne together.

Use of the airport will be $600 for six hours.

Ricard will give us $4,000 (after completion) and a press party.

The GTC Lab came down in price even more.

Now the onerous chore of my first letter to the accountant in New York. Gerard's careful receipts help greatly.

Thursday, September 22, 8:00 A.M.: Paris

Wayne was up at 6:00 A.M. yesterday. He jogged to the Eiffel Tower and back, which gave me an idea for a shot. We breakfasted across the street in "my" tabac. My routine seems to be juice and vitamins and cold cereal here, and then coffee and croissant in the corner store.

Living in such close proximity with your star can be good and/or bad. Yesterday morning it was good. He had questions about his role and the script, and I was able to deal with them.

Orson Welles's candidate for the woman's role came by in the afternoon. She looked smashing, but the reading was distant, surface.

The cold had Wayne walking about the apartment in his overcoat.

Friday, September 23, 9:15 A.M.: Paris

Wayne and I carried the cans of film submitted by a prospective cinematographer to the projection room on Lauriston. We got there, cans in hand, via the métro. Wayne delights in such chores, which some actors would see as demeaning.

Black Jack was off because of Yom Kippur, so I took a cab to Orly Sud to meet Gayle's plane from Tunis. On the ride here, she chattered in a slightly affected English way that worried me. But her reading with Wayne was tasteful, honest, and moving.

I told her we had one more actress to read and would call with definite word by 6:00 P.M.

The next contestant no threat.

I called Gayle, told her she had the part. She, Wayne, and I celebrated with dinner at Procope, where Wayne ordered two great wines and still the meal was $50.

Gayle will return for rehearsal on October 3 and begin to shoot October 17.

Peugeot is giving us a car, and Moet will supply champagne for the party scene.

After a talk, I hired Claude Saunier as cinematographer.

Saturday, September 24, 10:30 A.M.: Paris

I phoned Gayle Hunnicutt's agent in London to confirm our deal. He did not return the call.

We can shoot at Auteuil racetrack.

We have promoted a Citroen car needed in one scene.

Wayne and I went to visit his cousin Chouky, married to Pierre Sergent, who was high up in the OAS, the right-wing force that challenged De Gaulle after his about-face in Algeria. The Sergents were underground with their children all over Europe for seven years until amnesty. A most engaging family. The shared danger reflected in their unity. In parting, Pierre gave me a copy of his book *Je ne regrete rien.*

Sunday, September 25, 9:00 A.M.: Paris

Breakfasted with Wayne. He discourses over a wide range of topics that his myriad business dealings have demanded knowledge of.

We had another productive character-probing session.

I took a walk through the Bois. Found a location for the montage—the lake and boats. Made a decision: I will use English subtitles where needed so as not to deprive the French actors of their life.

Monday, September 26, 8:30 A.M.: Paris

Jack drove Wayne, François, and me to Marta Andras's[9] country place in Fontainaille. As usual, we got lost because Jack somehow feels diminished if he has to consult a map.

François so pessimistic in his contemplation of all we have to do that it is now a joke in which he shares.

Marta and Aimé (Phillipe de Marche) greeted us warmly. Had two friends in—one an actress that might be good as Madame Farny. But Black Jack objects: Told me in private the woman was not attractive enough to be his mistress. Once again he confuses life and art.

Wayne and Jack exhibit much life together in the car. Can I capture it and serve the story simultaneously?

Tuesday, September 27, 8:15 A.M.: Paris

Bob Lovett and Maurice Schell (assistant editor) arrived. Maurice was met by a cousin. We brought Bob back here, where he'll be staying.

Another good rehearsal with Jack and Wayne. I was right to have them get acquainted.

Gayle Hunnicutt's deal finalized.

Wayne treated Jack, Maurice, Bob, and me at a tourist place Jack selected on the Left Bank called Roger the Frog.

Waitresses goosing customers and desserts in phallic shapes suggest the ambiance.

Wednesday, September 28, 8:15 A.M.: Paris

Bob and Maurice went off to seek a cutting room and a movieola, which everyone says is not to be found in Paris. Jack's nose out of joint because I told him when he sings "Granada" in the picnic scene, there will not be any orchestra. Jack is also disturbed lest his apartment (in the film) not be grand enough.

I lunched alone with Claude Saunier, the cinematographer, to be sure we can converse without the presence of an interpreter. It works.

9. My friend and European play agent. I attended her marriage to Phillipe de Marche, actor (now deceased) shortly after my arrival in Paris to work on *Only Game* in 1968. It was a party at their country place, to which I brought Black Jack, that inspired a similar scene in *Once in Paris*.

Bob's wife is coming over next week. Because I expressly said no wives till after the first week of shooting, he is moving to a hotel.

Oh yes—he and Maurice found *two* movieolas.

Thursday, September 29, 5:15 A.M.: Paris

I went to see a prospective accountant, who said Gerard's records and preparation are so excellent that his services were unneeded.

In scouting locations, we encountered the champion *pétanque* player in all of France. His name is something like Babbet de Cannes. It occurred to me to have him do the actual *pétanque* playing in the picture.

Back at the apartment later, in discussing this, the trouble that had been brewing between Black Jack and François came to a head. I barely parted them short of blows.

Friday, September 30, 7:15 A.M.: Paris

Wayne and Jack rehearsed excellently. Their characters deepen.

I let the trouble between Jack and François resolve itself. They gave each other wide berth all day. Spoke to each other when necessary with extra politeness.

Accompanied Lois Peyser,[10] in Paris collecting recipes for a cookbook, to a swanky nightclub opening she'd been invited to. She and I the only ones of some two thousand guests not in formal clothes. Lois refused to check her shopping bag containing the recipes even when pressed by the Shah of Iran's cousin, whose hauteur suggests revolution might not only be possible but mandatory.

Saturday, October 1, 7:30 A.M.: Paris

No booze of any kind for several days. No mean feat since one imbibes so continuously and naturally here.

Rehearsing yesterday, Jack experienced a real emotion—a sense of fear as he and Wayne got into the denunciation scene. It was as though he realized for the first time that acting was serious and affecting business when done correctly. He kept saying the moment gave him butterflies. I worked with them all morning in our

10. She and her husband, Arnold, a writing team, age-old Hollywood friends. Her cookbook (*How to Beat Those Cordon Bleus*) did well.

living room, pausing only to interview actors who came by for minor roles.

Jack, Wayne, François, and I went to get clothes at a well-known place that was giving us a discount in exchange for publicity. Things began to unravel when François (delegated to watch Jack's car, which was illegally parked) came inside to report that it had been ticketed by a meter maid.

Moments later, all activity in the store was halted by Jack's bellowing, "*These clothes are shit! You expect me to wear this shit?*"

In a private chat with Jack, I told him he was going to be feeling a lot of new and strange emotions that he must recognize and admit (fear primarily) or they would come out in destructive ways. He nodded, but I doubt it penetrated.

Sunday, October 2, 8:15 A.M.: Paris

Jack arrived for rehearsal in an elegant dark suit of his own—announced he had canceled his clothes at the shop we visited. If he insists on that suit, it will make a chauffeur's cap, which he violently objects to, a necessity to denote his status.

All this would be intolerable if his work wasn't so good.

I worked all afternoon getting notes in order, writing a new scene, pasting maps of Paris to the wall—like preparing for a military campaign.

Dined out with Bob. Another great meal. It's surprising how much conversation each day is devoted to food.

I'm told we'll spend under $200,000 in France—at least that's the estimate on paper.

Monday, October 3, 6:15 A.M.: Paris

Of all the things I never expected to be tripped up on, Jack's goodwill and cooperation, increasingly in doubt, tops the list. If despite my best efforts his demon succeeds, who can I get to replace him? The film *must* be made, or I lose everything I own.

Tuesday, October 4, 6:45 A.M.: Paris

Marshal Tito's coming to Paris next week presents a problem because in the interest of his safety, they have decreed no exterior movie shooting during his stay.

Regarding Jack's disruptive behavior, Gerard said, "A star is born," signifying all are onto him.

Wednesday, October 5, 5:00 A.M.: Paris

Awake since 4:00 A.M. A new low, attributable to Jack draining the fun from the project (the enmity between him and François blazed anew yesterday) and our apparent inability to accomodate the schedule changes that Tito's visit necessitates.

On the up side, Gayle and Wayne rehearsed all yesterday and will be fine.

Claude Saunier, cinematographer, shows favorable signs. Patrick Aubree, the script supervisor who began work yesterday, sat in on a lengthy rehearsal and was a most positive and contributing presence.

Went to Dr. Dax for an insurance physical yesterday, 11 rue Franklin. Recognized him from September 1968 when I went to him while doing *The Only Game in Town.*

I told François he had to avoid all friction with Jack or quit because he was dispensable and Jack wasn't.

Gerard wisely counseled me against firing François, which would have further fueled Black Jack's megalomania.

Thursday, October 6, 6:30 A.M.: Paris

If the picture proves successful, I cracked it yesterday when after four hours' sleep I shoved all anxieties aside and wrote a beautiful ending to Michael and Susan's last scene. Wayne, Gayle, and I breakfasted across the street—rehearsed well.

François said he wanted to stay. I said only if he was going to manifest a new attitude. He agreed.

Rehearsed Aimé after shooting some available light tests in the street. The camera galvanized us all—the picture suddenly real.

I gave the crew a taste of my quick pace. They kept up. I sensed a new respect. Perhaps it was the first appearance of my director's hat.

More rehearsal, then to the Hotel Regina to shoot tests. I spent hours on Gayle's clothes. Selected from her own wardrobe, which she delights in showing.

When Jack saw Wayne and Gayle using their own clothes, he said, "Frank, wait. I'll bring my clothes for you to pick, like you did it with them."

I took Wayne, Mitzi (his wife), and Gayle to dinner.

Friday, October 7, 8:00 A.M.: Paris

D minus 3.

Gayle arrived with Patrick at 7:00 A.M.

Marlo Thomas called, wanted Wayne back one weekend to loop a television movie they did in New York. Gerard convinced them he could set it all up for them here. Another favor I am indebted for.

I began rehearsal with Wayne and Gayle, which went well. Jack arrived. I rehearsed his scenes with both of them. Made it a policy that when an actor was not in the scene, he or she was excluded from the room—this mainly to get rid of Jack, who begins to bother Wayne by remembering his lines for him.

Wayne almost in tears as he played the last moments of the farewell scene with Gayle.

Jack has appropriated one of my jackets to wear in the film. He sees it as a tribute of some sort, which seems to pacify him.

He balked again at the chauffeur's cap. I told him it was a must. But I see a plus in his dislike of the cap and will use it in the film by letting him ask Michael if he might dispense with it.

The broken-arm cast Jack had made is excellent.

Came back from scouting to meet a large jovial man representing Ricard, who brought booze for the house. Had drinks with us. Told jokes. I said something complimentary, which was translated to him. He said back, "I'm admired wherever I go."

Saturday, October 8, 7:30 A.M.: Paris

D minus 2.

How nice to be all alone here. The calm before the storm.

With Claude and Michel, I drove to the kiosk in the Bois where the *pétanque* scene takes place. A drizzling day, only two players. A man named Levy, speaking perfect English, materialized. We told him our problem. A call from us, and he will deliver some players when needed. An easy give-and-take between Claude and me as we discussed shots.

The Ricard man, Mr. Campiglia, drove Manny, Claude, and me to the Ricard Chateau, which he generously offered as site for the party scene. It's magnificent. I will do the party indoors there, thus erasing any rain fears. We had an excellent lunch: blanquette of veal after a plate of some seven different cold meats, three wines, and Ricard, of course. Mr. C. is Italian, which explains something of his warm volubility and our immediate rapport. He said he'd feed the crew and supply a buffet for the guests. When I volunteered I had insurance against any damage, he was injured that I should think he'd want such a thing.

Without asking, Jack has had my good suit jacket altered to fit him. I love it. He's like a delighted pussycat. I told him to rest till Monday (the first day of shooting) and to call me with any questions. He will drive the Peugeot to the airport (where we shoot the first day) with no passengers, by his own request. This is to affirm that he is no longer a chauffeur.

Sunday, October 9, 8:30 A.M.: Paris

D minus 1.

While scouting locations, I was told that in shooting a crowded market area on the left bank, we will be restricted to hand-held camera only. This because the government fears the setting up of a tripod might somehow stimulate the students to eruption. In that edict you read more worry about the coming election than is evident on the surface.

We had lunch on the Île de Cité, where I picked shots for the tour-bus scene. Will use the upstream *bateau mouche* because the ones that leave from the Île are enclosed.

10:15 A.M.

Just had an anxiety call (as I knew I would) from Black Jack. I'm glad. It shows he will be malleable. He admitted to great fear yesterday, which I said we all, regardless of experience, felt.

He offered to pick up Wayne (returning from Monaco) at the airport; offered to rehearse with the actress playing his wife; wanted to come here and show me his new "cheap" blue suit. All three suggestions I vetoed. He said he'd show me the suit at 6:30 A.M. tomorrow. I said 7:00 A.M. The poor fellow. It's the chance he begged me for, but God knows how this all ends for him.

11:40 A.M.

François just phoned to assure me that he and Jack are going to get along fine. He volunteered to share his production manager's credit with Gerard. Of course he too is venting pregame tension, but I appreciate it. He said, "I don't want you to think you brought me for nothing." I thanked him. He said, "We are well prepared. What falls on our heads falls on our heads." I agreed.

François said Jack called him this morning and they had a good talk.

As we near the front, see how we cling.

Yesterday's first day of shooting began like a dream and concluded as nightmare.

Got off to a quick start at the airport. Shot the arrival, the first ramp, the passport being stamped, the tubes, the scene where writer and chauffeur meet. Then lunch.

We prepared the car for interior shooting. Me at the feet of Aimé and Wayne in the backseat, Jack driving, and Claude with camera beside him in front; the sound man in the trunk.

Nothing worked. Wayne fighting a cold that now bloomed.

Suddenly the sun was a problem. We turned the car and headed away from the airport to avoid light on faces directly. Now the sun was directly on the camera. Things began to slide. The sun set. The day gone, and I was several pages behind what I'd planned to accomplish.

Did the failure to wear my director's hat (an oversight) jinx me? I'll wear it today.

Wednesday, October 12, 7:00 A.M.: Paris

Had one of my very good shooting days. Despite the sound man arriving an hour late, I finished the previous day's work; got some additional car shots; got, *I think,* a fine scene with Jack and Wayne; picked up points of view and other bits on the ride to the next location.

After lunch, I got all the stuff in the family scene at the chauffeur's apartment. Gerard pronounced me "champion."

To rushes—all a bit giddy at the day's achievement.

Adhered to my open-dailies policy in which everyone connected with the film is invited.

Dailies looked good. Bob Lovett (thank God) detected the cameraman framing with the wrong mat, which will require blowing up what we've done so far.

Black Jack had a memorable day. He almost wept with joy at the feeling of doing good work. *But* at the end of the day, he complained the apartment was not equal to his station in real life.

11:00 P.M.

Arriving at the Bois this morning, I was told no players would be there till 2:00 P.M., so I did the scene where Michael breaks Jean-Paul's arm.

As Wayne prepared for his emotional outburst, Jack was non-chalantly eating a croissant, which I asked him to refrain from in the interest of concentration.

Action: As Wayne and Jack moved toward the camera from a distance, I said, "Cut." Offered to bet Black Jack that he had a bit of croissant stuck in his tooth, which his tongue worked to dislodge as they approached. Jack confirmed my suspicion and for the rest of the day hailed me as "the greatest director in the world." Boasted my ability to spot a piece of croissant at thirty yards.

Despite Wayne's usual "I could have done it better," I got what I wanted. Will have to get more *pétanque* playing another day.

Thursday, October 13, 11:15 P.M.: Paris

Today the fourth day of shooting. I did five pages at the Coupe-Chou restaurant. The grip who was to do the "tough guy" part backed out at the last minute because, from what I could gather, he seemed to think acting was a step down. This necessitated pressing one of the drivers into the role, which started Jack complaining. He said he didn't feel the other driver was equal to the task. But it was clear he felt it somehow demeaned his own transformation.

Camera moves in that small room were not easy. I barely made it as the owner was ready to throw us out.

Rushes fine.

Saturday, October 15, 6:30 A.M.: Paris

Yesterday will go down as the battle of "Granada."

Manny Fuchs picked me up at 8:30 A.M. We drove to the recording studio in Pigalle where Gerard met us with three musicians: guitar, violin, and bass. They would do several public-domain songs as playback for the party.

That's all I expected of them, but my enthusiasm grew as they proceeded from song to song. Then they played the "slow"—a fox-trot. It was an old French song, simple and touching. As they played, the Frenchmen in the booth with me began to sing the words. I was moved to the point of tears. It hit me that I had possibly stumbled on the lyrical theme this film needs. I had them do a melancholy version, a slow version, then a joyous version.

And then Black Jack appeared, earlier than scheduled, and renewed the argument to have music behind his singing of "Granada." I went to take a leak. When I returned, he had stirred up a storm—said something to Gerard so infuriating that Gerard, wild with anger, was screaming, "A man is not an animal!"

Manny sagely took Jack out for coffee while I finished with the musicians. Then Jack was back, still angrily resistant. He said all he wanted was an instrument playing in his ear, which would not be heard on screen. I said no. Made an inspired, if strained, analogy: "A man on a high wire with a net does not inspire the same feeling as a man on a high wire without a net." Jack said, "You always convince me." I said that was my job.

Sunday, October 16, 7:30 A.M.: Paris

Arrived at Notre-Dame yesterday without a single extra, knowing I would have to steal shots of Wayne midst a lot of unpaid bodies to make the day work.

Only a few tour buses at first. And then abruptly there was an avalanche, so that Notre-Dame was all but invisible and the vehicles parked so close together that there was barely room to shoot. A moment of panic. Then I plunged ahead. The first shot accomplished demanded the second and so on.

When I needed extras, I displayed Wayne prominently. Invariably, American tourists came swimming in for his autograph and ended up in the film, to their delight.

We accomplished the heart of the scene, then filled in the edges and background. Claude caught my tempo and mood, suggested shots, enjoyed the scramble to get them.

In the midst of shooting, someone pointed to a solitary figure watching our operation, identified as Sterling Hayden. Having always admired his work, I sent someone to him with the message that it was a pleasure to have his company, whereupon he abruptly turned and walked away.

After lunch, we began to pick up material for the first montage: the Centre Pompidou, the Eiffel Tower, the Arc de Triomphe, where Wayne, risking life and limb, ran through traffic and back several times to get a desired shot.

We concluded the day, which seemed to stretch languidly, an hour early; all hands parted with a sense of pleasure and achievement at the first week's work.

Monday, October 17, 6:50 A.M.: Paris

Today begins the second week.

   11:00 P.M.

This morning at the tierce bar went well. But the next move and those damned car shots on the Champs strung us out. Result: We did not get the traffic jam or the flirtation scene. Barely made a few POVs at the Étoile before we lost the sun.

Then to dailies. Again the colors didn't seem right. They blame it on the lab. I'm having two shots reprinted down several points to see the effect.

Wednesday, October 19, 6:30 A.M.: Paris

I shot *twelve* pages at the Eclair Studio.

The day began slow, and at 11:00 A.M. I would have bet against myself. Wayne gave me a good idea—cutting to him at the window watching Jack and other drivers. That suggested another shot. We started to gain momentum.

The electrician erupted at something François said and started to quit in the midst of the party section. Black Jack pacified him. So everyone got to play a scene.

Thursday, October 20, 7:30 A.M.: Paris

The cops came by yesterday morning as we were about to shoot the rowboat scene in Lac Inférieur. They asked for our authorization, which, trying to save $300, we had failed to get.

I dispatched François and Michel to the police station where they obtained the needed document.

We got the first shot by noon. Got all the boat stuff and a walk in the woods by 2:00 P.M. The crew expressing deep concern about the lateness of the lunch hour.

Note that the first decision made each day is where we will have lunch, which requires negotiation. These lunches are rarely less than an hour and a half, and always full course.

Usually, around the cheese course I exit conspicuously and pace outside in an effort to speed things.

From lunch to Yuki's fashion show at Le Jardin. Wayne and Gayle took front-row seats with almost no one aware they were acting, given the number of other cameras covering the event.

Claude showed a passion for this scene that made him shoot and shoot despite my urgings to cut.

The dailies most encouraging. The scenes done quickly at the end of the day especially good.

Friday, October 21, 7:30 A.M.: Paris

We don't start till noon today.

Seven and a half pages yesterday. It was a uniquely mild day for this time of the year. A stolen day that brought hordes of *pétanque* players to the Bois. The leaves in midchange. The weather balmy. We had an apéritif for the crew at the kiosk where we'd been shooting all day. The sun almost gone as we left. The *pétanque* players still at it. The sense of a hard day's work well done. A moment I'll never forget.

I just sent for $35,000 more, which will bring the total brought to France to $110,000. That should see us well into the fourth week.

Saturday, October 22, 8:00 A.M.: Paris

If you asked for a perfect day to photograph Paris, your request could not be better filled than mine was yesterday. Wayne tells us he controls the weather, and after the past two weeks we begin to believe him.

I stole shots and people in volume. In the markets at rue Mouffetard I positioned the actors and was photographing a second after the shot was concocted. There was no time to ask for permission. What I got in less than an hour could take a day if it was laid out beforehand with all the resultant red tape.

We finished the week's shooting in a happy frame of mind at a cafe near the Pompidou. And then angry voices: François and Jack at it again.

Wayne, coming out of our apartment house last night, was hailed by a middle-aged man in a business suit who asked if he was Wayne Rogers. When he said yes, the man asked for his autograph on a piece of pink paper. As Wayne signed it, two other men appeared, one with a flash camera, and took his picture, whereupon all vanished. Very strange, and vaguely disturbing.

Now to the cutting room, then to check Monday's location and the racetrack for next Saturday.

Sunday, October 23, 8:00 A.M.: Paris

The racetrack people were accomodating, but the procedures we must adhere to when we shoot are strict.

Wayne and I went to have drinks with Princess Grace, who is a friend of his. She lives on a private court with an entrance on avenue Foch. Marcel Pagnol is her neighbor on one side. Artur Rubenstein lives on the other side. The latter, ninety or thereabouts and barely able to see, has run off with his young secretary. Grace thought it was the effect of dictating his amorous memoirs that stimulated him to one last fling.

What does a glamorous princess do on a Saturday night in Paris? She was taking her daughter to see *Mary Poppins*.

Monday, October 24, 8:00 A.M.: Paris

Worked nonstop yesterday, from 10:00 A.M. to 6:00 P.M., preparing for this week at the Hotel Regina. We are vulnerable to weather since entrances and exits must match nice days previously established.

Doris Roberts (actress) called to say she and her husband, William Goyen (the novelist), were in town. Under the impression they were friends of Wayne's, I invited them to dinner with him and me. Turns out that while Wayne knows them (her) better than I do, he thought they were close friends of mine. In any case, we had a most enjoyable meal.

Doris, as a lark, will be included in the racetrack scene.

Again that sense one is prone to while shooting, of continuous fever and delerium. Last night's sleep riddled with pursuit of phantom shots.

Tuesday, October 25, 7:40 A.M.: Paris

Rain began as I did the drive-home sequence after the party. Not enough rain to register on screen.

Switched the tire-blowout scene to a little town where Pasteur was born. I incorporated his statue in the declaration-of-love scene between Michael and Susan.

Had our biggest audience at the dailies, which were well received.

Wayne said I must be more tactful dealing with Gayle's unfounded concerns about her appearance. When she refers to her "big ass" on screen, I must not say "Stop eating" and "Don't worry, I'll protect you."

As of Friday, we've shot almost thirty thousand feet and printed about eighteen thousand, which is what we planned.

Wednesday, October 26, 6:00 A.M.: Paris

Got some beautiful stuff for the montage. We will have to edit cold-bloodedly. No shots included because they're pretty. The story must be served.

Thursday, October 27, 10:45 A.M.: Paris

Pierre came by for me at 6:30 A.M. We drove through a considerable fog on our way to the airport. Ruth, with Jim and Jean McLaughlin, landed a few minutes late.

We dropped the McLaughlins at the Ritz. On meeting Ruth, Wayne said that he hoped her presence would be a buffer since I "wake up like a gorilla."

We began shooting at the place de la Concorde at 6:00 P.M. Broke for dinner at 10:00 P.M. With Gerard and me off scouting, everyone ordered a la carte, so the meal took almost two hours. Enough wine consumed so that Wayne and Jack were not quite so sharp après—which fortunately works for the scene.

Quit at 2:00 A.M.

Friday, October 28, 10:45 A.M.: Paris

Ruth and I brought back a varied feast from the *charcuterie*, which we shared with Wayne.

Wayne and I were picked up at 5:30 P.M. I felt well prepared, all shots in mind. And then strike one—we had no permission to shoot the exterior of the restaurant I needed. We found another place that gave us permission. Strike two—Wayne suddenly found fault with a scene that has gone well every time he did it in rehearsal. His objections were phantom and no problem ultimately.

We broke for dinner at 10:00 P.M. Again the crew took almost two hours, and there was grumbling about the insufficiency of wine. Black Jack said the standard quota is one bottle for each two men.

We finished up at 2:00 A.M. at place Vendome with a U-turn that eluded us for five takes.

We parted tired and testy, making me glad we have today off.
The lab admitted destroying two of my Sacré Coeur shots.

Saturday, October 29, 8:10 A.M.: Paris

Nous allons à le champs de course aujourd'hui.

A crisis yesterday when the racetrack people called to say our electricians never showed up to install power lines. Gerard took appropriate steps, and all is in readiness.

Manny, Gerard, and I met at 4:00 P.M. Went over next week's work. Manny is more help every day.

Wayne ill—a fever, but he had to put in an appearance at his cousin's party last night.

After dailies, we (the McLaughlins, Jack and Juliette, François, Ruth, Wayne, and I) drove to the Sergents'. Eight of us in the Peugeot 604.

Jack insisted on cooking Algerian sausage he'd brought on a barbecue in the living room.

A memorable time had by all.

Sunday, October 30, 11:15 A.M.: Paris

We rendezvoused here—the actors, that is (Doris Roberts, Matt Carney [expatriate of some renown], Gayle, Wayne, and Jack)—at 9:30 A.M. On to the track. Ruth stayed behind. Would follow later with Nolan (Gayle's son) and his nanny. At Auteuil, we found the others waiting.

We got our gear upstairs to the clubhouse. Picked tables to shoot. The crew and we dined from 11:00 A.M. to about 12:15 P.M. People were arriving now. We only had one or two hired extras, so it was most fortunate that the McLaughlins arrived with two couples, friends from the States. I put them all to work as extras and used them all day. Ruth arrived and was pressed into similar service.

I began with Wayne and Jack spotting Gayle. Rolled well despite a lack of cooperation from gamblers who walked through several shots in their zeal to wager.

Now I was at the major table scene. Really cruising despite a couple of minor delays, which included getting a waiter's outfit for François when the real waiter couldn't speak sufficient English.

I got the legs-playing-footsie-under-the-table shot.

Manny Fuchs (his acting debut) did well in the improvisations.

Doris was excellent. Then suddenly time was running out.

There was only one race left to get the shot of Jack and Wayne losing the tierce. Could we get downstairs to the rail in time? Too late! The race had started without our knowing. We rushed Wayne and Jack to a window overlooking the track in the clubhouse. Claude put the camera on his back. We got something, but not much, of the finish of the race, which (hopefully) is tied to Jack and Wayne.

Urgency turned to panic as the crowd began to leave and I was trying to grab inserts (torn pari-mutuel tickets, the program, etc.) which might make it all cuttable. Then a scramble downstairs to get the arrival and departure shots skipped earlier. Light fading. The electrical gear didn't arrive. I moved both shots inside where night and day can't be distinguished. A little tiff, quickly patched up, with Claude, who is a fine worker. I had my eight and a half pages.

I need an establishing shot of the track and know I missed other things, but overall I felt good. The McLaughlins and their friends had an unforgettable day. Jean, touted by gamblers seated nearby, won a tidy sum.

The crew in revolt at the end of the day, but so far I haven't heard they won't be there tomorrow when we start to shoot at the Hotel Regina.

I've shot about forty thousand feet and printed about twenty-five thousand in the first fifteen days (three weeks) of shooting.

Monday, October 31, 9:30 A.M.: Paris

Good news from Gerard and Manny: As of the end of three weeks, we've spent a total in France of $92,000. On that basis, you can project getting out of France for about $150,000 plus shipping costs. Manny said, "I see it happening, I know it's happening, but I still can't believe it."

Tuesday, November 1, 9:30 A.M.: Paris

Today is a national holiday (All Saints' Day). Will the crew show up? They were told when signing-on that working today was a must. They all agreed but now find a loophole in our having worked three Saturdays instead of the planned two, plus some night work they claim was not part of the deal. So there was grumbling last night (it always starts with the electrician) when

I went twenty minutes past 7:30 P.M. to get the last shot. Intermittent rain didn't help.

Wednesday, November 2, 8:00 A.M.: Paris

Gerard got the crew there despite yesterday being All Saints' Day, but their discontent was palpable. The electrician arrived an hour late and only after being summoned by a special phone call that appeased his honor.

By late afternoon, I was behind and fighting to get all the material in the elevator. Six of us crammed in the small cage, and Wayne picks that moment to take huge exception to a minor change I was forced to make out of physical necessity. This problem superseded by the elevator conking out between floors in the middle of a take. Nervous jokes at first and then mounting commotion. Some guests, already pissed at being diverted to the other elevator, complained vociferously to the hotel director, who keeps saying, "Mr. Gilroy, this can't continue."

After some fifteen minutes, elevator service restored.

The rest of the day a scramble.

To give the electrician his due, I note Manny's report he almost socked some mug at the track who threatened to louse up our shooting.

Called Weissberg in New York about Leigh's note, due yesterday. He'd forgotten. Will get right on it.

Thursday, November 3, 8:00 A.M.: Paris

It rains and rains. Thank God we're shooting inside. All day in suite 117 yesterday—the heart of the picture. The first two scenes, Wayne's and Jack's first arrival, went well. As did the Gayle-Wayne apres lovemaking. *Very* well. But it will be impossible to finish in four days as I promised the hotel director.

To the dailies at 6:30 P.M. Dave and Ruth Harmon, visiting from L.A., present. Every seat taken. I feared the racetrack material needlessly. A bullish air prevails except for Bob Lovett who, backed by the sound man, insists almost all dialogue will have to be looped. The everyday noises of Paris, which I hear as music, they interpret as interference.

A meeting with Gerard and Manny after dailies. A budget blow. My fault. I had forgotten that the lab cost was predicated on one color print only of each scene, so we are over a good bit, as much as $12,000. It will now be a tight squeeze to get out of Paris for $200,000, and I may need two extra days.

I told them that the man in New York (Mitch Leigh) was depositing $100,000 to our account and I could take $10,000 or so if it was needed.

Arrived back here, where a call from Marsha Brooks in New York informed that Mitch Leigh refuses to make good on his note till I'm back in the States with the film. And this after my underwriting his goddamned note. In short, once he is assured of zero risk, he will (or so he says) put in the $100,000. When Marsha reminded him of the signed note, he said, "Sue me."

I told her to stand by. Woke Wayne. Told him all. He has enough dough to get us out of France. Once back in the States with the film, we can regroup and refinance. I called Weissberg and Marsha and told them to tell Leigh to make good on the note at once or he's out.

Friday, November 4, 7:30 A.M.: Paris

The crew, who had agreed to work today (a promised day off since we work tomorrow) for extra pay, changed their mind.

So we are off today, which is probably a blessing since I need rest and time to prepare.

It looks like I will have to shoot six weeks instead of five.

Gayle and Wayne worked excellently yesterday. At one point in the bedroom scene, I thought Wayne had forgotten his lines and was about to say "cut" when I realized he was so choked with emotion that it was difficult for him to speak. Look for that moment.

On to dailies. More racetrack stuff that proves excellent.

Gayle and Wayne quibbled about a take or two, but overall they were delighted. I think that is how actors try to appease the gods: They do good work and know it's good and then focus on some minor flaw as a sacrificial offering.

At lunch yesterday, debate about working or not working today raged from the far end of the table to the middle. The stop line of these almost daily eruptions seems to be one person away from me. Through all, I remain aloof. The language barrier helps me maintain dignity and an amiable relationship overall with the crew. It is the first mate, Gerard, who bears the brunt.

After dailies, Black Jack took the Harmons, Wayne, Ruth, and me to a Jewish delicatessen, Goldenberg's. David Harmon said, "My God, I came six thousand miles from L.A. to eat at Nate and Al's."

Marsha said she conveyed my ultimatum to Leigh, who now claims it was a misunderstanding. Bottom line—the money is to be in Marsha's hands by Monday.

Sunday, November 6, 8:15 A.M.: Paris

On Friday I prepared for the party section. Put each scene on a separate piece of paper, which I tacked to a board. That way I can size up what's to be done at a glance. Must shield this board from the crew lest they be discouraged by all I plan to accomplish.

Went to the editing room. Bob Lovett, suffering an awful cough and cold, needed bolstering. I invited him to lunch, during which he repeated his grim forecast that we would have to loop almost everything in the picture.

I said if his estimate proved true, I would deal with it but there was nothing I could do now. I said overall I felt we were winning the game, though I knew he didn't share my feeling.

He said Jack was hanging around the editing room gifting him with booze in the naive assumption it would gain him some advantage.

Ruth leaves today. Wayne's daughter, Laura, arrives today.

Monday, November 7, 8:45 A.M.: Paris

Saturday was a maelstrom, a kaleidoscope. Jack eventually got Wayne, Ruth, and me to La Voisine, the Ricard mansion. Sans Wayne as navigator, we would never have gotten there.

Some sixty invited guests, in addition to cast and crew. I went immediately for arrivals and departures to give me a frame in the face of uncertain weather. Was ready to shoot inside by the time we broke for lunch at 1:00 P.M. Our fear of too few people proved misplaced. We had so many that we had to shuttle half of them to a nearby town to eat. When I saw the group split up and contemplated the huge amount of work that had to be done by sundown, I recalled Kipling: "If you can keep your head when all about you are losing theirs, etc."

Thanks to a logistical miracle accomplished by Gerard, the people who went to town got back cheerful and contented at almost exactly the same time the crew and other guests rose from the table at La Voisine.

By 2:30 P.M., I was shooting. Knew at once I wouldn't get all fourteen pages. Abandoned the plan of shooting in all three rooms and confined myself to one area.

Going for the vital shots, I began to achieve the fire-storm rhythm that feeds on itself, sweeps all before it. The crew caught my tempo. We rushed from setup to setup. I gave lines to people who had never been in front of a camera. Almost all came through fine.

It's 5:00 P.M. and miles to go: the musicians telling me they must leave to play a job in Paris; the violinist adamant and angry at not being used earlier. I have to get the musicians established in the film. They will give me ten minutes only. I throw them in a different corner of the room. Turn on the playback and start shooting. I beg for five minutes more. I put dancers on the floor where fortunately the rug had been rolled back earlier for a dolly shot. It's the wrong playback. No time to change it. Shoot, shoot, shoot! The violinist leaves. The guitar and bass remain a bit longer. I shove people in and out. Mr. Campiglia is very sorry, but I *must* stop shooting at 6:00 P.M. Leo Fuchs's producer's heart responds to my predicament. He comes to me at 5:45 P.M. and asks if I can finish in another hour. I said maybe. He went off and tried to negotiate it for me (talk about empathy!). But at 6:00 P.M. we were forced to stop.

Of the fourteen pages, we shot eleven.

On the ride home, Jack began to complain about the music. I cut him off. Sensing my extreme fatigue, he said no more.

On Sunday, Manny and Gerard arrived for a financial meeting to which Wayne was invited. The estimate is seven more shooting days needed. It means we will need $25,000 above the $200,000 in hand to get out of France. If Mitch Leigh comes through with his $100,000 today, there is no problem. If not, I'm in a jam. Stay tuned.

Wednesday, November 9, 8:15 A.M.: Paris

On Monday, I told François he was through at the end of this week, for budgetary reasons. He evinced neither surprise nor disappointment.

Took Wayne and his daughter to dinner. Hanging over the day was uncertainty whether Mitch Leigh would come through as promised. My anxiety reduced by a call from Manny Fuchs inviting me to his and Leo's office where (knowing I was having trouble with the last $100,000) he, Manny, told me that Leo was willing to post a bond for my lab costs, which would allow me to get out of the country and pay later if we came up short. In addition, Manny offered me personal assistance, his own dough, $17,000 if we get stuck.

It's a tribute to the picture as well as his generosity because as he said, "I've seen what's on the screen."

Marsha Brooks reported receipt of Leigh's check.

Tuesday, yesterday, we were back in suite 117 at the Regina with M. De la Russie (the hotel director) hot and heavy on our necks.

It began slowly—two days off making everyone languid.

We went to the dailies at 6:30 P.M., which began on an anxious note when Laura, Wayne's daughter, failed to meet us there as planned. She had been out on her own most of the day. Wayne called the apartment. No answer. Fear sprouted. We began the dailies—a big crowd composed of people from the party scene.

The party stuff looks rushed and rough. For the first time it occurred to me we might fail, despite every allowance for fatigue, anxiety about Laura, etc. What a mistake to have all those people present on the worst night of dailies.

Wayne's daughter still not there when we concluded. Fear deepened. We went back to the apartment, found her crying in the concierge's office. She had been followed by a man. In flight, she got lost. Finally got back here.

I dined with Lee Konitz and then went to a jazz club where Lynn and Bob Lovett joined us. Shelly Manne, traveling with Lee, sat in. Was introduced to Kenny "Klook" Clarke, the expatriate drummer who was there when bop began.

Thursday, November 10, 8:45 A.M.: Paris

Wayne overreacts to any alteration of what we rehearsed. He has a muscle pain where the camera fell on him last week.

The crew listless yesterday, as though it was the last day before vacation. Still I got a great deal done.

Wayne volunteered to give one of his points to Manny. I shall match it with one for Gerard.

No croissants!!! Bakeries closed to protest a government edict reducing the price of croissants. It sends a nervous ripple through the city.

If I can get three big scenes today (lobby, balcony, breakfast room), I will be done with the hotel, which will be an enormous relief to the hotel director.

Friday, November 11, 9:15 A.M.: Paris

I may have had rougher shooting days, but yesterday is surely a contender.

We began at the hotel with the confrontation scene. His first meeting with Her after she slept with the chauffeur. We knew it would be difficult emotionally, and tension built while the crew prepared the lobby for a late-night scene requiring black covers over the windows.

Gayle was disturbed that her character had irretrievably lost audience sympathy by sleeping with the chauffeur. She quoted Wayne quoting his thirteen-year-old daughter, who on being told the story, said, "But Gayle seems like such a nice person." I told her the film was intended for more mature audiences but acknowledged that for her character to regain sympathy, she would have to let us know the pain and anguish it cost her.

I had intended a slow build through the various sections of the sequence. But Gayle and Wayne came out of the gate so supercharged and emotional that we were flying from the top. The emotion I was getting was real. If I tried to orchestrate or restrain it, it could vanish. I turned them loose.

We did the lobby, the desk, the elevator. Now we came to the up-the-stairs section. It was 5:00 P.M. or later. Wayne had strong objection to continuing the sequence as written. He claimed, and rightly so, that the emotional level achieved earlier made it unnecessary and even impossible to say some of the original lines. I agreed, but still wanted a few of the lines as a saver in case the audience was not convinced she had suffered enough to redeem herself. Wayne would not give me the lines. Spent and tired, he began to say things like "Let's stop, and I'll pay for another day."

Oh yes—this crisis preceded by going some fifteen takes to get Gayle, who suddenly went dry, to say the key line, "What I felt for you frightened me."

Ultimately I got what I wanted plus a bonus (not in the script) when Wayne instinctively turned his back on her and walked away.

On that note, at 7:00 P.M. we wrapped.

The hotel will allow me in the little room and the balcony of the suite on Monday, but the hotel director has ordered that we will not be allowed anywhere else, including the breakfast room.

Came back here fast. Got cleaned up. To dailies, which looked fine. Then to Princess Grace's for dinner.

Among those present were André Voutsinas, who directed the successful Paris stage production of *The Only Game in Town*. I spent much time talking to Prince Rainier, who exhibited an interest in films that seemed genuine, although I'm sure he has to feign interest in a great many things that bore him.

Saturday, November 12, 11:00 A.M.: Paris

Bob and Lynn Lovett picked me up in a rented car, and we three drove first to Versailles and then to the suburban site of the Shelly Manne–Lee Konitz concert. A nightmarish place. A government-built complex of modern apartment dwellings around a combination shopping mall and culture complex, all in the middle of nowhere.

Sunday, November 13, 9:30 A.M.: Paris

Manny and Gerard arrived at noon. A most productive meeting as we went over the schedule of needs for next week, made plans for a wrap party next Friday night. I told them I was making them coproducers in acknowledgment of their contribution above and beyond the call.

We then went to the Regina. A good meeting with the hotel director, who agreed to let us back into the breakfast room. This after we paid our bills (gracefully), though they were a bit above the agreed-on rate.

Monday, November 14, 7:45 A.M.: Paris

The last week, *j'espére.*

We went back to Auteuil and picked up some racing footage.

Also tracked down a red-and-white bus to match what we shot previously at Notre-Dame.

It rains hard right now, which could louse up the balcony scene tonight. Have we exhausted our luck?

Tuesday, November 15, 9:30 A.M.: Paris

After three days off, being the last week, it was very difficult starting yesterday.

Finally got into the small-hotel-room scene. I did two masters and moved in for close-ups, despite Claude assuring me it was unnecessary and my fatigue urging me to agree with him.

Note to new directors: Never look to, or listen to, the crew for accurate appraisal of your overall work because each department is properly focused on its contribution.

Did four pages in the little room. Then did two-plus pages in the breakfast room. M. De la Russie was looking on, and I was encouraged by his genuine delight at the scene where Wayne attempts to order breakfast in French.

We moved to the balcony. It was night. Heavy rain and wind made us postpone till today.

It is abruptly colder.

Wednesday, November 16, 6:30 A.M.: Paris

Felt flu-ish, chills, yesterday morning. Intermittent rain all day. We did two big car scenes, the balcony finale, and a night arrival at the hotel after the party scene, plus a couple of traffic and establishing shots. Work seemed to improve my condition.

Jack erupted at the end of the bone-wearying day. Claimed I betrayed him by not having Susan (Gayle's character) say "It was no fun for him or for me." He said it made him look like "a shitty lover." Manny, Gayle, and Wayne tried to make him see the difference between the character and himself, but he went on brooding. I'm really too weary to go into it.

Dailies fine.

Thursday, November 17, 9:30 A.M.: Paris

Got to La Voisine (the Ricard mansion) by 8:30 A.M.—Wayne, Jack, and I. Of course we got lost again. Got the picnic scene and Jack singing "Granada." Despite cold and intermittent showers, there was enough sun to make you think it's summer or fall.

Started on pickup party shots after lunch. Scrambling for my life by 5:00 P.M. The crew, fearful of missing a big soccer match on TV, grumbled.

The rushes looked fine.

Gayle and Wayne liked themselves in the climactic balcony scene. For the first time, Wayne didn't say "I could have done it better," which I suggested should be his epitaph.

Friday, November 18, 4:10 P.M.: Paris

We wrapped the picture at 10:45 this morning! Tonight the wrap party!

Saturday, November 19, 12:30 P.M.: Paris

Manny, Gerard, et moi just loaded Wayne's things into the car that drives him to the airport.

A most moving scene: Gerard repressed tears till we came back up here. Then when I let him and Manny out, I felt the moisture on his hand where he had rubbed his eyes. Such a grand fellow. Manny the same. The sadness hasn't hit fully because it won't be over for me for a long time. Fatigue deadens response, but I know that a wonderful chapter is concluded.

The wrap party at 77 Champs Élysée was a grand success; even the electrician had a good time. Much press. Many photographers. Moscowitz, the longtime Paris correspondent for *Variety*, was amazed that we had shot an entire movie in Paris without his being aware of our presence—a first in his experience.

Sunday, November 20, 9:20 A.M.: Paris

Felt disoriented yesterday with the apartment to myself.

Hovering over the day was the magnitude of Sadat's gamble. He arrived in Israel last night.

Gerard and Manny brought good news: I don't have to send for more money. Will get the details this morning, but it looks like we get out of France for under $200,000.

Incidentally, at the wrap party when Marion Segal (wife of George Segal, who is here doing a film) asked our budget, Wayne said we'd get out of here for about a million and a half, which astonished her to the point of disbelief.

In my sleep, I tracked that phantom shot and asked Steve Sondheim to do the music.

Tuesday, November 22, 8:00 A.M.: Paris

I have just returned from my *dernier jus d'orange, presse double, deux croissant et confiture fraise, et café au lait* in the tabac across the street. Told them I was leaving, and we (the owner, the cherubic bartender, and I) exchanged small but sincere emotion.

And so it's over. Gerard and Manny come to fetch me shortly.

I am numb to my achievement. Feel drained of surface emotion. But at bottom I feel great.

Jack made no offer to drive me to the airport, which I was prepared to decline. He has graduated from driver to actor. Fine.

Au revoir, Paris, and all who shared this adventure.

1978
Sunday, February 26, 10:00 A.M.: Home

My last entry was made on the day of departure from Paris. I arrived home two days before Thanksgiving.

I took a sublet in the city.

On Monday, December 9, we began editing at 1619 Broadway, the Brill Building. Irene Bowers, Bob's assistant editor, had started work the week before. There was a delay in arrival of the work print (and subsequently the negative) from Paris due to strikes over there.

How to summarize the editing to date?

We have worked twelve weeks. Strictly five-day workweeks, with no overtime due to our limited budget.

We are on the tenth reel. I figure eleven reels will see us done with about one hour and forty-five minutes of film.

My appraisal to date (not shared by Bob) is sanguine.

I disabused Mitch Leigh of the notion (his) that he was the injured party. His version: He had made this purely selfless gesture and been shat on. I reminded him of the letter he had me sign that put my house on the line if I abandoned the film for any reason. "I never would have taken your house," he assured me.

Tuesday, February 28, 8:10 A.M.: New York Apartment

We approach the area of the story that has always been suspect in my mind: Susan's bedding with the chauffeur and the subsequent reconciliation between the two men. We'll soon know if the emotional arc is there.

A lovely letter from Wayne reprising his delight with the experience.

Wednesday, March 1, 9:00 A.M.: New York Apartment

We're using the scene at Louis Pasteur's statue that everyone predicted would be unusable—too noisy to hear the dialogue.

There *is* noise, but the dialogue is audible and the background enriched with true ambiance.

It costs $2,500 for the right to use eight bars of "Granada" a cappella—more than we can afford. Sorry, Jack.

Thursday, March 2, 6:00 A.M.: New York Apartment

I realize again how vital it is to be in the editing room every day. You must live and breathe it as the editor does (aware of every resource) to be inside the process. If you merely drop in now and then to review and suggest, you have abdicated your vision to some extent.

Wednesday, March 8, 8:00 A.M.: New York Apartment

We begin work today on the last scene. Should be through with the first cut of the picture by lunch. It is six months since the day I left for Paris. Took special pains not to rush the editing of the last few pages in my eagerness to complete.

Bob did good work yesterday on the studio-party scene: my excesses neatly excised and gaps imaginatively filled.

The balcony scene and what follows plays well.

Thursday, March 9, 6:00 A.M.: New York Apartment

I have been awake since 4:00 A.M. as the enormity of what is still to be done (the selling of the picture) really hits me. Hits me because we completed the first cut yesterday.

Friday, March 10, 6:00 A.M.: New York Apartment

Panic yesterday as the chateau-party sequence, upon reexamination, failed to work or submit to correction. Went over and over it. All perspective lost, and dissatisfaction spread to the reels that followed. Radical and ultimately impractical solutions began to suggest themselves by quitting time.

Saturday, March 11, 9:00 A.M.: Home

Began yesterday by polishing the party scene. Broke at 2:30 P.M. with some sense of achievement. Walked. Ate. Got myself psyched for my first view of the entire picture at 4:00 P.M.

Met Bob and Irene in the fourth-floor screening room. Sat far forward of them. Had that hooky-playing sense—alone in a movie theater in the afternoon.

We began. I was really into it when the projector broke down about halfway. A ten-minute wait hurt my appraisal of the rest. But despite many flaws, it worked overall. The film timed at one hour and forty-eight minutes. Seeing it in its entirety exposes areas that work independently but impede the flow. I will bet that we take close to ten minutes out. What works best are the people, their relationships. You resent any screen time away from them. Too many voice-overs. Establishing shots, ditto.

The racetrack sequence the biggest surprise: Viewed alone, all that lovely horse-racing stuff is fine. But not in context! You don't want to see horses. You want to see the characters, which is a tribute to how well their relationship works. We have much work to do, but I feel optimistic.

Thursday, March 16, 8:15 A.M.: New York Apartment

We cut five minutes from the version I saw last week. Still a few things to do this morning in preparation for today's screening. For temporary music over the montage, we're using Fats Waller's "Jitterbug Waltz," played by Ralph Sutton, which fits nicely.

Friday, March 17, 8:15 A.M.: New York Apartment

St. Patrick's Day. A great day for one Irishman—because yesterday's screening was successful.

Still some changes and polishing to do, but it's there. Tommy Mason (who played Archie in my "Nero Wolfe"), invited on the spur of the moment to join Ruth and the boys, knew nothing about the story but was able to catch every point.

Irene volunteered it was the first time the story worked for her. Bob offered no comment, *comme d'habitude.*

Tuesday, March 21, 8:00 A.M.: New York Apartment

There is a moral to yesterday: Don't be present the first time an actor (sans audience) sees himself in a movie. In short, I ran the picture for Manny Fuchs and Wayne, and it was a disaster. Manny anxiously watching Wayne and Wayne watching himself. Both taut. No response. No laughter at all—zero. Polite appreciation at the end. Much talk of music and those extraneous things that people discuss when they wish to avoid the heart of the matter.

Reluctant to let them leave New York with those low opinions, I'm trying to arrange for a large screening on Thursday.

Wednesday, March 22, 8:45 A.M.: New York Apartment

Wayne gave me his notes, many of which involved mechanical items that will be remedied when we mix. Some of his points that lend themselves to immediate correction are being worked on.

I called people all day to invite them to the screening. Figure we'll have about thirty or so. It will be the most crucial screening this picture ever has. It's a shame it must be done with a work print. But there it is.

Thursday, March 23, 8:15 A.M.: New York Apartment

How do I feel about tonight's screening? Nervously confident.

Wayne sees no humor or life till several reels into the picture. I'm sure he's wrong.

Friday, March 24, 9:15 A.M.: New York Apartment

Good Friday indeed!

We did it! A minor triumph!

Worked in cutting room till 2:00 P.M. yesterday. We implemented Wayne's suggestions, plus things that Bob and I saw.

Long walk. Lunch. Then came back here and lounged. Wayne called. Confessed his anxiety about the screening.

Ruth and I by cab to 1600 Broadway at 7:40 P.M. People began to arrive. Gayle Hunnicutt looking fine and chipper. Manny Fuchs looking nervous. Wayne looking trapped. Enter Mitch Leigh and party. Milt Kurtz and family. Jim and Jean McLaughlin with son J.C. At 8:10 P.M. I stepped before our audience of some thirty-five, noted the deficiencies of a work print for the uninitiated.

We began.

Almost immediately a whisper of laughter, and from then on, with the exception of a moment or two, we had them all the way. Strong and spontaneous applause at end. They lingered and lingered until I had to put the last ones out.

Mitch Leigh was ecstatic. Manny Fuchs was his old self. Wayne looked overwhelmed. Gayle happy. Bill Goldman offered to buy up the points of any backer who wanted out. Dennis Smith, who drove us home in a fire-red car, winked deep approval as the lights came up. Ulu pronounced it "excellent." Eleanor Perry said it was a privilege to be there.

Saturday, March 25, 10:00 A.M.: Home

Calls all day yesterday, like after the successful opening of a play. Lila Ehrenbard, the first phoner, to say how wonderful the film made her feel.

I walked to work. Arrived at the editing room where congratulatory calls from Mitch Leigh, Rick Shaine, Rose Gregorio, and Jim McLaughlin awaited.

Bob Lovett congratulated me on the "successful screening." He said that Lynn (his wife) and Maurice Schell, who had come to the screening prepared for total disaster (based on their assessment of the dailies in Paris), liked it enormously.

Bob volunteered that Lynn was so high on the film that when they got home, she called Jerry Greenberg, editing *Apocalypse Now* in San Francisco, to spread the word. As he said this, it occurred to me that the total cost of our picture is probably less than Coppola's spent on movieola rentals.

Wayne and I lunched at Sardi's. Spotting someone he knew across the room, he all but shouted that we'd made a wonderful movie.

Met Mitch Leigh, who said he'd be glad to do the song I need. I said I'd be delighted to have him do it, but he'd be risking rejection since I wouldn't accept anything just because he was an investor. All of this discussed with amiable candor since he's as direct as I am.

He's going to work on the song over this weekend, and it will be our secret that he's auditioning for me.

Wednesday, March 29, 8:45 A.M.: New York Apartment

Resumed a reel-by-reel inspection for sound needs and picture polish. The film is now a little over ninety-eight minutes.

Saturday, April 1, 9:30 A.M.: Home

On Thursday I went to Mitch Leigh's office to hear his song. He bursts with enthusiasm for the film, embraced me, saying, "You will never again want for money as long as I'm alive."

Before he played the song, I told him that even if it was the greatest song in the world, I would have to live with it a while before I made a decision. He said he understood.

The song was written in 1974 for the musical *Odyssey*. A simple lyric melody that I responded to favorably. He gave me lead sheet and cassette. The melody was in my head as I departed. It's a definite contender.

Bob and I went to the sound-effects library of Sound One and picked out effects, at $45 an hour, for two hours.

At 6:00 P.M. we screened for Dick Vorisek. As with *Desperate Characters*, I felt immediately comfortable in his hands.

Dick liked the film. More than that, he liked the sound tracks. Seemed impressed I'd achieved them with a French crew. He saw no reason why we'd need more than four or five days to mix. And then a bombshell: He thought he had five days between big jobs, starting two weeks from Monday. I leaped at the possibility, while Bob recoiled, began a recital of all the things that would have to be done by then. I told him we would hire whomever we needed to meet Vorisek's schedule.

Friday (yesterday): Arriving at the editing room, I outlined a game plan: We would go over our list of sound needs, and I would veto any that I felt were not vital. The essential work isolated, we could decide if we needed more help. En route to the editing room, I'd stopped at the accountant's where I learned I was closer to the financial edge than I thought. I announced this to Bob so he could understand my concern about not hiring anyone we didn't really need. Suddenly he and I were in a heated dispute about the premix work that needed to be done.

End result: He quit.

George Bowers, Irene's husband, will complete the job.

Wednesday, April 19, 9:15 A.M.: New York Apartment.

After auditioning the work of several other composers, I decided on Mitch's song. When I called to tell him, he said, "That proves you have no taste."

He wants to do all the arranging, conducting, etc. Fine.

At 10:00 A.M. this morning we will go over the film reel by reel to spot music needs.

Friday, April 21, 8:15 A.M.: New York Apartment

Began the mix yesterday. Did two and one-third reels.

Saturday, April 22, 9:30 A.M.: New York Apartment

As of last night, we mixed four reels.

Again I see that the director (representing the audience) is the only one who appraises the picture as a whole. Everyone else, including Dick Vorisek, focuses on his field of expertise, which is as it should be.

Editors hold Vorisek in highest regard and treasure any good word from him regarding their preparation.

I think I don't have enough money to complete the film.

Wednesday, April 26, 8:10 A.M.: New York Apartment

We still have reels nine and ten, plus a review, to do today. Got bogged down yesterday when Dick tried a device that ferrets out and kills a particular frequency. The result miraculously cleaner, but in removing the noise, some of the life was tempered. I did not like the trade, and we reverted to the original.

Thursday, April 27, 8:25 A.M.: New York Apartment

By lunchtime yesterday, we had mixed all reels. Took Dick Vorisek and the Bowers to Gallagher's. Learned that Dick, like me, graduated from DeWitt Clinton High School.

After lunch we reviewed. Found very little to alter. Next Friday we mix in the music.

Saturday, April 29, 8:45 A.M.: Home

We spotted titles yesterday. Went to the optical house to put them in the works.

A big blow, unexpected, in cost: After we get the answer print, the next step is to get a dupe negative with color corrections incorporated. That last step (which I thought was included elsewhere) will cost an additional $9,000 or thereabouts. I will not, cannot, have this done. Will defer it till we get a distributor.

Mitch Leigh, working hard in preparation for Tuesday's recording session, said (amiably), "You are the bane of my existence." I reminded him that he volunteered for the job.

Sunday, April 30, 10:00 A.M.: Home

Here is how the movie stands financially:

> I have $22,000 left.
> I owe over $10,000 for mixing.
> I owe $1,500 to the negative cutter.
> I owe $1,500 to editors.
> I owe $? for titles.
> I owe about $4,000 for music.
> I owe about $3,500 for answer print.
> I owe $? to accountant.
> I owe $? for insurance.
> Plus miscellaneous debts like cutting room and severance and vacation pay for the Bowers.

Tuesday, May 2, 8:30 A.M.: Wyndham Hotel

To TVC to screen for Dan Sandburg and his timer.

Tuesday, May 3, 9:00 A.M.: Wyndham

With Mitch conducting (sax, harpsichord, flute, and harmonica), we recorded the music in two sessions yesterday. I like the music by itself; now let's see if the picture concurs.

Saturday, May 6, 10:00 A.M.: Wyndham

We screened with music on Thursday to test it before the mix. All agreed the balcony scene (their last moment together) wants no music. Discarded another cue entirely and shortened another. It appears the film wants no music in dialogue scenes where faces can be seen.

Took the picture away from the title man, who attempted to overcharge us outrageously.

Yesterday, Friday, we mixed the music. It took eight hours.

I asked Jack, Dick's brother, what discount he would give if I paid cash on the spot. He laughed and said there was no need to give me a discount since "you are as good as gold."

"Maybe I'll stiff you this time, so you'll give me a discount next time," I said. He didn't seem worried.

Tuesday, May 9, 9:00 A.M.: Wyndham

Went to the Colton office. Told Marsha Brooks I would have to borrow $25,000 to complete the film. Turns out I must first get

Mitch Leigh to waive the letter wherein I agree not to borrow any money.

> *1:30 P.M.*

I have the pleasure to report that Mitch Leigh not only waived the prohibition against borrowing but is putting up the $25,000 (not without recompense), which is especially heartening since it reflects his estimate of the picture.

Regarding music rights, I told him to draw up a deal that he would deem fair as an investor.

Friday, May 12, 9:20 A.M.: Wyndham

A reshoot needed of the subtitles. Our fault for selecting the wrong type size. Additional cost? The man said $500. I winced. He said $350. Must learn to wince more.

Friday, May 26, 9:00 A.M.: Wyndham

To TVC yesterday to see the first answer print, which has to be done over. The faces too pink. I told the timer that I used no makeup. Now he undercuts me by applying "rouge."

Tuesday, June 6, 9:10 A.M.: Wyndham

Apropos the screening, I asked Pepe for one of the lucky beard trims reserved for special days.

Booted two people from some magazine who tried to crash. A full house, so Wayne and I had to stand. Giving him a stick of gum as the lights went down, I noted his moist hand.

Unwavering attention. Much laughter. All went smoothly. A couple of people fled at the end, but the overwhelming response was excellent.

Julian Schlossberg feels that if the film is brought out small and allowed to grow, it can ultimately play any theater in the country. He mentioned the Sixty-eighth Street Playhouse as a good launchpad. Julian's overall plan, with which we concur, is (1) show it to the majors in Hollywood; (2) try the minor distributors; (3) go our own independent way.

For his assistance (past and future) I insisted Julian take one point of mine so he had more than a rooting interest. He said he'd rather have the guilt. I said I couldn't afford that. He accepted the point.

We booked the DGA Theatre in L.A. for June 20. I leave for L.A. next Thursday.

Sunday, June 11, 9:30 A.M.: Home

Julian said my name is associated with "artistic ventures in commercial spheres."

I diet and exercise in anticipation of the Beverly Hills Hotel swimming pool.

Thursday, June 15, 7:15 A.M.: Home

Off to Hollywood today, the picture tucked neath my arm as usual.

Friday, June 16, 9:00 A.M.: Beverly Hills Hotel, L.A

Ruth drove me to the noon flight I've been taking for years (American 3).

A year ago I was in that barren $6-a-day room on the Left Bank close to junking the project as the enormity of the risk and attendant difficulties loomed. Now I was bound for Hollywood with the finished product. A sense of achievement dawned.

Harry Keller met me at the airport, shared a favorable intuition he has about the film.

Tuesday, June 20, 9:00 A.M.: Beverly Hills Hotel

D-Day.

What will I be writing here tomorrow? I don't want to know. It would spoil the pleasureful pain of uncertainty.

All studios except Universal and United Artists say they will have someone there. Most of the minors will be represented as well.

George Bowers, checking the reels to be sure, found a piece of tape on one reel; needless changeover marks on the last reel; and a reel incorrectly rewound, which the projectionist probably would have caught. But suppose he didn't?

A phone call from Jim McLaughlin wishing me luck raised my spirits.

Wednesday, June 21, 9:30 A.M.: Beverly Hills Hotel

Walked from the hotel to the center of Beverly Hills, noting again that the many times I've done this, I've never encountered anyone but Japanese gardeners. Had coffee with Mann Rubin, who is most soothing company in times of stress.

Followed my usual day-of-the-fight routine: isolation, rest, beard trim, reading.

Met Paddy Chayefsky. Invited him and Howie Gottfried (his partner) to the screening.

Invited almost everyone I bumped into to the screening.

George Bowers picked me and the film up at 5:45 P.M.

We went to the Cock 'n' Bull. Had a Pimms Cup #1 and a beer with dinner. To the DGA theatre at 7:00 P.M. We tested a reel; set the sound level.

At ten after eight, I felt we had almost all who would be there, and with some three hundred present, I said, "Let's go."

My reaction is derived from the audience reaction, and except maybe for fifteen seconds (I don't recall where), it never flagged. At several points there was spontaneous applause.

An enthusiastic lingering afterwards.

Paddy said he liked it despite his dislike for the French.

Met Wayne, Marlo Thomas, Shirley MacLaine, Elaine May, Paddy, Julian Schlossberg, and Howard Gottfried at the Cock 'n' Bull. They applauded my entrance. Elaine said there were only two very minor cuts she would have made. Surprisingly, they were two alterations, amounting to no more than ten seconds, that I regretted not making.

Swanie (H. N. Swanson) called me from his hospital bed to report hearing that I had "the best love story seen here in years."

Numerous congratulatory calls, but will they translate into a distribution offer?

Thursday, June 22, 9:20 A.M.: Beverly Hills Hotel

Despite all the accolades, no one is seriously interested except Columbia, who want their top people to see it. We are arranging a screening for them.

The consensus seems to be that the picture will have to be too carefully nursed to make it worth their while.

AVCO, a smaller firm, said they would be interested if the majors passed, but they are not passionate.

I asked Julian what sort of a deal we might expect from Columbia. His answer was not pleasing.

Thank God for this journal, which provides immediate relief

and long-rage (I meant to write *range*) hope.

Walter Mirisch called to say how much he loved the film, but he wished I'd made it with a couple of big names. Of course, if I'd done so, it might not be the picture he likes.

Friday, June 23, 10:30 A.M.: Beverly Hills Hotel

With George Bowers to a cocktail party at the French Consul's house honoring the head of the Deauville film festival.

Frank Moreno (First Artists), who was at the screening, lauded the film. Said First Artists had three meetings about it but concluded they were not equipped to give it the slow build and personal attention successful marketing requires. He counseled that none of the majors were geared for that route. He also warned against very small distributors with no nation-wide apparatus to follow up a successful opening.

An actor phoned to say he liked the picture better than he liked Wayne. He allowed that his criticism might derive from wanting to play the part himself.

An editor who had worked for me previously phoned. His only criticism was "Why the one fade-out?"

Interesting how each critiques according to his own discipline.

Saturday, June 24, 10:00 A.M.: On Flight 2

George Bowers returned from the Columbia screening at 6:30 P.M. He said six people saw the entire film, but keeping himself at a discreet remove, he had no clue to their reaction.

Monday, June 26, 9:15 A.M.: Home

In this morning's *Times*, Norman Levy, in charge of acquiring independent films for Columbia, said the least important consideration is whether he likes it or not.

Thursday, July 6, 8:30 A.M.: Home

Today's screening will sound the last of the distributors. If no acceptable offer is forthcoming, it's do-it-yourself time, with all that entails.

Friday, July 7, 8:30 A.M.: Home

The screening went excellently, the best so far. Not so much laughter, but deep attention and identification with the characters. No one moved at the end until the final fade-out and then strong general applause. "*Champignon*" for "champion" is a much bigger laugh in New York than L.A. Allied, Quartet, Reade, and Rugoff were represented.

A call from Julian later. He said Rugoff's people were high on it and Rugoff wanted to see it himself. Julian also had a call from the head of Allied in L.A., who'd received a glowing report from his people and wanted to see it.

Monday, July 10, 8:30 A.M.: Home

Jim McLaughlin called. Said if I decided to open the picture myself, I could count on him.

Wednesday, July 12, 9:00 A.M.: Home

Film in the trunk, I drove to the city. Cab to Cinema II. Arrived at 9:30 A.M. Set a sound level that the projectionist told me to put on the high side because Rugoff had trouble hearing.

At 9:50 Rugoff's secretary arrived with two Cinema 5 board members. At 10:00 A.M. Rugoff called to say that we should start the film and that he'd be there in a half hour. Informed of this by his secretary, I said I wouldn't start till Rugoff appeared.

Now two other board members arrived. Told of the situation, they became agitated. I suspect they were fearful of Rugoff's reaction to his orders not being carried out.

One of the board members all but pleaded with me to start the film.

The latest we could begin was 10:20 without running into the first show at noon. I said I did not want to disappoint the board members so I would show it to them, but not before 10:20. At 10:19 Rugoff entered. He seemed surprised we'd waited.

While they watched the film, I went to the Plaza and had breakfast in the Edwardian Room. When I returned to the theater, some minutes before the end of the film, the usher said no one had left. I told him to fetch me from the bar next door when it was over. He did, saying the six were in earnest conversation at the rear of the theater, which was in his opinion a good sign.

The six disbanded saying nice but deliberately restrained things to me in passing. Rugoff wants me to show the picture to a man named Duncan who owns the Paris Theatre. Since that is the theater where I most want to be, I agreed.

When I related all this to Julian, he read it as favorable.

Wednesday, July 19, 8:30 A.M.: Home

Neither Rugoff nor Allied has gotten back to us. Julian as puzzled as I am. He will explore theater availability in New York in the growing likelihood we have to open the picture ourselves.

Thursday, July 20, 8:00 A.M.: Home

Thayer David's[11] obituary in this morning's *Times*.

He was the most widely educated and best-read actor I've ever encountered.

Each day during the shooting of "Nero Wolfe," I picked him up and drove him to the studio. One morning, en route, we were trading classic lines about Hollywood (Saul Bellow's, Dorothy Parker's, etc.) when he said, "Everything in Los Angeles is on the way to the airport." I asked whose line that was. Thayer said he'd just made it up. I said whenever I quoted it, I would give him credit.

Incidentally, that morning (as on two other mornings) we got so caught up in conversation that we drove past the studio.

Thursday, July 27, 7:45 A.M.: Home

I phoned Marsha Brooks and asked her to prepare the letter to investors (per Paragraph 8 of the limited partnership agreement) that allows me to sell points in the event we have to open ourselves. God, how I loathe soliciting again. It's a nightmare to find myself doing exactly what I was doing a year ago.

11. When Orson Welles bowed out of playing Nero Wolfe, which I was enticed to write and direct with assurance they had Welles signed, I was told to discover someone for the role since no other name actors were acceptable to them (ABC/Paramount) or to me. After a bicoastal search, which acquainted me with just about every corpulent middle-aged actor available, I, close to giving up, encountered Thayer David. No sooner did he start to read than Emmett Lavery, the producer, and I exchanged a look: We'd found our man. Why *The Doorbell Rang* has yet to be seen in prime time, despite critical accolades, is a mystery Rex Stout would appreciate. That the story involves the humbling of J. Edgar Hoover and the FBI is a possible factor. Suffice to say that Thayer David's is acknowledged the best portrayal of Wolfe by the Nero Wolfe fan club, who show the film repeatedly.

Saturday, July 29, 8:00 A.M.: Home

Julian will try to tie up the Sixty-eighth Street Playhouse, Little Carnegie, or Paris for late September or early October.

Calls from Bill Goldman and Joe Johnston (lawyer, classmate of Wayne's at Princeton) volunteering money toward the opening. Since they've seen the picture, this cheers me enormously.

Saturday, August 5, 8:30 A.M.: Home

Thanks to Jim McLaughlin and Milt Kurtz, I have half of what I need to open.

Monday, August 7, 8:00 A.M.: Home

I phoned Mitch Leigh. He will join our meeting with Julian. He sounds supportive, said, "They'll never take us alive."

Wednesday, August 8, 8:00 A.M.: Home

Meetings, meetings, meetings. Talk, talk, talk. At 1:30 P.M. yesterday, I lunched with Mitch Leigh, Julian, Wayne, Jim McLaughlin, and a representative of Gray Advertising.

Bringing these disparate elements together was risky but necessary. Julian acquitted himself well. Mitch had good questions and amiable comments. That *Man of La Mancha* just did over $450,000 in Boston doesn't hurt. Jim mostly listened and observed since it's not his field. A good meeting overall.

At 3:30 P.M. the same group, less the ad man, repaired to Julian's office where Meyer Ackerman, owner of the Sixty-eighth Street Playhouse, awaited us. He has seen the film and likes it, which is important since he has a personal regard for what plays his house. Ackerman feels his theater will be available by the middle of October.

After this meeting, Wayne, Mitch, and Jim decided we, less Julian, should meet again. On to Mitch's apartment, where after two hours of chat we got to money: Mitch said he'd supply whatever part of the $100,000 we need for New York that I am unable to raise.

Thursday, August 9, 8:15 A.M.: Home

New York newspaper strike began this morning.

Friday, August 11, 7:50 A.M.: Home

The newspaper strike (they once went 170 days) looms long. We, of course, can't open the film without them.

A call from Mitch Leigh to inform that he will have no cash for us till January.

The newspaper strike hangs over all.

Sunday, August 13, 8:30 A.M.: Home

Julian says the contract with Ackerman for the Sixty-eighth Street Playhouse will be ready for inspection this week. He said two weeks' advance would be required.

Tuesday, August 15, 8:00 A.M.: Home

The mail brought a big vote of confidence from Joe Johnston via his check not for $5000 (as pledged) but for *$10,000!*

The paper strike continues.

Wednesday, August 16, 8:00 A.M.: Home

Another lovely surprise—an additional investment from John Gay of $5,000.

The newspaper strike appears to deepen.

Friday, August 18, 8:00 A.M.: Home

The newspaper strike shows no weakening.

Bob Ehrenbard volunteered $10,000. That gives me $60,000 for sure.

Friday, September 1, 7:45 A.M.: Home

Newspaper strike news bleaker than ever.

Saturday, September 2, 8:30 A.M.: Home

Black Jack called from Paris. For a change, he was calm and rational. He's met people who have seen the film and liked it. I again assured him his work is excellent.

Spoke to Meyer Ackerman. The theater is ours, *but* we must let him know by Thursday if we will open regardless of the strike. If not, then we lose it.

Monday, September 4, 8:30 A.M.: Home

Begin, Carter, and Sadat meet at Camp David. I don't expect anything major to result. How could it, absent the *New York Times*?

Friday, September 8, 8:30 A.M.: Home

The plunger has been pushed. The dice are rolling; the ship has sailed: We open at the Sixty-eighth Street Playhouse after the next picture closes, newspaper strike or no.

Julian counsels against opening during the strike but sees my point—namely, that things will unravel if opening is deferred too long.

Thursday, September 21, 8:30 A.M.: Home

Met Renee Furst, the press agent, at Sardi's for lunch. She seems well connected, promises to deliver the necessary people (critics) to screenings.

Monday, October 2, 8:30 A.M.: Home

Marsha Brooks called with so many points to insert in the theater contract that fearful they'd sink the deal, I complimented her zeal but reduced the list to salient matters.

Friday, October 13, 8:30 A.M: Home

Julian phoned to say Ackerman was accepting all terms of the contract and sending them back signed. Almost immediately another call saying I could open November 1, 3, or 5. I requested Wednesday, November 8, the day after Election Day.

Saturday, October 14, 8:30 A.M.: Home

Carrying film cans, I got a cab to TVC. The driver deduced I had something to do with movies. He knew who Wayne Rogers was. Despite not liking the title *Once in Paris* ("Is that the title you're going to open with?"), he assured me it would be a success.

Rick Shaine will handle the critics' screenings for me. He and I went to look at the Rizzoli screening room. Individual plush velvet chairs but a smaller screen than I'd like.

Sunday, October 15, 9:00 A.M.: Home

I wrote the news release announcing the opening of the film. Ruth lettered the photo that will be our poster.

Tuesday, October 17, 8:30 A.M.: Home

Learned that Manufacturers has a branch one block from the Sixty-eighth Street Playhouse, which will be convenient for night deposit of box-office receipts.

To Renee Furst's office. She approved the news release and biography sketches. We arrived at a press-kit format, fixed screening dates for critics. She and I to the theater to check display cases. There is a flagpole from which we will hang a banner.

Friday, October 20, 9:30 A.M.: Home

Gray Advertising called yesterday to tell me that a high-ranking executive at Warner Brothers (their No. 1 client) forbade them to work on my picture.

What to do? Thought of Matty Serino, who used to be with Ingram Ashe at Blaine Thompson and recently opened his own agency. Phoned him. Met with his staff within thirty minutes. We are in business. Will finalize today.

Newspaper strike talks bogged down again as we near the waterfall.

Am still not satisfied with the Rizzoli screening room. Made the projectionist get a new mat, but still the borders aren't right. Amazing, with all the pictures screened there, no one ever complained.

Saw Vincent Canby's play (*End of War*) at the Ensemble Studio Theatre last night. Good dialogue but unfocused through line. Ducked out without speaking to him because anything I might say would be suspect in light of my impending opening.

Tuesday, October 24, 8:30 A.M.: Wyndham

Renee reports the first screening tomorrow is already "sold out." She has set up several interviews for Wayne and me. One of them is a tentative luncheon date with Judith Crist the day after she views the film.

"If she thinks it's a stinker, she won't come," Renee informed in the easy parlance of the trade.

Our picture will be Serino, Coyne, Nappi's first movie-ad account. Must go to Colton office to clear up music-rights contract. Suddenly Mitch's lawyer wants $20,000 deferred.

Wednesday, October 25, 8:30 A.M.: Wyndham

Newspaper strike talks broke off again.

Thursday, October 26, 9:15 A.M.: Wyndham

About the screening last night: Rick Shaine said a heavy guy (a critic) talked throughout and the audience filed out quietly at the end. He said it seemed warm to him. This apropos of my almost getting into a fistfight with the Rizzoli manager because when I checked the room at 5:00 P.M., I found it overheated. Was informed the air-conditioning had been permanently disconnected. After much Sturm und Drang, they brought out two fans.

Renee said she had nothing to report about critics' reactions. But I suspect she's had some hints and they're negative. Witness her remark: "We may have the kind of film that the public likes but the critics don't."

Friday, October 27, 8:30 A.M.: Wyndham

At a Dramatists Guild Council meeting, Betty Comden said she had heard I had a good film via a relative of hers who'd attended the previous night's screening with Archer Winston (New York *Post* critic), who, she reported, did not seem displeased by the film. Oh, how we cling.

After the meeting, Edward Albee, Marc Connelly, and I rode down in the same elevator. Max Eisen, the press agent on *Roses*, entered at an intermediate floor and noting me, said something to his aide about the honor of riding with a Pulitzer Prize winner. As we exited the building, Albee said, "You should have told him he was riding with the winners of four Pulitzers." I know he has two, so Marc must have one.

Went to Serino's. He had various sizes of the ad laid out and the cost schedule. Nick Nappi and Nancy Coyne joined the discussion.

Saturday, October 28, 9:00 A.M.: Home

Gil Weist (Michael's Pub) delighted to have the opening-night party in the Bird Cage Room. I asked how much, eliciting, in a tone of grievous injury, "Frank—please." He said he'd arrange "surprises," which I assume will be in the area of entertainment and not cost.

If the newspaper strike isn't over by Monday, it precludes next Sunday's ad in the *New York Times* (330 lines costing $2,500). I almost hope that is the case. I could then enlarge the opening-day ad, which is currently 180 lines.

Tuesday, October 31, 6:30 A.M.: Home

The newspaper strike was almost ended yesterday—but no. A last-minute hitch.

Two more screenings today are fully booked.

I went to Rick's cutting room to select a ninety-second clip for TV use.

Wednesday, November 1, 8:30 A.M.: Home

At one of yesterday's screenings, Rick reported a man seated beside him who after quietly watching the picture for more than half its length, launched into a negative commentary from that point on.

Thursday, November 2, 9:00 A.M.: Home

Our first review in "Our Town." Renee read an advance copy over the phone. Quite perceptive and most laudatory.

The two screenings yesterday went excellently. Rick left notes to that effect in my box.

Five interviews today. Must run.

Friday, November 3, 8:15 A.M.: Home

Met Wayne at WOR radio at 10:00 A.M., where John Gambling ("Rambling with Gambling") received us graciously. We did a joint interview with their film critic.

Wayne and I did a luncheon interview at Sardi's with Richard Freedman for the Newhouse chain.

On to the Regency where Wayne and I did separate and joint interviews in the restaurant. Some distraction occasioned by the entrance of Moshe Dayan and party. Dayan ordered consommé; his three aides ordered sandwiches, while the bodyguards—dark suits, young, alert—sat vigilant at nearby tables.

The fellow interviewing me, awed by Dayan's presence, called out, "Shalom, shalom." "Shalom," Dayan answered.

There is the distinct impression by all hands that our screenings are going better and better. Are the actors improving or what?

Saturday, November 7, 9:40 A.M.: Home

Julian said Meyer Ackerman (Quartet Films) wants to distribute the film. I said thanks but not now. He said, "It's my duty to warn you that if you open and don't do well, you won't get any offers." I said I was aware of that but as mother taught me, "When you sense a hot hand, press."

I told Julian the most favorable portent is that I now have Renee Furst's complete attention.

Monday, November 6, 8:30 A.M.: Wyndham

The *New York Times* is back. I feel better for it, unrelated to the film.

Black Jack called from Paris. I told him I would let him know how the opening went. He sounded oddly tranquil. I'm sure it must all seem unreal to him by now.

Tuesday, November 7, 9:00 A.M.: Wyndham

Interviewed by Chris Farlekas (Middletown (N. Y.) *Times Herald Record*, my local paper). Chris, who has interviewed me many times over the years, said my answers were better. I said it was his questions that had improved.

A call from Renee: Vincent Canby can see the film only on Tuesday. So at double-pay rates because it is Election Day, we are having a one-man screening at Rizzoli.

Rick Shaine and Renee both contacted me after last night's screening to say it went the best so far and that David Denby, the *New York* magazine critic, announced at the end that he "loved every bit of it."

Wednesday, November 8, 8:00 A.M.: Wyndham

Canby, as reported by Renee, arrived on time. He sat in the last row of the empty room. Renee absented herself, of course. And so until tomorrow's paper we have no inkling.

They have restored air-conditioning to Rizzoli. Will that be my major accomplishment in all this?

Lunched with Judith Crist, Wayne, and Renee at the Regency. This followed by several other interviews.

Note: The smaller the publication, the longer the interview.

While we were being interviewed, a photographer came in from *Cue*, brought a copy of the new issue (the first review seen in print), and it is murderous. Absolutely scathing, and this from the guy who talked all through the first screening. I told the photographer to convey my enmity to the critic—not for the negative review but for the gross behavior.

Called home, where I got the startling news that Black Jack would arrive in New York today—the guest of another American he'd met in Paris. Wayne went pale. "I'll be out of town all weekend," he said, "and I'm busy tomorrow night." It's a shame we feel thus about Jack, but there it is.

Thursday, November 9, 8:00 A.M.: Wyndham

The *Daily News* and *New York Times* panned the film.

To counterbalance, there are six fine reviews, including *Variety* and the *Village Voice*.

I took David Leone (who will be overseeing the Sixty-eighth Street Playhouse for me) to the bank to establish procedures.

We tested the film at the theater and found the number-two projecter defective, plus a sound problem. Mechanics have since repaired things.

Rick Shaine has done a fine and most supportive job.

While I was supervising the lettering of the marquee last night, Black Jack appeared with his American friend. I felt an initial rush of good feeling, but by the time he left, he had undone it: Complaining that his name be spaced differently, etc.

Friday, November 10, 9:00 A.M.: Wyndham

A call from Renee. The *Post* a rave! "*Once in Paris* is a delight" the headline. More interviews. David Leone, at the theater all day, reported that people exiting liked it enormously.

The party last night at Michael's Pub was excellent. Sylvia Sims gifted us with several songs.

Black Jack finally got to sing "Granada."

At the theater we did $1,104.

Saturday, November 11, 7:30 A.M.: Home

We did $2,075 yesterday. Not record-breaking but lively, especially considering how little we've advertised.

Yesterday morning we heard a fine review of the film by Walter Spencer on WOR, followed by an enthusiastic discussion of the film by him and John Gambling.

Wayne and I did a joint interview for the *Christian Science Monitor*. We work well together.

I walked to the theater, found David Leone in a nearby coffee shop surrounded by notebooks, a calculator, and tally sheets. He's really into it.

Ruth and I walked by the theater last night. David told us the 8:00 P.M. show was big and we would surely go over $2,000. He also informed that Gene Shallit (NBC) had arrived to review the picture well after it started.

Tuesday, November 14, 8:00 A.M.: Wyndham

We did $3,548 on Saturday and $2,336 on Sunday, which gives reason to hope.

Wayne and I lunched with Ackerman, who would like us to advertise more. He assumes our financial resources are considerable. If he only knew.

David called to tell me the capsule in *New York* magazine labels us "the only truly adult film in New York."

Wayne and I dined with Jack and his friend at Peter Luger's. Jack has been recognized a couple of times on the street. Even been asked for an autograph. "I never forget what you did for me," he said last night, pressing my arm to emphasize his gratitude. I only hope that what I've done works ultimately to his benefit. In any case, he's getting the shot he dreamed of all his life.

Wednesday, November 15, 9:00 A.M.: Wyndham

The first real test will be the response to our one-third-of-a-page ad (some $6,000) in this Friday's *Times*.

We've had offers of theaters in Boston and Philadelphia. Wayne goes back to the coast where he'll concentrate on an L.A. theater.

Thursday, November 16, 9:00 A.M.: Wyndham

The sad note of the day was a call from Wayne, about to get a plane, reporting on a cataclysmic two hours he'd just spent with Black Jack.

As a parting gesture of goodwill, Wayne had taken Black Jack to lunch at La Caravelle (one of the most elegant restaurants in the city). Wayne said that Jack sent the meat back and created a scene, prompting the maitre d' to say, "Don't ever come back." Jack's response was a vow that when he became a star, he would return and make the fellow eat shit.

Wayne said Jack complained I wasn't doing enough for him; wondered if I could be trusted with the money, et cetera.

Jack insisted on accompanying Wayne to the airport where Wayne told the driver to take Jack back to the city.

Two hours after this call from Wayne, I am crossing Fifty-seventh when someone hails me. It's Jack in the rear of a chauffeured limousine—Wayne's obviously. Jack jumps out, tips the driver, comes to me. "It's a little town," he said. I asked whose car it was. He said, "A friend's." He wanted to get coffee. I said I was on my way to an appointment. "You can't have coffee with your old friend?" he wheedled.

Boiling from what Wayne had told me (which I'd promised not to repeat), I said no. Jack said he'd walk with me. His every word was a petition. "You make the critics say nice things about me— please, Frank," etc. Then he asked if Gerard Croce had points in the film. I said yes, Wayne and I gave him a point. Jack's lip dropped poutingly, prompting me to say, *"Without Gerard, there would have been no picture! You wouldn't be standing here!"*

Unaware I'd spoken to Wayne, Jack was puzzled by my passion. "I think I walked far enough," he said. "Behave yourself," I called as he turned away.

Informed of this, Ruth prophesied, "He'll end up suing you."

We did $11,593 for the week.

Friday, November 17, 9:00 A.M.: Wyndham

Wayne received a TV plug from Liz Smith, who hasn't seen the film.

Renee called breathless with excitement to say that Rona Barrett just gave the film a big plug on TV. She too has not seen it.

Saturday, November 18, 9:00 A.M.: Home

We did $2,905 last night! Up $835 from last Friday. Had calls from six more minor distributors and theater owners.

Renee reported Jack's arrival at her place in a chauffeured limousine (Wayne's?) with more flowers.

I bumped into Bob Fosse en route home after a day of shooting *All That Jazz*. He looked spent but happy. Was carrying an open wine bottle and glass.

"Want a drink?" he invited. I declined. "How's it going?" I asked. "Great," he said with a joy that was almost reverent.

Sunday, November 19, 9:00 A.M.: Home

Now hear this: WE DID *$5,108* yesterday! UP $1560 from last Saturday's $3,548.

David said they turned away people at the 9:10 show. *WOW!*

Wayne saw Julian about getting a theatre in L.A. Julian predicts doom if we open before Christmas. Cited the dead weeks after Thanksgiving, plus all the big pictures that will be opening. Wayne, thinking as one with me, told Julian that the dead weeks are exactly right for us. No competition for press, and the theater owner is vulnerable to a deal.

On Friday night the theater manager and David Leone found a wallet with $2,000 in $100 bills belonging to Bess Meyerson. They phoned her. She raced back, took the wallet, and left with naught but curt thanks.

Monday, November 20, 9:00 A.M.: Home

We're up $3,600 over same time last week.

Tuesday, November 21, 9:00 A.M.: Home

Tony, my eldest son, learning the mechanics of the theater operation from David, and will occasionally spell him.

Thursday, November 23, 9:00 A.M.: Home

We are preparing a blowup of David Denby's *New York* magazine review (a rave) to be mounted on an A-frame (40 by 30) in front of the theater.

Variety lists us among the top fifty grossers.

David, Tony, and I went to the accountants. Established a once-a-week procedure for deposit slips and tally sheets from the theater.

Meyer Ackerman again complained about our minimal advertising, said it would be better to shoot our entire budget at the outset.

"Look," he said, "you've got about a million in the film, right?" I said we would not disclose the figure. How surprised he'd be to know the real numbers.

Wayne called. We open in L.A. at the Westland Laemmle Theatre, 260 seats, for one week, December 20 through 26, to qualify for Academy eligibilty. I told the family it probably meant my absence at Christmas. All went glum. My monomania wears them down.

Total second week was $16,448.

Sunday, November 26, 9:00 A.M.: Home

We did $5,304 yesterday. Are up $3,200 on the week.

Thursday, November 30, 8:45 A.M.: Home

The phone interview I did with *Variety* (the lead story on page 5 of yesterday's weekly edition) mistakenly suggests that it is my hope and intention to distribute the film on my own.

We ended our third week at $18,448.

I go to L.A. next Thursday, will live in Wayne's guest house.

I phoned Black Jack to alert him to the full-page ad we ran in *Variety*. He asked how we were doing. I told him we were gradually growing. "Whatever you do, Frank, I know it's the best."

Wayne spoke to John Cassavetes, who having tried to distribute, expressed a sympathy so great that I felt its impact even secondhand. Cassavetes offered to share his knowledge with us.

Marsha notified Ackerman (by letter, per four-wall agreement) that we're extending through the seventh and eighth weeks. I signed another letter (extending the ninth and tenth weeks) that she'll hold ready in my absence.

I had Marsha draw up a power-of-attorney authorization for Tony, who will be in charge while I'm in California. Tony said he'd meet me in Bolivia. I said our bankroll wouldn't get him to Trenton.

Note for others who travel this road: Get your hands (somehow) on those Diener Hauser reports, which track what every movie theater is doing on a daily basis. They will usually show that when your grosses dip, everyone else's do the same, which can be very comforting.

Monday, December 4, 8:00 A.M.: Home

Tony was robbed at gunpoint of $2,100 as he was about to make the bank drop after the matinee. A guy, obviously a junkie, shoved a gun in his face.

As the cops drove Tony around the neighborhood in an attempt to spot the robber, one of the cops said, "Get yourself a piece and blow him away next time."

Needless to say, Ruth and I are in shock at what might have been.

Friday, December 8, 7:15 A.M.: Wayne's Guest Cottage, Beverly Hills

I flew out yesterday bearing prints three and four. It's a short walk to the Beverly Hills Hotel, which makes it convenient for breakfast.

Charles Champlin, the *Los Angeles Times* critic will see the film December 18 at 3:00 P.M. at the Royale Theatre—over five hundred seats. He expressed a refreshing desire to see it with an audience, has no objection to the presence of other critics.

Saturday, December 9, 10:15 A.M.: Los Angeles

Wayne and I encountered Max Baer, Jr., on the street. Since "Beverly Hillbillies," he has emerged as a successful producer of small wide-market-appeal films. Wayne told him our situation and asked his advice. He was instructive and encouraging. We must have talked for forty minutes. As we parted, I told him I remembered the Star of David on his dad's boxing trunks. "1934," he said.

I set up shop in one of Wayne's offices.

A note marked "urgent" to call John Gerstad, actor-director, in New York. I could not conceive the reason since he and I know each other only slightly. I phoned him. He raved about the film, then told me that I was being "robbed." Reported going to the show the other night and the ticket taker, besides not tearing the tickets, reluctant to give them to John when he asked for them. I thanked him for the advisement. Said I'd look into it.

I spoke to Tony about this. He dropped a friendly word on the theater manager.

We've hired Rogers and Cowan to handle publicity out here.

Sunday, December 10, 9:00 A.M.: Los Angeles

This is our fifth week in New York, and I think we might triple that number ultimately.

Monday, December 11, 6:15 A.M.: Los Angeles

I went to the Gays' in midafternoon. John took me on a walking tour of the recent fire damage. The entire canyon burned black.

As we began our walk, Ronald and Nancy Reagan appeared at the foot of their driveway with their dogs. Reagan wore a bright green jumpsuit and boots that triggered a Green Beret image. He is taller than I supposed. We said hello as we passed. They returned the greeting guardedly.

Tony called. We did $2,784. A very good day.

Larry Gay will handle the theater for me here.

Tuesday, December 12, 8:00 A.M.: Los Angeles

We did $562 in New York yesterday, the lowest gross to date. Of course, I know it's Monday of the acknowledged worst week of the year, but still it hurts because the thread we hang by is so delicate.

Breakfasted yesterday with Gloria (Rogers and Cowan) the publicist. Her constant air of excitation sets me trilling. Evidently that frenetic air is something most clients require or they don't think they're getting their money's worth.

Wayne and I lunched with Max Laemmle and his son Bob. We got on nicely.

I told Wayne I felt he'd done well on the Carson show. His response, *comme d'habitude*, was "I could have done it better."

Wednesday, December 13, 7:00 A.M.: Los Angeles

Arthur Gregory, Wayne's manager, requested a screening for twenty-five people last night. Nine turned up, including Max Laemmle, who impresses me increasingly.

Gloria suggested the Golden Globe Awards, which I gather is an association of foreign-press film people. They have a New Actor category that Black Jack might win.

Wayne and I met a foreign distributor who estimated "conservatively" that the film, including TV, would do a million. After the meeting Wayne regretted not asking what advance he'd offer. I said a man who wore shirts like that (garish red stripes and slightly frayed) would never give advances.

Friday, December 15, 7:30 A.M.: Los Angeles

Was breakfasting at the Beverly Hills Hotel yesterday when a well-known producer stopped to tell me that what I was doing was "beautiful, but crazy." I sensed he found my activities vaguely threatening.

New York box-office figures slide.

Saturday, December 16, 8:30 A.M.: Los Angeles

Harry Keller took me to Harry Gelbart (Larry's father) for a beard trim and haircut. Gelbart, seventy-two, who's coming to the screening on Monday, is considered one of the best joke tellers in town.

Sample: "Guy dies and goes to heaven. God says, 'Are you hungry?' Guy says he could eat something. God makes him a tuna-fish sandwich and one for himself. God says he has to do something. 'While I'm away, you can look around. Over there you can see hell.' God goes off. The guy looks down at hell and sees them having a feast—gourmet food, the works. God comes back. Says, 'Are you hungry?' Guy says, 'I could eat.' God makes them each another tuna sandwich. The guy says, 'God, why are they having a banquet in hell and here it's tuna-fish sandwiches?' God replies, 'For just the two of us, it doesn't pay to cook.'"

Sunday, December 17, 6:10 A.M.: Los Angeles

Tony called. Reported Black Jack, at the theater last night, seemed disoriented.

When I cast Jack, I had no inkling what I was touching off. If I had known, I don't think I would have proceeded. I say, "think" because he's so excellent in the role. My hope is that he returns to France without doing serious damage to himself or anyone else.

Went to Tom Laughlin's annual Christmas bash with Wayne and Mitzi. Laughlin has the reputation for being difficult, in good measure due to distributing *Billy Jack* on his own, which of course strikes a sympathetic chord.

Anne Bancroft, Darryl Hickman, and I got into a religious discussion appropriate to three ex-Catholics who have coughed up the hook to varying degrees.

Monday, December 18, 10:00 A.M.: Los Angeles

Went to the Woman's Press Club party at the Beverly Wilshire with Wayne and Mitzi. Vestiges of old Hollywood. Numerous photographers taking hundreds of pictures that will never appear. The clicks and flashes imparting a reassuring sense of moment.

We shared a table with Rita Hayworth, who remained inside herself, shyly. She received by far the loudest and longest applause.

Larry Gay and his girlfriend passed out a thousand flyers on Saturday night. Some people saw the *New York* magazine "adult movie" quote and thinking it a porno flick, refused to accept.

Tuesday, December 19, 10:00 A.M.: Los Angeles

I arrived at the Royale Theatre (for the Champlin screening) at 2:15 P.M. Larry, waiting, took the print from my car. We ran a bit of reels one and two to set focus on both projectors.

It required an eight-block walk to locate a saloon for my pre-screening apéritif. The crowded bar I found was a neighborhood place. A cozy feel. I resisted the urge to invite them all to the theater.

Some two hundred people, including thirty critics and movie writers, showed up. It seemed to go well.

Wednesday, December 20, 6:30 A.M.: Los Angeles

Did I note moving to the Gays' because Wayne's mother and sister are using his guest house?

John Gay knocked at my door a few moments ago to tell me that Gloria was on the phone. When I picked up, she said, "I've been waiting since four a.m. to make this call." She then read a most glowing review by Champlin.

Thursday, December 21, 8:00 A.M.: Los Angeles

In the midst of lunch with Wayne (everyone enthused about the Champlin review) I realized I was sick and came back to the Gays'.

Wayne will take my place at the theater tonight and see that Larry is launched.

Word from the theater that there was a line at 6:00 P.M. The 8:00 P.M. sold out.

Feel on the road to recovery this morning, but weak.

A call from Jack's American friend, who made threatening reference to a lawsuit. "About what?" I asked. He became evasive but insinuated Jack felt entitled to compensation because of the similarities between him and the character in the film. I said that beyond Jack having driven me, all else was invention. "Why did you hire Jack to play the part?" he asked suspiciously.

My God I, can see the law suit now—the fact that I gave him the chance of his life being used against me!

The friend also told me that Jack was traveling in jet-set circles. Said some wealthy woman had invited him to Palm Beach. I wince.

Friday, December 22, 8:30 A.M.: Los Angeles

This flu bout may be a blessing—respite without guilt.

The $1,550 we did opening day at Westland broke their house record!

Saturday, December 23, 9:00 A.M.: Los Angeles

Drove to the Boutique at LaScala at 5:30 P.M. to meet John Cassavetes and Wayne.

I found Cassavetes genuine and sound. He has been through the entire independent-distribution gamut. He said if Wayne and I were willing to devote the next three years of our lives exclusively to distribution, then he would advise us to continue as we have to date. We of course said that was out of the question.

Cassavetes is sure there is a conspiracy to keep the independent filmmaker out of the game. He cited abuses he's been subjected to. The fact he has never had a concrete TV offer on *Woman under the Influence*, despite Peter Falk's name, not the least of them.

It seems that anyone who bucks the system and makes the slightest dent is labeled crazy: Tom Laughlin, Max Baer, Jr., Cassavetes. I suspect I may be joining them.

In addition to sympathetic support, Cassavetes offered us access to his distribution material.

We did over $1,700 out here—another record.

Monday, December 25, Christmas Day, 11:00 A.M.: Los Angeles

First Christmas away from home in twenty-five years.

We did $12,400, breaking the one-week house record at Westland!

Went to H. N. Swanson's office on Sunset Strip. The memory of my first visit in 1954 as I climb the stairs.

Swanie, as always, in that dusty paneled office that has been his lair for so many years.

I noted how often his name cropped up in books about Hollywood, including S. N. Berman's, which I had just read. Swanie said, "Berman did very poor work out here."

We spoke of Fitzgerald, whom he'd represented. Swanie said he was going to serialize *Gatsby* in *College Humor* (his magazine) for $10 grand but the deal was killed at the last minute lest it hurt book sales.

Swanie's coming to see my film last week, given his various ills, was touching. Once again I urged him to record his memories of Fitzgerald, Faulkner, O'Hara, et al. But I doubt he will since it would be tacit admission of his own mortality.

The Shah of Iran appears to be going under. But why pretend my interests at the moment are global?

Friday, December 29, 8:30 A.M.: Los Angeles

Frank Price, head of Columbia, phoned. Would like to see the film on the basis of Sherry Lansing's recommendation. He said next week, perhaps Thursday. I said we were screening for the Directors Guild that night, suggested he might want to see it with an audience. He said that might be advantageous, will get back to me.

Story in today's *Daily Variety* about our breaking the house record at Westland.

Saturday, December 30, 8:45 A.M.: Los Angeles

I am out here over three weeks.

We succeeded both critically and at the box office, and yet the prize (a distribution deal) eludes.

1979
Monday, January 1, 9:45 A.M.: Los Angeles

Will move back to Wayne's bungalow today.

Wednesday, January 3, 8:50 A.M.: Los Angeles

Met with Tom Coleman of Atlantic Releasing. He has money and an organization that so far has been devoted to foreign films. He wants to break into the American market, sees our picture as the perfect vehicle.

The world leaked into Beverly Hills yesterday via Iranians rioting outside the Shah's sister's house where their ninety-year-old mother is staying.

Friday, January 5, 9:00 A.M.: Los Angeles

Wayne and I met with Coleman, who offered an advance that he would recoup three-for-one out of theater rentals. After that, we would split 70-30 (us on the short end), plus he wants to participate in ancillary rights.

Another meeting scheduled, to which we will bring Julian.

Accompanied Wayne and Mitzi to a screening at Charlton Heston's home. Among the guests was Franklin Schaffner, who directed Heston in the "Playhouse 90" version of John Marquand's *Point of No Return*, which I'd scripted in the days when I was known as "the Marquand man," Marquand having insisted no one but me adapt his work for television.

Two screenings for the Directors Guild last night (some four hundred people at each), went excellently.

Saturday, January 6, 8:30 A.M.: Los Angeles

Wayne, Julian, and I met with Coleman. Result inconclusive.

The Directors Guild screenings spurred interest by other distributors, including Warner and Twentieth.

A delightful dinner with the Gays and Edward Vilella, whose story John is adapting for television. Entering the restaurant, I noted Vilella's limp, which miraculously disappears when he dances.

Sunday, January 7, 8:45 A.M.: Los Angeles

Four screenings at the Writers Guild today (11;00, 2:00, 5:00, and 8:00).

Julian said the deals made by distributors and exhibitors really don't mean much because after the run, according to business done, they renegotiate.

Called Mitch Leigh. Read him Champlin's favorable quote about his music.

Good news from New York where we did $3,092 yesterday. David reported Ackerman's surprise, compounded by the absence of any advertising.

Monday, January 8, 8:00 A.M.: Los Angeles

Gloria reports, "The Writers Guild screenings could not have gone better." She said there was talk of Black Jack for a supporting nomination. But only actors can nominate actors, so we must hope for a big SAG turnout on the 25th.

Tuesday, January 9, 8:35 A.M.: Los Angeles

Pete Meyers, head of distribution at Twentieth, saw the picture yesterday and called to express serious interest. I went to his office at 3:00 P.M. Haven't walked those Fox corridors in ten years, and it's twenty since my introduction there via Dick Powell.

Meyers said Twentieth is interested in all rights. Was sending two of his assistants to last night's screening.

Ate at the Kellers'. Harry, seeing how tired I was, covered the 9:30 show for me—reported excellent reaction and brought the film back here.

    10:00 A.M.

Meyers called. Reiterated "serious interest" but wants twenty-four hours to allow their TV sales expert in New York to make an evaluation. "If our TV man has a favorable response, we will jump in with both feet," he concluded.

Related this to Wayne, who is about to leave for a meeting with Coleman and Julian, from which I've excluded myself so they can talk purely as businessmen.

Thursday, January 11, 7:00 A.M.: Los Angeles

Warner still on the fence. Twentieth vamping.

Friday, January 12, 6:30 A.M.: Los Angeles

Coleman, Wayne, and I met. We resolved almost all major points, are close on others, and left the reversionary clause (how we part if he is derelict) for the lawyers.

Exiting a restaurant, Wayne and I encountered Orson Welles.

Wayne introduced us. Welles and I acknowledged prior contact on "Nero Wolfe." He congratulated us on *Once in Paris*. I told him we had seen and read the actress he recommended. "And cheapened yourselves by not using her," he riposted.

Saturday, January 13, 9:00 A.M.: Los Angeles

The deal with Atlantic is made. Coleman eager to start a campaign for Oscar nominations.

Variety reports the Las Vegas betting line on Academy Award nominations lists Wayne at 2–1 over Laurence Olivier at 3–1!

Sunday, January 14, 9:30 A.M.: Los Angeles

In this morning's *L.A. Times*, Champlin lists me and six others as logical Oscar nominees for Best Original Screenplay. Tony reports Black Jack at the theater with a photographer who snapped him getting a standing ovation from the audience leaving the nine o'clock show.

Friday, January 19, 8:15 A.M.: Los Angeles

Coleman had papers delivered that contradict some of what we agreed on; alters other things, ignores some points. In short, the deal is in jeopardy.

Saturday, January 20, 6:40 A.M.: Los Angeles

The deal is back on the tracks.

The women in Wayne's office (where I've become a fixture) opened wine and had a cake to toast my departure.

Harry will pick me up in a few minutes to drive me to the airport.

Wednesday, January 24, 9:45 A.M.: Wyndham, New York

Frank Weissberg received the redrafted papers from Coleman yesterday. Some calls and revisions back and forth.

I phoned Black Jack to tell him it looked like we had a distribution deal. He said he was leaving for California tomorrow. I suggested lunch today. He agreed.

Time magazine gave us a bad review. Coming twelve weeks after we opened, I characterize it "a late hit after a touchdown."

Gayle Hunnicutt and Wayne Rogers during or between takes.

Michael Moore (Wayne Rogers) and Jean-Paul (Black Jack Lenoir) nearing the climactic moment in the *pétanque* game. Photo by Bernard Couzinet

I am having a good day. Manny Fuchs (with the camera) is at my side as always.

Wayne and Black Jack in a characteristic moment. Photo by Bernard
Couzinet

Black Jack and moi. Photo by Bernard Couzinet

Left to right: Jean-Paul (Black Jack), Michael (Wayne Rogers), and Susan (Gayle Hunnicutt) moments after Jack sings "Granada."

Went to the apartment where Jack has been living. We talked for an hour and a half. I briefed him on all that's happened.

I tried to prepare him for Los Angeles: Counseled that if he played the star, made demands, or was difficult, he would abort his career before he started. He seemed to listen.

He fears talk shows because he isn't as smooth and glib as other performers. I told him his appeal was that he *wasn't* like the others, that no one expects a man plunged into a new life at fifty-two to be smooth.

He apologized for his friend's phone call in which there were veiled threats of a lawsuit. I said it was such a foolish notion that I never took it seriously.

"No matter what happens, I never forget the chance you give me," he said for the umpteenth time. I said it would please me greatly to see him prosper and pain me to see him fail. And so we parted, with, I suspect, relief on both sides.

The deal with Atlantic is official.

Am renewing our lease of the Sixty-eighth Street Playhouse for the fifteenth and sixteenth weeks.

P.S.

We closed in New York in March after a run of seventeen weeks.

Atlantic's theatrical distribution proved unsuccessful, and eventually the picture reverted to us and was turned over to Julian Schlossberg's company (Castle Hill) with Walter Manley handling foreign rights.

The Writers Guild of America nominated the picture for Best Comedy Written Directly for the Screen.

Black Jack cut a wide swath during the four months he was in the United States: In Los Angeles, he frequented the Playboy mansion, escorted Rita Hayworth, and had a host of adventures I heard rumor of.

After he returned to France, there were phone calls accusing Wayne and me of making money from the film and refusing to give him his two-point share, these calls culminating in an accusation that the robbery in which my son was held up at gunpoint was faked.

"We've just had our last conversation," I told Jack, and invited him, if he really believed he was being cheated, to sue me. Which he did, or tried to, a lawyer he'd met in New York sending me a letter of claimed injustices, all of which were refuted to the lawyer's satisfaction.

Some two years later, and long after it happened, I learned Jack had died of a heart attack.

Ironically, *Once In Paris* eventually returned a modest profit but despite many efforts I have been unable to track down Jack's legal heirs. It's my hope this book will accomplish that so the account can be settled.

I understand the Hotel Regina has done a lot of business attributable to the film. It's at place de Pyramides if you're curious.

Wayne, at some point, asked about future plans, said, "All I want to do is *Once in Paris* the way we did it—over and over."

A final word about Black Jack:

Gloria, the press agent who shepherded him in Los Angeles, said he was the most unforgettable character she'd ever met.

I suspect many who met him (myself included) feel the same.

Asked what I learned from the experience, I'd say, "It's dangerous to make someone's dreams come true, especially at an age when they'd abandoned them."

Asked if I'd undo the experience if I could, I'd say no. I suspect Black Jack would say the same.

Two's Company   by David Denby

Sometimes a few small details are enough to tell us that we've fallen into good hands. At the beginning of *Once in Paris*, a low-budget, independent feature written, directed, and produced by Frank D. Gilroy, an American screenwriter named Michael Moore (Wayne Rogers) arrives in Paris to do some work and is checked into his posh hotel by Jean-Paul (Jack Lenoir), an alarmingly friendly and competent chauffeur. As Jean-Paul boldly demands a bigger room for Michael and then tries to unpack his bags and show him around town, Gilroy brings out Michael's increasing irritation with the man's bullying hospitality. This is exactly right: Official greeters never realize that people getting off an airplane want nothing more than an empty room and a bathtub. Gilroy, who is a screenwriter, playwright (*The Subject Was Roses*), and occasional movie director (*Desperate Characters*, *From Noon Till Three*), has made a movie that is as sharply observed and perfectly structured as a first-rate short story. Don't be misled by the disparaging review in the *Times*: This is no frothy, gay-Paree romance but a surprisingly tough-minded tale—perhaps the only true "adult movie" in town.

Gilroy's theme is a familiar but inexhaustible one—the innocent abroad. Michael Moore, an all-American boy perhaps forty years old (but more like twenty in terms of experience), is a cocky, irritable prig, hiding in his happy marriage as if it were a fortress designed to keep out the rest of the world. That scoundrel Jean-Paul takes him in hand. A cunning, amazingly resourceful jack-of-all-trades, a "man with a past" who has done time for manslaughter, Jean-Paul is the kind of earthy, wised-up proletarian that Jean Gabin would have played with irresistible glamour and authority thirty years ago. Jack Lenoir is not a professional actor, but he doesn't do badly. Born in Algiers, he actually worked in Paris as a movie-studio chauffeur (also as a stunt man) for twenty years, and although he lacks acting technique and flair, he draws on his experience and his self-assurance as a man to get him through. Swarthy, a little crude, even slightly oily in a menacing way, Lenoir's Jean-Paul is a very convincing Mediterranean male, loving both his wife and all other women, drawn to larceny of every kind and also to a private but very strict ideal of honor. And Lenoir shows us something Gabin couldn't—a natural con man's baffling mixture of servility and pride. As cautious Michael finally realizes, Jean-Paul's exuberant contradictions express a love of life greater than his own. Lenoir and Wayne Rogers work well together, maintaining an edgy give-and-take relationship that isn't resolved until the last frame of the movie.

Jean-Paul pimpishly encourages Michael's affair with a beautiful English woman, Susan (Texas-born Gayle Hunnicutt), who is some sort of international fashion designer. Susan isn't created with the same kind of detail as Jean-Paul. A woman of mysterious swank, she remains regally proud even as she goes to bed with this second-rate American; clearly the most interesting thing about her for Gilroy is her luxurious availability. Dark-haired and imposing, Gayle Hunnicutt (she starred in the Masterpiece Theatre version of *The Golden Bowl*) is one of the most convincingly adult women to appear on the screen in years. Despite a few lyrical views of the lovers gazing at the Eiffel Tower, which the charitable will overlook, the affair of Michael and Susan is presented in remarkably unromantic terms—each is looking for a bed partner.

Frank Gilroy's direction has improved immensely since his first movie, *Desperate Characters*, a tense, constricted exercise in urban anguish shot in punishing close-up. He may never be a master of film rhythm and texture (most of *Once in Paris* is extremely simple visually), but his work is clear and sharply pointed. His only serious failure as a director—and it's the reason the movie isn't a minor classic—is his inability to coax a warmer, more interesting performance out of Wayne Rogers. Maybe Rogers spent too many years playing Trapper John in *M*A*S*H*: When he tries to act sexy and debonair it comes out crass and rather unpleasant, as if he were still hacking around with the guys on the base. He doesn't show us the charm under Michael's frightened aggressiveness (it's there in the script but not in the performance), and so it's never clear enough why Jean-Paul and Susan find him attractive rather than merely surly.

Still, the movie works quite well. Living in a more dangerous world than Michael, both Jean-Paul and Susan come to fear that he will be destroyed if he tries to live as they do, so they join forces and send him back home with his self-righteousness intact. The movie's ironic final twist is as brutally nonchalant as the close of a great short story. *Once in Paris* is a bittersweet fable (with an emphasis on the bitter) that keeps going one step further than you expect. In a season of feeble big clinkers, it's a little movie with clout.

When was the last time you did something you really wanted?

McLAUGHLIN, PIVEN, VOGEL INC. present a Frank D. Gilroy film

THE
GiG

STARRING
Wayne Rogers ▪ Cleavon Little

Andrew Duncan ▪ Jerry Matz ▪ Daniel Nalbach ▪ Warren Vaché

featuring **Joe Silver** as Mitgang with **Jay Thomas**

Director of Photography **JERI SOPANEN**   Editor **RICK SHAINE**   Sound **ERIC TAYLOR**

Produced by **Norman I. Cohen**   Written and Directed by **Frank D. Gilroy**

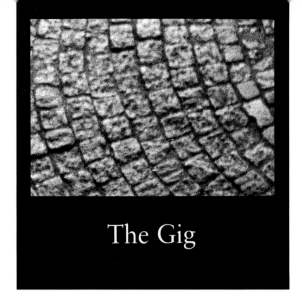

The Gig

Blessed, or cursed, with a memory that allows me to recall only the good of an experience, I ventured into the independent film area again.

The script traceable to the summer of 1950 when the Dartmouth Dixieland Band played at Zuk's Castle Grill in northern New Jersey and my hopes of becoming a first-rate trumpet player died with nightly reminders of my limitations.

At the end of that summer, I packed my horn away, the writer-jazzman split forever healed.

But what of those who don't sound their dreams (in whatever field) and regret what might have been.

Suppose in middle age they got a second chance? And suppose they took it?

Such speculation spawned *The Gig*.

1984
Tuesday, February 21, 9:45 A.M.: Los Angeles

At dinner I told Sarah and Norman Cohen I intended to proceed with *The Gig*.

I just breakfasted with Wayne Rogers. Offered him the role of the used-car dealer–trombonist.

Wednesday, February 22, 10:30 A.M.: American Flight 40

Headed home.

Horton Foote[1] aboard. We congratulated ourselves on finding a way of making films that allows us to control our destinies.

Wednesday, February 29, 8:30 A.M.: Home, Upstate New York

Norman (Cohen) phoned with preliminary breakdown: We can do it two or more hours outside New York for $500,000. This based on shooting six days a week for three weeks. *Or we could do it in Montreal, with a 25 percent rate-of-exchange gain, for $400,000.*

Thursday, March 1, 7:10 A.M.: Home

I've booked into the Wyndham next Tuesday, Wednesday, and Thursday in an effort to prime the production pump, get myself started. What that means, of course, is raising the money.

Friday, March 2, 8:30 A.M.: Home

Wayne wants to do the car-dealer role in *Gig*. He volunteered that if I had any trouble raising money in New York, I should call him. "I'll come flying in," he said. I alerted Norman, who will now attack the budget seriously.

Sunday, March 4, 9:00 A.M.: Home

I started compiling cast lists. Intend to bring the six lead actors only to Montreal, find everyone else there. I will try and get a black bass player, a genuine musician, to play that role.

Friday, March 9, 10:00 A.M.: Wyndham Hotel, New York City

At the Hanover Square (India House) restaurant (where I spent many Saturdays as a kid while my father rolled poker dice for drinks), I outlined the *Gig* deal to Jim McLaughlin.

Saturday, March 10, 8:30 A.M.: Home

I made an appointment to meet a young man (characterized by Dennis Smith as "a wealthy ex-hippy scion") who might invest.

1. Playwright, screenwriter (*Trip to Bountiful*) involved in independent film production.

Sunday, March 11, 8:30 A.M.: Home

Julian Schlossberg called from L.A. to say how much he liked *The Gig* script.

He is seeing his "deep pocket" investors at Hillcrest on Thursday.

Tuesday, March 13, 8:00 A.M.: Home

Meyer Ackerman phoned echoing Julian's enthusiasm for *The Gig*.

Wednesday, March 14, 9:00 A.M.: Home

Wayne got Norman together with Harold Greenberg, who owns a lab in Montreal. Greenberg can't produce directly anymore because he owns a Canadian cable system, but he would like to arrange a production package for us and be our Canadian representative.

Saturday, March 17, 8:00 A.M.: Home

The "wealthy scion" arrived forty-five minutes late for our appointment.

He and his associates like the script, will get back to me.

Thursday, March 22, 9:00 A.M.: Home

J. C. McLaughlin (Jim's son) phoned. He loves *The Gig*. We will meet tomorrow.

The scion wants an "artistic conference." I said that was agreeable but should be preceded by a letter outlining business details: what they sought in the way of points and controls, etc.

Saturday, March 24, 9:10 A.M.: Home

Julian and Meyer took me to a Chinese restaurant where we had a wide-ranging conversation studded with anecdotes and asides.

The business portion came to this: Meyer is embarrassed to raise $750,000 because it seems unrealistic.

"No one believes you can make a film for that," he said.

They (he and Julian) want to raise $1 million. If we do it for $750,000, the remaining money will be contingency in lieu of completion bond and for prints and advertising if we don't get a suitable buyout offer and have to distribute ourselves.

I noted the novelty of the director asking for $750,000 and the money sources insisting on $1 million.

Julian will put their proposal in a letter.

J. C. McLaughlin is in. I like his succinct way of dealing.

Tuesday, March 27, 9:15 A.M.: Wyndham

Wayne studied Julian and Meyer's proposal. We then met them for lunch.

In discussing the deal, Wayne said he couldn't see why, since he and I and all the other talent were working for scale, they, Julian and Meyer as distributors, should get their usual fees prior to the investors being repaid, which would make the profit goal that much harder to achieve.

Julian and Meyer responded that we would have the same situation with any distributor, alerting me they would be partners to the point of distribution, whereupon they went in business for themselves.

When I noted that Julian and Walter Manley have made more money from *Once in Paris* than I will ever see, Meyer (as though such inequity was ordained from on high) could not understand my dissatisfaction.

The meeting concluded ambiguously.

Thursday, March 29, 9:15 A.M.: Wyndham

Julian phoned to say he and Meyer had contacted their (Meyer's) money guy, who knew my work and was enthused at the prospect of involvement. He also said he was calling to establish his interest as distinct from Meyer's, to make sure he and I didn't lose touch.

Saturday, March 31, 8:20 A.M.: Home

I breakfasted with Julian. Gave him my definition of *partnership*, which meant sharing the risk from beginning to end. I told him (and he agreed) that at the mention of "risk," his eyes glaze.

I inspired him sufficiently that he will try to bring Meyer around to their taking only the barest profit (equivalent to Wayne and me working for scale) until the investors are paid back.

Thursday, April 5, 9:30 A.M.: Wyndham

Julian, Meyer, and I met for an hour and a half, during which they offered three deals. In the most attractive one they get nothing but expenses until the investors get their money back.

I said I'd get back to them today and if there was a deal, Norman and I would immediately proceed to scout Montreal. I said I'd pay half of our (Norman and mine) expenses but they (Julian and Meyer) must pay the rest. Whereupon, as though they'd rehearsed it, they threw up their hands in mock horror at the suggestion of even so modest an outlay, which will be a gauge of their intention.

Tuesday, April 10, 6:30 A.M.: Wyndham

There appears to be a *major* misunderstanding: When Julian and Meyer said they would take nothing until recoupment, I assumed "nothing" included distribution fees. Not so, according to a memo Julian sent me.

Wednesday, April 11, 8:30 A.M.: Wyndham

As feared, it was a misunderstanding.

Meyer and Julian rejected Wayne's proposal aimed at "getting us all on the same side of the table." They just can't abide the notion of sharing risk.

Tuesday, April 17, 10:00 A.M.: Wyndham

Wayne and I, in a last-ditch effort, to Julian's office where Meyer and he awaited with plates, utensils, and a bowl of fruit and cheese.

Wayne volunteered to go halvies with me on the preproduction outlay of $10,000. When I said there must be a matching $10,000 from Julian and Meyer, they swallowed hard but agreed.

Since, by Meyer's admission, they have never put a dollar in the risk area, we must be gentle with them.

Wednesday, April 18, 8:30 A.M.: Wyndham

Norman met Bob Boyar about film insurance and had a productive visit with Julie Gottfried, who will be the film accountant.

Norman and I to TVC to see what inducement Dan Sandburg can offer to lure our postproduction to New York vis-à-vis Montreal.

Dan did his beguiling nonstop, non sequitur monologue, touching on prices, philosophy, and love for me, concluding, as always, with his eternal gratitude for my inviting him to have a drink at the Polo Lounge when he was new to Hollywood years ago.

What it all adds up to financially I leave to Norman because they speak a language ("Here's the rate card but of course it doesn't mean anything") I don't grasp.

So much for picture needs. Norman and I now proceeded to Trans Audio (sound) and its owner, Ralph Friedman.

Again that secret language as Norman and Ralph spoke.

We made a bet: Ralph was sure I'd use ADR[2]. Norman said, knowing me, I wouldn't. I took part of the bet without knowing what an ADR is.

Good Friday, April 20, 7:00 A.M.: Home

Up since 5:30 A.M. Anxiety dreams—director's dreams: On a set I couldn't seem to gain control of, I was making bad concessions to stars.

Norman called from Montreal. He's scouting five resort locations today.

Tuesday, April 24, 9:00 A.M.: Hotel de la Montaigne, Montreal

I felt tense and melancholy during the flight here. Had a drink. No help. Since it is my enthusiasm and energy that brings these ventures to fruition, I feared appearing down.

Norman met me at the airport.

After checking in, we went to meet the casting people—Vera and Nadia, identical twins.

Charlie Biddle, in his sixties, a black bass man and former boxer from Philadelphia who has his own jazz club, came by. He could be a useful contact.

Norman and I inspected the Chanticleer and several other resorts (potential locations) he'd lined up.

By supper, I was in full stride.

Wednesday, April 25, 8:30 A.M.: Montreal

Phoned Ruth, who asked me what exactly the financial founda-

---

2. ADR stands for automated dialogue replacement—in common parlance, *looping*. I never looped a syllable, so Ralph Friedman (deceased) still owes us.

tion of *The Gig* was. Since the query tapped my fears and doubts, I blew my top, told her there isn't a dime in the bank, that I'm gambling on futures, dealing in smoke.

Jeudi, April 26, 10:10 A.M.: Montreal

Norman and I arrived at the casting office in a building next door to Moishe's Delicatessen.

The pleasant surprise of the day was how many interesting actors, appropriate to our needs, were seen. The result is that some eight to ten are coming in tomorrow to read.

Having seen a couple of young black actors, including Charlie Biddle's son—a larger, virile version of Michael Jackson but alas too young for the role—it occurred to me that Charlie Biddle, despite age, might be a candidate.

Phoned Julian to tell him that before long we'd have to make serious financial outlays. He said Meyer was most optimistic about raising the money.

Norman and I went to Charlie Biddle's club. He'd left, but we ran into him later downstairs in our hotel. Gave him a script. Judging by the way he is greeted, he knows and is known by everyone in Montreal.

Friday, April 27, 7:50 A.M.: Montreal

Norman seemed down. A Chinese meal and tales of previous adversities I've overcome revived him.

Saturday, April 28, 9:10 A.M.: Montreal

Found several actors I might use, including Daniel Nalbach, who (seeking the drummer's role) made the best impression.

All the black actors we read, including Charlie Biddle, were wide of the mark.

Phoned Ackerman with a full report. Reminded that commitments would soon have to be made to secure actors and crew, he, a bit defensively, said, "We're not letting any grass grow under our feet."

Norman and I scouted resorts and priced labs.

Sunday, April 29, 9:45 A.M.: Montreal

Norman suggests going to Toronto to look for actors since time is short, and *if* we are forced to the austerity budget (the one he's doing for me privately in case all other financing fails and I'm forced to mortgage the house), it would be best to get the six lead actors in Canada.

Monday, April 30, 8:50 A.M.: Montreal

These balmy days bring people into the streets with a festive air. Similarly affected, I went to the ballpark, saw Pete Rose get two hits (Expos 6–2 over Cards) while Norman wrestled with the budget.

I've decided the resort we saw on Saturday is the one I want. Begin to see the film in my head—a good sign.

Norman was discouraged by his first pass at the numbers, which brought us in at about $850,000.

At supper, I relieved him by reducing and adjusting various categories and requirements. He will now make it come out to $750,000 or less, demonstrating my "accordian budget" concept: the same song, regardless of the number of octaves.

Tuesday, May 1, 10:10 A.M.: Montreal

Just back from meeting with the owner of the resort that seems the most likely candidate.

Major terms agreed on, he extracted a photo of his wife and asked if there was any chance of finding a part, no matter how small, for her. "That's the problem when you marry a woman twenty years younger," he said ingratiatingly.

Wednesday, May 2, 8:10 A.M.: Montreal

We leave Montreal in three hours. Went to Sono Lab yesterday at the invitation of André Fleury, the owner. Bottom line is they would give us good prices on services but no investment.

Ditto the Greenberg connection, which has come to naught.

Norman and I spent several hours on the budget.

We saw Charlie Biddle. If we shoot in Montreal, he will most likely be a consultant.

Rick Shaine (editor) called. Likes the script, is eager to come aboard.

Thursday, May 3, 8:10 A.M.: Wyndham

Norman and I to Julian's office. At the sight of his and Meyer's faces, I knew they didn't have the money.

They make their annual pilgrimage to Cannes next week, where they would like to do presales for no commission. I told them if I halted activity till they got the money in Cannes, it would be too late to start shooting as scheduled on June 17.

I said I'd let them do presales if they put up a sum of money that would allow Norman and me to commit people and make other production arrangements.

At this, they became defensive and put-upon.

Saturday, May 5, 9:30 A.M.: Home

Andy Duncan wants to play the piano player. I told him there was no need to read and we hoped to make him an offer next Friday.

Wednesday, May 9, 6:30 A.M.: Home

Julian and Meyer crapped out definitively yesterday after the usual chat about potential investors who would ante up as soon as other deals were consummated, etc.

About the preproduction tab, Julian said if the picture isn't made, he and Meyer will reimburse me for their pledged share.

Informed that Julian and Meyer were out, Wayne asked, "What can I do for you?" I said, "Get me five hundred fifty thousand to go with what's been pledged so far."

I sincerely doubt I'll be able to pull this one off.

Friday, May 11, 8:55 A.M.: Wyndham

Rick Shaine phoned. His research, coupled with Norman's, makes shooting in super 16 millimeter for blowup to 35 millimeter feasible.

Rick spoke to the man in New Jersey (John Allen) who is supposed to be the best at blowup work.

Will Wayne go for 16 mm? I haven't asked him, and won't till the 35-mm possibility is dead for sure.

Saturday, May 12, 8:30 A.M.: Wyndham

Hal Gaba, representing Embassy (Perenchio's company), continues to dance about me with various but as yet vague proposals re *The Gig*.

I, on impulse, entered a tent in Central Park where people were invited to have their blood pressure checked.

"You're not going to ruin my day, are you?" I asked the woman as she wrapped the paraphernalia about my arm. She found my pressure excellent, depriving me of a legitimate reason for abandoning the picture.

Phoned Wayne. Alluded to my "Alamo" position if all else failed: the movie shot in super 16 for $500,000. His reaction, less than enthusiastic, was akin to when I told him I might use my real-life chauffeur in *Once in Paris*. To complicate things further, he informed me of various acting commitments that might conflict with our schedule.

Tuesday, May 15, 8:30 A.M.: Wyndham

Wayne doing a Canadian TV movie that makes him unavailable until June 26 or 27.

Julie Gottfried (my accountant) read the riot act when I suggested using my pension fund to help back the movie. He said mortgaging the house (long term with interest deductible, which he also opposed) is preferable.

Thursday, May 17, 8:30 A.M.: Home

Wayne said he'd take trumpet lessons if I'd let him play that part instead of the trombonist. I said no.

Friday, June 1, 8:00 A.M.: Home

Meyer Ackerman called to say that he and Julian felt "extremely close" to me.

Tuesday, June 26, 7:45 A.M.: Home

A great inertia seizes me at the prospect of going to the city today and resuming the money quest. How I loathe this part of the game.

Wednesday, June 27, 8:15 A.M.: Wyndham

Called Bob Ehrenbard, who insisted on being involved—will let me know how much.

Dennis Smith gave me a big lift by saying he and his partner would take a point each.

Friday, June 29, 9:15 A.M.: Wyndham

Arrived at Wall Street early for my meeting with the McLaughlins. Entered Trinity Church—the quiet midst all the financial district tumult like the eye of a hurricane.

The McLaughlins (Jim and J. C.) reaffirmed their pledge.

Bad news: Norman can't get the budget down to $500,000. It looks like $575,000 to do it *very* tightly.

Saturday, June 30, 8:30 A.M.: Home

Bob Ehrenbard phoned to say that he and Lila were taking two points. I told him how encouraging his call was.

I phoned Frank Weissberg, who said if I get all the money from ten or fewer people and they were all New Yorkers, he thought it would constitute a private offering and not require that SEC procedure.

Norman still can't get the budget below $575,000, even with my deferring everything. Shooting in super 16 could be the answer.

Wednesday, July 4, 8:30 A.M.: Home

Norman had a talk with John Allen that makes him increasingly enthusiastic about super 16. I told him I hope to have the money in place by the end of next week.

Tuesday, July 10 , 8:00 A.M.: Home

Norman called to say Montreal humming with film activity, which will make it difficult if not impossible for us to get a crew. Alternatively, he has a locale to show me near his home in Woodstock.

Wednesday, July 11, 8:10 A.M.: Home

Drove to Woodstock where I met Norman and went with him to Rhinebeck to view Omega Center. Norman was right. It's ideal as the borscht-belt resort location. Being two hours outside New York, Norman is sure he can get concessions if we shoot in 16 mm that will see the film made for $500,000.

Shooting in the United States instead of Montreal would entitle investors to full tax credit.

Phoned Wayne about the possible switch from Montreal. He

likes it. I said I was investing $100,000. He said that in that case, he would invest $50,000. We now have $360,000 pledged.

Wednesday, July 18, 8:50 A.M.: Wyndham

The first thing I noticed was the way he perched at the end of the booth, alone, like a person grabbing a fast cup of coffee in a railroad terminal. I don't think the waiter or the other couple in the room realized it was Spiro Agnew.

Norman phoned. We can't house anyone at Omega because of no heat and a water problem after Labor Day.

Sunday, July 22, 9:00 A.M.: Home

By this time next week, I will press the *Go* or the *No* button on *Gig*.

Wednesday, July 25, 8:00 A.M.: Home

Meyer Ackerman phoned to put Bertrand Tavernier[3] on. Tavernier looking for a black saxophone player for a jazz film he is preparing. I made suggestions.

Meyer called again later to tell me that Tavernier spoke highly of *From Noon till Three* as well as *Desperate Characters*, which he'd championed in print.

Thursday, July 26, 7:40 A.M.: Wyndham

Met Meyer and laid out the situation explicitly: Rhinebeck, $500,000, 16mm. I told him I have $360,000 and wanted a minimum of $100,000 from him and Julian as straight investment, for which, besides points, I would give them screen credit, the option to premier at the Sixty-eighth Street Playhouse, first look at the film to make a distribution offer if they desired, and the chance to agent the film in a buyout deal.

Meyer loved the package, but then, like a compass needle returning to true north, he started in about presales. When I told him that ship had sailed, he said, "I can't help trying to hedge; it's my nature."

Julian phoned to say Meyer is "excited" about my proposal. I'm meeting Julian for breakfast in an hour to see what "excited" means.

---

3. Renowned French film director. He would eventually and inspiredly cast Dexter Gordon in *'Round Midnight*.

At noon yesterday, I thought I had all the money, causing Norman to say "yippee."

That proved the dawn before the dark, as all hopes now appear dashed.

I will recount the disappointing tale tomorrow, having neither the stomach nor energy to do so now.

Saturday, July 28. 8:15 A.M.: Home

Now hear this: The deal is made! The $500,000 pledged! The papers are being drawn!

Let me recap: On Thursday, Julian and I apparently cinched the deal, with his firm to put up $120,000 in exchange for points, executive producer credit, and the right to distribute if we didn't get a better offer. We shook hands at the Plaza (Julian picking up the tab, which underscored the seriousness of his intention) and agreed to meet at 4:00 P.M. to set terms by which his outfit would distribute.

At 4:00 P.M. I went to Julian's office.

"The part I like is this morning having breakfast and you telling stories," Julian said. "The part I don't like is this."

Julian now laid out his distribution terms. They were outrageous, even to my inexpert ear.

In low spirits, son John and I went to Eddie Condon's. Happened upon that exciting cornetist Warren Vaché, subbing for Billy Butterfield. Due to a kitchen accident, Vaché had his right arm in a sling. Played with such facility, I assumed he was left-handed and was amazed to learn he had never played with his left hand until that night.

"What an irony," I said to John, "that on the eve of the day when it looks like *The Gig* must be abandoned, I should stumble on a jazzman [Vaché] who could conceivably play the role of the trumpet player."

On Friday (yesterday) I informed the McLaughlins of Julian's terms, which if rejected meant aborting the picture.

I no sooner finished than J. C. said, "Forget Julian. We'll guarantee what's needed."

Took a cab to Frank Weissberg's office. Awaiting his return from lunch, I called Wayne in San Francisco (summoned him from a winemakers' conference). He approved the deal. I called Norman, who once again said "yippee."

Weissberg arrived. I outlined the whole thing. He thinks he can have the necessary papers in a week.

Tuesday, July 31, 9:45 A.M.: Wyndham

Norman and I went over the budget for a couple of hours.

He and I to Weissberg's where Frank introduced us to Tom Distler, the fourth fledgling lawyer I will be breaking in at the Colton office. It was Tom's first day with the firm. They are drawing up a private-offering letter in which each investor, per government regulation, must prove he has sufficient means to be part of such a risky venture.

Took Norman to Eddie Condon's. He was favorably impressed by Warren Vaché. Introducing myself to Warren, I asked if he'd ever acted. He said no in a way that suggested he was game for anything. Said he'd just taught Richard Gere to play cornet for *Cotton Club*. I gave him my number.

Wednesday, August 1, 9:30 A.M.: Wyndham

Jeri Sopanen, the cameraman who shot *My Dinner at Andre's* (in 16 mm) and worked with Norman years ago, arrived for lunch. I sensed competence and dependability, gave him a script.

As he was leaving, he asked if he could attend rehearsals. I said I'd be delighted.

Warren Vaché smoked four cigarettes to the nub in the time he was here. I gave him a script.

Jerry Matz came by. Looks perfect for the clarinetist. I gave him a script.

As I exited the hotel, the phone operator intercepted me in the lobby with a call from Warren Vaché, who'd read the script immediately.

"It's every band I ever played with," he said. "Only you've got one thing wrong." Asked what that was, he said, "It's the drummer, not the trumpet player, who always gets laid."

Passed a movie shooting on Fifth Avenue. Rick Waite, the cinematographer on "Nero Wolfe," introduced me to Walter Hill, the director, who spoke as in the midst of a dream—the cocoon of absorption that envelops directors in the fever of a shoot.

Thursday, August 2, 9:30 A.M.: Wyndham

Susan Egbert, my daughter-in-law, arrived to read with Warren Vaché.

They forced a bit initially but made a nice adjustment.

Jerry Matz, who has been a maitre d' at the Village Vanguard between acting jobs for many years, read with Warren. They'll be fine. I want them both, and I want Susan to play Warren's wife.

Warren Vaché just phoned "to prove that jazzmen don't all sleep till after noon." He has contacted a black bass player, who will call me.

Friday, August 3, 8:45 A.M.: Home

Norman made a deal with Jeri Sopanen.

Warren is going to try to get out of his last week touring Wales after the Edinburgh Jazz Festival. If he does so, the role is his.

Andrew Duncan came in. A long chat and a deal made. He asked if I wanted him to play it funny. To his enormous relief, I said it was the last thing I wanted. My goal, as always, is absolute credibility, and let the humor speak for itself.

Duncan knows Jerry Matz and loves the idea of working with him. As for improvising, which Duncan, one of the founders of Second City, is expert at, he warned it only works if all participants are gifted that way.

Enter Reggie Johnson, the black bassist suggested by Warren. He's on the nose physically. Gave him a script.

Sunday, August 5, 8:45 A.M.: Home

Norman phoned last night to say he'd found another location: Sacks Lodge in Saugerties (Upstate New York).

The draft of *The Gig* offering circular arrived by express.

Monday, August 6, 7:00 A.M.: Wyndham

Dan, my son, drove me to Saugerties where Norman showed us Sacks Lodge.

In contrast to the script, where the resort is depicted as run-down and inferior to the brochure, Sacks Lodge is a charming, well-maintained place. Best of all, there is a little half-bungalow (that's the only way to describe it) apart from the main buildings that could house the band exactly as the script depicts.

Demonstrating the advantage of having the writer along when you scout locations, I made an immediate adjustment: Instead of the band complaining about the resort at first sight, they will laud it, only to find that the pool, tennis courts, etc., are off-limits to employees. Thus they will still be able to gripe, as the story requires.

Introduced to Ann Sacks, who has owned and run the place for many years, I asked if anyone had ever done a movie there. "No," she said, "we've been waiting." "Well," I said, "we're here."

A deal looks likely.

Tuesday, August 7, 7:00 P.M.: Wyndham

Norman and Sarah picked Danny and me up at 10:00 A.M. We drove to John Allen's place in New Jersey to acquaint ourselves with his blowup process.

I see now that I will need a professional actor rather than a converted musician for the bass player's role.

Wednesday, August 8, 10:00 A.M.: Wyndham

Breakfasted with Norman, Sarah, and Abigail McGrath, whom the Cohens met as a fellow student at Bard. Owner of the Off-Center Theatre, she will do our casting.

At 11:00 A.M. Warren Vaché and Dick Wellstood[4] arrived to discuss music needs.

Quintessential jazzmen whose stated idea of the perfect gig is to be paid in cash at the end of the night, they all but fled at the mention of contracts and paperwork. The upshot is we will hire a contractor, with them just handling the music.

How to guarantee that a song is public domain is crucial.

Forgot to mention that at the meeting with Abigail McGrath, she suggested Cleavon Little as ideal for the bass player. When I told her that Cleavon was high on my list but that I didn't know how to reach him, she said she'd recently met him and would see to it.

---

4. Stride pianist (now deceased), one of my favorites since I first heard him with the Jimmy Archey band at Jimmy Ryan's in 1950. The insert of his hands at the keyboard in the montage band scenes gives me a shiver. Can this be his only appearance on film?

Now, at 5:00 P.M., Cleavon Little arrived with Abigail. He'd read the script and wants the part. Would he read? Yes.

Thursday, August 9, 8:45 A.M.: Wyndham

Met Irwin Young, head of DuArt Lab. A man passionately invested in his work, he laid out the pros and cons of the 16-mm blowup procedure.

One drawback is that you can't print selected takes, must (in seeing dailies) view everything you shoot, which besides taking time, compels you to face all your mistakes.

He said that for pictures budgeted over $500,000, he sees no economic advantages to 16 mm. But below that, yes.

To Abigail's Off-Center Theatre on Eighteenth Street (with Norman and Dan) at 7:00 P.M. to meet and read actors she'd lined up for the bass-player role.

Cleavon Little and Arthur French the best, but I learned that I don't have a firm fix on that part—am searching.

Friday, August 10, 9:00 A.M.: Wyndham

Norman and I met Herb Harris, who will be the music contractor for Vaché.

Abigail called to say Cleavon is pressing for word since he's been offered a play in Los Angeles but would rather do *The Gig*.

Saturday, August 11, 8:30 A.M.: Home

When I called Cleavon at 9:30 A.M., he answered the phone drowsily, prompting me to say, "Sorry if I woke you."

To which he responded, "He wakes me, and then he says he's sorry."

When I said I was seriously interested in him for the part and proposed lunch, he cheered up considerably.

We met at 12:30 and spoke for two hours and twenty minutes. I told him I had no idea what he would do in the role. Nor was I locked into a concept. In other words, if we worked together, it would be in the spirit of joint exploration.

We spoke candidly. Left it that his agent would contact Norman to make a deal.

A month from today I should be shooting—the first day.

Tuesday, August 14, 8:15 A.M.: Wyndham

Abigail contacted Joe Silver,[5] who is reading the script.

Wednesday, August 15, 7:50 A.M.: Wyndham

We made a deal with Cleavon Little and Joe Silver (to play the resort owner) yesterday.

A long probing talk with Herb Harris, the music contractor.

Thursday, August 16, 8:15 A.M.: Home

Having found no actor as right for the drummer's role as Daniel Nalbach, we decided to see if he could make it down from Canada, given all the red tape involved.

Friday, August 17, 8:00 A.M.: Home

One should do a movie about location scouting, which provides momentary contact with people and situations you would never encounter otherwise.

We stopped for lunch. Norman, exhibiting the hallmark of the true production manager, summoned up a nice restaurant in the middle of a forest.

On to Sacks Lodge. As a right location should, it looked even better on second inspection.

Monday, August 20, 7:00 A.M.: Home

The deal with Sacks Lodge (all but made) will include twenty rooms for cast and crew and the right to shoot there for seventeen days—breakfast included.

Tuesday, August 21, 8:30 A.M.: Home

As always, when the most is happening, you have the least time to record.

I drove to Sacks Lodge where Norman and Scott Hancock, his location manager, awaited.

Norman said he'd spoken to Weissberg, who advised we meet John Maguire (head of the East Coast Screen Actors Guild) to ar-

5. Now deceased. He seemed one of the last of the borscht-belt breed, but surprisingly that was no part of his background. While shooting, he got an offer to play Falstaff at Yale. "To see you in that role, I'd travel anywhere," I said, but despite my urging, he turned them down.

rive at accommodation, and hopefully relief, by stating our case.

Jeri Sopanen arrived with his 16-mm camera. We made a tour of the Sacks premises, noting areas that could be used.

In the dining room, Jeri suggested the bandstand be placed against the back wall instead of the windowed wall, as I'd planned, to facilitate lighting.

He shot available light footage in the dining room, kitchen, rehearsal hall, and lounge.

In each location I submitted my intention for comment, which will save us many hours when we shoot.

We drove to Kingston to see vans in which there will be much shooting of the band en route to the resort. Decided a Volkswagen van best suited our needs.

Jeri asked how we accounted for the choice seat beside the driver being so conveniently left free for the cameraman. An excellent question, which Norman solved: The bass player will not allow them to put his bass on top of the van, and there is no room in the back, so the bass gets the seat beside the driver, which the cameraman can then occupy with only the sawed-off neck of a bass showing.

Like all good suggestions, it satisfies more than one need by in this case giving further evidence of the bass player's salty nature.

A most rewarding trip because everyone was able to contribute something.

Thursday, August 23, 6:15 A.M.: Wyndham

Norman said, "We are near the point of no return," alluding to moneys that must be paid out even though only $30,000 of the $500,000 is in hand and none of it can be touched until the entire $500,000 is in the bank.

"You've got it wrong," I informed. "We passed the point of no return a week ago." Told him I'd supply the $15,000 or so needed immediately for the music session and other items.

From 5:00 P.M. to 10:00 P.M., I met and read actors for some of the smaller parts at Abigail's theater.

Friday, August 24, 7:45 A.M.: Wyndham

Norman and I met Jeri Sopanen at DuArt to screen the available-light test reel we shot at Sacks.

Norman and I to Tape House, one of whose owners is Mark Polycan, an old friend of Norman's. The most attractive editing facilities I've ever seen.

Wayne and I missed each other's calls. His sudden expression of "serious reservations" about the script weights the day.

Norman arrived early for our meeting with Herb Harris and Dick Wellstood (Warren away on tour) to finalize the songs for Tuesday's recording session.

Before they arrived, Norman informed we were in trouble with the Directors Guild for registering so late, said we had a 5:00 P.M. appointment with Stanley Ackerman, the East Coast president.

Enter Dick Wellstood with more bad news: None of the suggested songs had been cleared for public-domain status.

Herb Harris phoned a lady in California who was supposed to be clearing public-domain titles.

At 5:00 P.M., Norman and I raced to the DGA office where I gave Ackerman a candid account of our situation.

We left a script and budget with Ackerman for his board to review. No problem envisioned.

Back here for more talks with Herb Harris about the music.

Got Wayne on the phone. His serious script reservations proved minor. His jacket size (the band will wear matching blazers) is 39 long.

Saturday, August 25, 8:30 A.M.: Home

Too many meetings to record.

Relieved by an early call from Herb Harris reporting "Saints," "Bill Bailey," and several other Dixieland songs have been established as public domain.

Sunday, August 26, 9:00 A.M.: Home

Herb Harris phoned. We still need a fox-trot or two and more Dixieland tunes.

I began to refine and polish the script.

Monday, August 27, 8:00 A.M.: Home

I rewrite with my directorial eye and eliminate what, if shot, would end on the cutting-room floor.

Abe Lastvogel, head of William Morris, died at eighty-six. Did I ever record him late in the afternoon (a daily occurrence) floating in a tube at the old Beverly Wilshire pool as subordinates reported while circling the perimeter?

Phoned Harris and pinpointed music needs.

Tuesday, August 28, 7:00 A.M.: Wyndham

Worked well on the script, especially the new speech for George (Stan Lachow) when he convinces the other guys to accept the gig.

We started seeing actors for the part of Rick Valentine, the has-been singer. Jay Thomas, an FM disc jockey, stood out.

Deirdre O'Connell, the daughter of Tom, my Dartmouth classmate, came in to read for Lucy. A nice reading, but unforunately she's too young.

Herb Harris arrived at 6:00 P.M., but Warren Vaché, running a 102 fever, didn't come. When we called Warren, he said he felt better, vowed to make the recording session.

Norman, Herb, and I went over music cues. The woman on the West Coast added a few more public-domain numbers, including "Frankie and Johnny" and "La Cucaracha."

J. C. McLaughlin's check came in for *more* than he promised!

If I get the flu, don't tell me.

Wednesday, August 29, 9:00 A.M.: Wyndham

To Chelsea Sound Studios at 11:00 A.M.

Daniel Nalbach (Arthur) already there. He seems as perfect as I recall from Montreal.

Warren Vaché arrived, sweaty and ill.

George Masso on trombone; Dick Wellstood, piano: Kenny Davern, clarinet: Reggie Johnson, bass; and Herb Harris on drums.

We did eight cues when Warren all but collapsed with 104 fever—still had to be ordered to leave.

There was a panicked hunt for a cornetist while we recorded solo work. By luck, we got Bob Bernard, a fine Australian player who happened to be passing through New York, his last day before going home.

The actors all showed up, got to meet each other and watch the musicians ply their trade.

We had food and beverages sent in. A grand day, done by 6:00 P.M.—only forgot a polka.

For me, who once aspired to be a jazzman, the day was more than grand. And it did not end there. At night I went to Hanratty's East where Dick Wellstood and Kenny Davern played, with Bob Bernard sitting in.

Friday, August 31, 9:00 A.M.: Home

Norman and I came to terms with the Screen Actors Guild— must give them a $22,000 certified check as bond on Tuesday.

We inspected rehearsal spaces. Decided on the No Smoking Theatre. Decided on Jay Thomas and Michael Fischetti as Rick Valentine and his manager.

Listened to the music we recorded on a cassette Scott Hancock brought me. Will edit it to specific cues and give each actor a cassette so he can acquaint himself with it for better faking.

Saturday, September 1, 8:00 A.M.: Home

Working slow-but-sure on rewrites.

Sunday, September 2, 7:15 A.M.: Home

Phoned Warren. He has viral pneumonia but is recovering nicely. I told him to bring his horn (his security blanket) to rehearsal.

I begin to close out all concerns not related to *The Gig*—one of the dividends of directing, and why so many directors run from one picture to another.

Monday, September 3, 8:15 A.M.: Home

Sixty pages of script remain to be polished.

Spent six hours with Scott and John[6] going over music cues plus location and prop needs. Scott becoming increasingly valuable.

Tuesday, September 4, 8:00 A.M.: Home

Worked without pause (except meals) from 8:15 A.M. to 8:30 P.M., Ruth typing behind me, and completed the rewrite.

6. My son, an assistant film editor back from working for Coppola in San Francisco. He would cover until Rick Shaine, the editor, completed his current assignment, and then be first assistant.

Norman called to inform that SAG has cleared all actors to work except Cleavon. Apparently a money matter, which hopefully will be resolved today.

Wednesday, September 5, 8:00 A.M.: Wyndham

We commence rehearsal in two hours. Brand-new blue-covered scripts ready for the actors.

Jim McLaughlin sent a check to cover the sum pledged by an investor who fell out.

Cleavon Little has been cleared to work by SAG.

Thursday, September 6, 5:00 A.M.: Wyndham

First day of rehearsals excellent overall. Many sparks of life in the first reading, with Susan playing all the women.

I must get Wayne and Cleavon to use more of themselves instead of relying on extreme characterizations.

Several script weaknesses surfaced, which is why I'm up at this hour.

Friday, September 7, 7:30 A.M.: Wyndham

Another fine rehearsal day
During breaks, Warren entertains with his horn.
Checks have all cleared.
The rewrite worked.

Saturday, September 8, 9:00 A.M.: Home

Rehearsed till 3:30 P.M. yesterday. Went well despite some soft parts in the script that have to be inspected.

Susan rehearsed with Warren and was so excellent that he was unsettled by "her" ultimatum.

Broke at point of maximum harmony.

Sunday, September 9, 4:30 A.M.: Home

Worked on script till 4:00 P.M. yesterday—some seven new pages.

Monday, September 10, 6:30 A.M.: Sacks Lodge, Saugerties, N.Y.

All guests gone, we have the place to ourselves.

Housed in bungalows and buildings on the site of our main location blends reality and movie.

As always, I let the actors outfit themselves.

As almost always, they come up with things I never would have thought of. Wayne perfect in bright yellow polyester pants, matching T-shirt with a Desert Inn logo, gold chains, and a mustache.

Norman, fearful of using the Desert Inn logo without permission, had Wayne call the owner in Vegas, who said, "You can use it, provided you write 'I got laid at the Desert Inn' on the soles of your shoes and show it in the film."

We rehearsed in the areas of the lodge we'll be using.

Mrs. Sacks provided a welcoming dinner.

Tuesday, September 11, 7:00 A.M.: Sacks Lodge

Joe Silver arrived with a full bag of schticks: "Hello Cleveland" on meeting Cleavon, etc.

One of the crew might be too accustomed to studio operations: When I asked him to strap the bass fiddle in the van, he said, "I'll get someone." Whereupon I did it, hoping the lesson wasn't wasted.

To get a jump on things, we are going to "shoot the rehearsal" of the band driving to the resort.

This means Wayne driving the van; Jeri shooting from the seat beside him; Daniel and Cleavon seated in the next row with me curled from sight at their feet; Warren, Jerry, and Andy in the back row; and Eric Taylor hidden behind them recording sound.

Wednesday, September 12, 7:00 A.M.: Sacks Lodge

Shot from about 1:30 P.M. to 5:45 P.M., got two and a half to three pages. Spirit fine. No camera mounts on the van, so we have to cover a lot for variety.

Two state troopers stopped us, but didn't request permits (which we didn't have). A good omen?

I think of the performances en masse rather than individually, which is a good sign.

Took the actors to dinner last night. A couple of our jolly band show a partiality for the grape that will have to be watched.

How did Cleavon's bass case get ripped?

Thursday, September 13, 6:45 A.M.: Sacks Lodge

Up since 5:00 A.M. rewriting.

Shot seven and a half pages. Excellent spirits all around. The work with Joe Silver felt splendid.

Saw dailies under adverse conditions. Projector broke down in the middle. All that bad stuff you're forced to print in 16 mm is distracting.

Nalbach gets a laugh whenever his face appears.

I hope Warren can give up his gig on the 19th, which would make him miss a day.

Friday, September 14 (already?), 6:45 A.M.: Sacks Lodge

I write from the midst of the delirium. In this case a sweet one because last night's dailies (Joe Silver greeting the band and their singing "Riverside" in the van) were well received. A great boost after a hard shooting day.

Andrew Duncan has a tendency to take any group criticism personally.

Warren, who initially was so anxious about acting, asked, "Is that all there is to it?" "Right," I said, "just keep doing what you're doing."

Jerry Matz notably more relaxed each day.

To insure harmony I must cover *everyone* as equally as possible.

Saturday, September 15, 7:30 A.M.: Sacks Lodge

It's the day of the big party scene.

Shot night-shack sections during day. Plus I got the dawn shot—Warren blowing reveille (sunset passing for sunrise). Have no idea how many pages I've done so far.

The kitchen shut down except for breakfast has inspired members of the cast and crew to a culinary contest. Last night Cleavon prepared his secret fried chicken recipe.

We eat in the recreation room, which is where we watch dailies and will eventually shoot, which compounds the seamless feel.

I begin to look forward to editing, which is a good sign.

Some 150 guests expected tonight when we *must* get all the scenes involving crowds and music.

Sunday, September 16, 10:00 A.M.: Sacks Lodge

The morning after!

Shot ten pages between 4:30 P.M. and 1:30 A.M., with an hour off for dining.

Jeri looked glassy, said it was the "wildest" shoot of his life.

The real musicians (Wellstood, Davern, et al.) alternating with the actors added a great deal to the picture and the festivities.

The crowd, completely caught up in the proceedings, was joyous, attentive, and responsive.

In the midst of shooting, I knew with piercing certainty I was at the top of my form.

I've done thirty pages so far, including a lot of the harder stuff.

Monday, September 17, 7:00 A.M.: Sacks Lodge.

Fifth shooting day.

We don't start shooting till 1:30 P.M. today, in compliance with union requirement of a thirty-six-hour turnaround.

I remain apart from the cast and crew after shooting (they deserve some respite from me) but glean that several location romances are in progress.

We all went to Norman's last night to eat leftover party food.

Tuesday, September 16, 6:45 A.M.: Sacks Lodge

Great success scouting locations yesterday before we started shooting. Approved five sites.

Started shooting in the band shack at 1:30 P.M. Exerted pressure to counteract the natural tendency to let down after the monstrous shoot on Saturday, which everyone is still awed by.

It was Warren Vaché's turn to make dinner. His wife, Jill, did most of it. Pork and red cabbage, etc. Very tasty. Mrs. Sacks, her son Victor, and her sister, who have become part of the tribe, ate and watched dailies with us.

Jeri lit and shot the shack night stuff excellently. Applause at the end.

Fatigue licking at my edges. Must rewrite a page before we resume at 8:30 A.M.

Norman has not given me the requested financial report, which makes me suspect trouble.

They say the world still turns and Mondale is behind by 18 percent.

Thirty-four pages shot as of last night.

Wednesday, September 19, 6:45 A.M.: Sacks Lodge

A struggle to get all the recreation-room material (nine pages) from 8:30 A.M. to 9:00 P.M.

A slight tiff with Jeri (the traditional cinematographer vs. director split), with him focused on appearance and me on content. Nothing serious.

Joe Silver made lasagna—everyone in high spirits.

Two hours of dailies as we viewed all the Saturday party stuff and some of what we got yesterday.

The crowd stuff is great. Sorry I didn't tie the band and crowd together more in dialogue shots.

Jeri overly critical of his work, which no one else found fault with.

Thursday, September 20, 6:45 A.M.: Sacks Lodge

Jay Thomas, Michael Fischetti, and Chuck Wepner (the "Bayonne Bleeder," who went the distance with Ali) arrived.

I shot their first appearance in the picture.

I'm behind about two days. Must plan—must run.

Daniel Nalbach's beef bourguignonne was excellent.

Friday, September 21, 7:00 A.M.: Sacks Lodge

Chuck Wepner ("If I had a nose like yours [to Joe Silver], I never would have got hit in the face") took Jay Thomas and Michael Fischetti on a tour (hair-raising, from all reports) of the countryside last night.

Jay and Michael were on time for shooting this morning, but Chuck and his car had vanished.

Since he was already established in the picture and central to the scene to be shot, anxious attempts were made to find him while I shot all the peripheral stuff not requiring his presence.

At noon, Chuck pulled up (license plate, *CHAMP*) with a story about his car breaking down.

I put him to work immediately and was pleasantly surprised, given his lack of experience, at how well he took direction.

The cast and crew awarded me the "Mr. Cool" award for how I handled the situation. Did they think I was going to hit him?

The grips made dinner last night—great steaks. Not only did they cook, but they donned formal attire to serve in.

Think I have the logo for the picture—a photo of the band with the shack in the background.

Saturday, September 22, 9:00 A.M.: Sacks Lodge

Shot till after 1:00 A.M.

I feel the picture unraveling via fatigue and my jaundiced view at 2:00 A.M. of the dailies.

I fear my montage concept won't work, and I sense money problems Norman isn't telling me about, which I fear to ask about.

It's "If you can keep your head when all about you . . ." time.

Sunday, September 23, 10:00 A.M.: Sacks Lodge

Did all the Saugerties bar stuff yesterday from noon till 7:00 P.M.—six pages.

I'd told cast and crew to take candid still shots that might be used in the montage, but so far I've not seen any results, though frequently aware of cameras clicking.

Relieved somewhat when Dan volunteered that the dailies (which I'd slept through) were good—later confirmed, without solicitation, by Eric Taylor, the sound man, whose work and demeanor I like increasingly.

More relief when I asked Nick Romanac about the candid photos and he showed me the first batch of some fifty to come.

By the time I get all the photos, I'll have several hundred to choose from.

Confidence restored, I prepared for Saugerties. We drew a cooperative crowd on the main street. Got off to a flying start. Ate on the street as we worked. The actors, lounging in the van between takes, besieged for autographs.

Got my first dolly shot of the picture at Corby's Bar.

Now to prepare for next week and determine remaining needs, including connective-tissue shots not in the script.

Wayne said, apropos his numerous female visitors, "I hope you're not keeping a journal."

Monday, September 24, 7:10 A.M.: Sacks Lodge

Norman says we'll be on budget if we wrap Friday, which gives me five days to get forty pages.

Discussing a member of the crew who has been irascible of late, Norman attributed it to "semen backup." Hopefully his wife's visit will be the remedy.

Tuesday, September 25, 7:00 A.M.: Sacks Lodge

The used-car-lot sequence went excellently. I hope so because last night's dailies (the band dining) were dull. Wayne, uncharacteristically, left without a word.

Wednesday, September 26: 7:00 A.M.: Sacks Lodge

Got several bits and pieces around the band's shack and began the scene in Marty's "basement" before we broke for lunch.

From 3:30 to 8:30, I got all nine pages of dialogue, including Georgie's long emotional speech that makes them decide to take the gig.

Stan Lachow (Georgie) so good, I did only one take, at the end of which he got a hand.

The dailies (amen) were fine. The coverage of their eating in kitchen redeems the previous day's dull masters.

Jeri apologized for dailies being too dark, or was it too bright? Can't recall because they were fine, which I told him.

After dailies, Wayne and I drove into Saugerties. Ended up at the Hunting Lodge Bar, a neighborhood Italian place where he was recognized. How strange it must be to have someone you know from television suddenly appear.

Thursday, September 27, 7:00 A.M.: Sacks Lodge

Great dailies last night (the used-car lot, opening-credit music montage, kid bouncing the ball, etc.).

Bad news is that I think I'll have to reshoot the very last moment of the film—the band playing beside the van.

Jeri happy because he's made an adjustment in the movie projector that makes the dailies look better.

The hot spell over, could use long johns. A lot to do to finish by Saturday.

Friday, September 28, 6:30 A.M.: Sacks Lodge

The fifteenth and next to last day of shooting. If all goes well today, only van pass-bys needed tomorrow.

Did lake fishing scene and Susan's scene plus a reshoot of the final scene.

Warren Vaché saved us by playing a bit of minor-key blues, then switching to a major key to give the upbeat feel wanted at the end.

A rugged little climb up the hill where Jeri, via zoom lens, got our "helicopter" shot.

I ran the picture in my head from 5:30 A.M. till a few minutes ago. It feels very nice.

Saturday, September 29, 8:00 A.M.: Sacks Lodge

Except for establishing shots to be picked up Tuesday in New York, today will be (should be) our last day of shooting.

Group improvisation doesn't work because no one has Andy's talent for it. But he is throwing in bits on his own that could be useful.

Shot from 9:00 A.M. till after midnight last night. We broke for dinner, which was a gift prepared by Mrs. Sacks at 9:00 P.M.

Saw dailies at 1:00 A.M.

Without telling Warren, I had Cleavon, in the fishing scene, say that his schedule included a European tour with Warren Vaché. On seeing and hearing this at dailies, Warren went about the room and kissed each of his fellow actors and me.

Susan's scene with Warren is fine.

Monday, October 1, 9:00 A.M.: Home

On Saturday, the final (sixteenth) day of shooting, the call was for noon since we shot till 1:00 A.M. the night before. At noon, we picked up shots at the shack and then out to the Thruway for van-passing shots.

From Kingston we leapfrogged (camera set up—van passes and stops; camera advances—van comes again, etc.) to the Saugerties exit.

Everyone glad to be crammed in the van again as we were at the outset of shooting.

At 6:30 P.M. we redid the shot of the band returning to the shack after the first night's playing.

Scott Hancock, in addition to everything else he's done, cooked the wrap-party meal. Barbecued chicken and ribs.

Awoke twice last night, certain that there was a scene to be shot. Ruth assured me it wasn't so. I asked for my script to check—eventually dozed.

Tuesday, October 2, 8:30 A.M.: Home

Last night, despite Ruth's assurances the picture was over, I was so certain there was a scene to be shot when I awoke that I went to my workroom and returned with the script, which I sat on the bed perusing until the realization sheepishly penetrated that she was right.

Wednesday, October 3, 8:50 A.M.: Wyndham

Jeri and Herb Forsberg, his assistant, picked me up in their van.

I detect a new respect from Jeri because my name was a clue in yesterday's *New York Times* crossword puzzle—he being a cross-word fanatic.

We met Scott and Norman at the Kwasha Lipton Building on the Jersey side of the George Washington Bridge, where Norman obtained permission to shoot the van crossing the bridge from the roof.

In quick succession, we picked up three other daytime establishing shots MOS (mit out sound).

And then to 30 Wall Street for the exterior night shot of the building in which McLaughlin, Piven, Vogel is housed.

The picture officially wrapped, we dined at the Fulton Fish Market. Good feelings all around.

Awoke at 2:00 A.M. and fought off the "missing" scene once again.

Thursday, October 4, 9:15 A.M.: Home

Final dailies screened last night.

Scott Hancock, for service above and beyond the call, will be given associate producer credit.

Awoke again last night to get that missing shot. But the spell was shorter.

Sunday, October 7, 9:30 A.M.: Home

Awoke again, certain I had to shoot a scene with the band in mounted-police uniforms.

Wednesday, October 10, 6:30 A.M.: Home

Scott arrived with no more than four rolls of snapshot film, and most of that useless, for my montage concept. This after my stressing how crucial the montage was and being assured there were innumerable photos in the works. Why did no one alert me so I could have covered myself?

Fortunately, unknown to anyone, I have always had a backup plan—combining stills interspersed with film.

We begin editing Tuesday.

Thursday, October 18, 7:45 A.M.: Wyndham

Rick Shaine showed me what he had so far. We worked till 6:00 P.M. when I sensed we'd passed the point of diminishing returns.

No lunch again yesterday in an attempt to lose the weight picked up during shooting when one feels entitled to eat anything and everything "for the sake of the film."

Friday, October 19, 8:00 A.M.: Wyndham

We seem to have established a modus operandi (Rick, John Gilroy, and I) that allows me to be on the scene without inhibiting their creativity.

Saturday, October 20, 9:00 A.M.: Home

By late afternoon we had the basement scene (six minutes) finely polished. Not a dead spot in it, and Georgie's pivotal speech is gold.

Rick, on another job till last week and therefore new to the material, was impressed by the actors' handling of their instruments, which makes it all but impossible to tell that with the exception of Warren, they're faking.

Now the downside: As Norman and Julie sort out the bills, it appears that I have less money left than anticipated.

Monday, October 22, 9:15 A.M.: Home

Why did I apparently get up during the night and unscrew my reading-light bulb, found on the floor this morning?

François Truffaut died at fifty-two. I subscribe to his "I like to work for myself because when I work for other people, I'm never busy enough."

Tuesday, October 23, 7:40 A.M.: Wyndham

We hit a snag in late afternoon. A solution may have occurred as I walked back to the hotel, which is when best ideas often suggest themselves.

Marilyn Zeigher has joined us as apprentice.

Wednesday, October 24, 8:00 A.M.: Wyndham

I note that the most productive days (like yesterday) are usually the ones we start early.

Thursday, October 25, 7:45 A.M.: Wyndham

Saw John Sayles's *Brother from Another Planet,* on which Eric Taylor, our sound man, worked. Sayles's 16-mm blowup to 35 mm gives me confidence, especially since we used *super* 16, which further enhances the process.

Saturday, October 27, 9:30 A.M.: Home

We have about twenty-five minutes of film cut.

Tuesday, October 30, 8:15 A.M.: Wyndham

A sluggish day — little progress.

Attended John and Suzanne Mados's (owners of the Wyndham) birthday party for Rady Harris. Present, among others, were John Huston, Lena Horne, Alec Guinness, Tammy Grimes, Kate Reid, Julie Wilson, Vincent Price, Al Hirschfeld, Hume Cronyn, Jessica Tandy, Bobby Short, David Susskind, et al. It's fatiguing to be in a room where there are so many people more famous than you.

Wednesday, October 31, 8:20 A.M.: Wyndham

Back to the reel world.

The day began shakily, with Rick's assemblage of Cleavon Little's entrance scene not up to expectation. The fault largely due to my selecting the wrong takes the night before.

I vowed no more selections at day's end when fatigue undermines judgement.

Herb Gardner called. He is considering Cleavon for his new play *I'm Not Rappaport* and wanted to know how I felt about him. I said it was a pleasure to recommend someone without qualification.

Friday, November 2, 8:50 A.M.: Wyndham

I was disappointed at yesterday's screening of the first twenty-five minutes. Fortunately, Rick and I are in perfect agreement on what has to be done.

Saturday, November 3, 10:00 A.M.: Home

We spent a rewarding day making changes affecting almost every scene.

I commissioned the first dissolve, noting it had gotten into the film the old-fashioned way: earning it after all other possibilities had been explored.

Sunday, November 4, 1:00 P.M.: Home

Winnowing the photos for montage scene.

Tuesday, November 6, 7:20 A.M.: Wyndham

Rick had a fine idea about splitting the first dialogue sequence in the van into separate scenes to give the feeling of distance and time passage.

Although he is free, as he admits, to execute any creative notion that occurs to him, I know my unorthodox approach to editing occasionally ruffles Rick.

Wednesday, November 7, 8:30 A.M.: Wyndham

A fine day for me yesterday—a terrible day for Walter Mondale.

I left Rick to assemble the next traveling-van section after we reviewed the material. He did well. In each new scene the characters bring a sense of prior life.

As of last Friday, I have $39,000 left. Which means I have barely enough to cover picture editing. It will require another $50,000 to $60,000 to complete the film, including blowup to 35 mm.

Friday, November 9, 8:00 A.M.: Wyndham

The picture continues to gain momentum.
We have thirty-three minutes of film.

Tuesday, November 13, 8:15 A.M.: Wyndham

Ruth and I dined at the Tuilleries (on Central Park South) where we saw Lady Bird Johnson several tables away. She spoke to her dinner companions with that total focus that distinguished her when she came to see *Roses* and later invited us to the White House. Not once did she look about to see who might be aware of her presence.

We have thirty-six minutes of film.

Wednesday, November 14, 8:00 A.M.: Wyndham

We hit a snag. The solution required surrendering a scene I particularly liked: "You've gotta kill those darlings."

Friday, November 16, 7:15 A.M.: Wyndham

We ran the arrival sequence, found dead moments.

I realized that my delight with Joe Silver had made me include too much of his guided tour.

Rick cut one and a half minutes out of a five-minute sequence, got things flowing again.

Sunday, November 18, 10:30 A.M.: Wyndham

From separate sources, I hear that Andy Duncan, Cleavon, and Joe Silver have been singing the praises of *The Gig* experience. Good publicity since in lieu of their usual salaries, it's one of the main inducements I offer.

Thursday, November 22, 10:00 A.M.: Wyndham

We have forty-four minutes of film as of yesterday.

Wednesday, November 28, 8:00 A.M.: Wyndham

No one seems to have definitive information on super 16, which will make us a source in future.

At 9:00 P.M. Rick said he had something to show me. Said it in a way that unfailingly tips me he is pleased with what he's done.

We viewed it, and it's excellent. A truly creative manipulation of the material by cutting to the band talking among themselves while Mitgang (Joe Silver) does his comedic routine.

Both Rick and John are more awake at 9:00 P.M. than at 9:00 A.M., which (my being a morning person) is a minor but continuing source of friction.

John walked me back to the hotel—a beer and snack en route. I can wish no father a greater joy than his child's company after a day of shared labor. What the Jews call *naches*.

Thursday, November 29, 7:45 A.M.: Wyndham

What we liked Tuesday night at 9:00 P.M. still looked good the next morning, which is not always the case.

Friday, November 30, 9:15 A.M.: Wyndham

After much trial and error, the party scene has the swirl and tumult envisioned.

Wayne phoned to see how things were going. I said, "If we were on a dead horse, we would know by now."

Sunday, December 2, 8:30 A.M.: Wyndham

Spoke to the Wolfe Pack, a group dedicated to Rex Stout's creations. Showed them the screen test of the late Thayer David, whose portrayal of Nero Wolfe in *The Doorbell Rang* they deem the greatest, bar none.

Monday, December 3, 10:00 A.M.: Wyndham

Rick doesn't want me in the editing room till noon while he, I hope, makes magic.

Tuesday, December 4, 9:00 A.M.: Wyndham

The director's idea of inserting dialogue before the band plays "Hava Negilah" is wrong. I should have listened to the writer.

Tuesday, December 11, 8:00 A.M.: Wyndham

Up betimes—after a weekend of leafing Pepys's *Diaries*.

We are at the band rehearsal scene. Have been there since 3:00 P.M. yesterday when I viewed Rick's assemblage, which, we agreed, is too long.

My failure to shoot the scene properly the basic flaw.

By 7:00 P.M. when I called a halt, we still didn't have it. Think the glimmer of a solution occurred to me at 5:00 A.M. this morning.

Wednesday, December 12, 9:00 A.M.: Wyndham

Rick clung to some of my directorial mistakes on the ground that the severe cuts I recommended might leave the audience confused.

I opted for confusion, saying, "When you bore the audience, they blame *you*. But when you confuse them, they blame themselves."

We are in the area of the story where the plot line is thinnest, making moment-to-moment life a vital necessity.

Just breakfasted with Wayne, who seemed to know I was over budget without my saying so.

Thursday, December 13, 8:15 A.M.: Wyndham

Rick's assemblage of the Warren-waitress scene was substantially to my liking. We polished it, then viewed material for the next sequence.

This seemed the right moment for introducing my fallback montage concept: bits of film interspersed with subliminal glimpses of stills, intended to convey the passage of a happy week.

Rick responded favorably. He, John, and I went to the optical house to launch it.

Again it was impressed on me that super 16 is pretty much virgin territory since the people at the optical house disagreed among themselves as to procedure.

Some forty slides and photos will be shot. When I hesitated at their asking price, they dropped it a bit; 16 mm facilitates such discounts since no one with money to spare would use it.

On our way back to the editing room, Rick, John, and I stopped for slices of Boychick's Kosher Pizzas, a first for me.

Friday, December 14, 8:15 A.M.: Wyndham

I felt euphoric about *The Gig* yesterday due to repeated expressions of pleasure from Rick as he worked.

Once again, the accumulation of credible moments seems to be winning the game.

Saturday, December 15, 9:10 A.M: Wyndham

Harry and Jeanne Keller stopped by the editing room. Harry told of the disastrous first preview of a film (*Kitten with a Whip*) that he produced. After the preview he returned to his limo and found a card under the windshield wiper with the message *Don't ever come back to Long Beach.*

Sunday, December 16, 9:30 A.M.: Home

Again some little thing Andy Duncan did (a look, a gesture) that went unnoticed while shooting proves valuable.

We hope to be through the first pass by New Year's—nine working days from now.

Must remember Harry's dictum: "No one ever walked out on a movie because it was too short."

Wednesday, December 19, 10:15 A.M.: Wyndham

We have seventy-three minutes and thirty-five seconds of film for eighty and one-third pages of script.

Marilyn, the apprentice, wears very well.

Norman reports that SAG still hasn't returned our bond, which means I will have to put in another $15,000 to ensure we get through our picture cut.

Thursday, December 20, 8:30 A.M.: Wyndham

Ruth and I went to hear Dick Wellstood at Hanratty's. Depressing to learn the dearth of work here compels him to Europe.

Friday, December 21, 9:20 A.M.: Wyndham

Now for the montage sequence, which, if the concept works, will be a nice Christmas present to myself.

Thursday, December 27, 7:40 A.M.: Wyndham

The montage eludes so far, which causes anxiety since it is the springboard for the finale.

Ulu Grosbard dropped in to the editing room. His eyes went to the screen. "Sixteen millimeter?" he asked, as though discovering something vaguely illicit.

We lunched and talked film, but I had the feeling we are not in the same business, reinforced by Ulu telling me the Teamster charges on his last film, which came to more than the total cost of my entire picture.

Friday, December 28, 8:45 A.M.: Wyndham

The montage, on review, seemed truncated.

We added twenty-three seconds to the end (the band playing "Maple Leaf"), which is how the montage began. And there it was—a lively swirl of film and photos blended so smoothly that many observers will not be aware of the mix involving some forty stills and a dozen bits of film totaling one minute and twenty-three seconds. Has this ever been done before?

We reviewed the material for the rowboat scene—Wayne, Cleavon, Andy fishing.

"That's the worst line in the movie," Rick asserted apropos of one of Wayne's speeches. As author, I started to bristle, but feeling good about the montage, I told him to cut the line. Immediately he relented, said he might have been "too harsh" about it. I'll be curious to see if he includes the line in his assemblage and whether the line ultimately makes the picture.

Marilyn, Rick, John, and I went to the Jewish Repertory Theatre to see Joe Silver and Jay Thomas in a revival of Ron Ribman's play *Cold Storage.*

They gave the play an emotional arc, a rewarding conclusion absent when I saw the play some six years ago on Broadway.

Saturday, December 29, 10:00 A.M.: Wyndham

Sam Peckinpah dead at fifty-nine.

We worked together for one week on *The Cincinnati Kid.* My exit followed by his two weeks later.

My most lasting memory is watching Sharon Tate screen-test with Steve McQueen.

1985
Thursday, January 3, 8:20 A.M.: Wyndham

The scene Rick promised to have ready at 11:30, then 12:30, then 1:30, then 2:00, I saw at 4:00 P.M.

Pacing that chilly corridor while he worked accounts for my irritability, though the film is going well.

Norman's financial report ($10,000 needed to get us to the rough-cut backers' screening) doesn't help my mood.

We have eighty-four minutes through page 90.

Friday, January 4, 8:45 A.M.: Wyndham

Norman, Rick, and I scheduled procedures from the end of picture cut through sound editing, titles, premix, mix, blowup to 35 mm., etc.

Saturday, January 5, 9:50 A.M.: Wyndham

Bill Goldman entered the editing room like a foreign land. His tentativeness attributable to the plight of most screenwriters (no matter how successful), whom the system wastefully contrives to distance from the filmmaking process. Rick showed him a bit of the scene he was working on. During the minute or so it ran, Bill laughed. Rick, John, and I buoyed by this first review.

Rick completed the scene at 10:00 P.M. When viewed, it seemed no more than thirty seconds passed. When measured, it proved to be three and a half minutes.

We now have ninety minutes of film.

Tuesday, January 8, 9:30 A.M.: Wyndham

Wayne's daughter, Laura, joined us today for several weeks of a college work program. I told her that to avoid artificial experience (which is what merely observing would be), we were going to treat her like a new apprentice: Marilyn will introduce her to the mundane world of tabs, trims, splices, and running errands.

Thursday, January 10, 9:15 A.M.: Wyndham

We worked till 11:30 P.M. last night. Sent out for Chinese food. The scheduled screening tomorrow has been postponed till Monday.

Friday, January 11, 8:30 A.M.: Wyndham

We completed the first cut last night at about 7:00 P.M.

Norman, Rick, and I lunched with Paul Barnes, an editor Rick knows, who had just completed a blowup at John Allen's, whom he recommended enthusiastically.

Saturday, January 12, 8:10 A.M.: Wyndham

Tried an end-credit idea that has been put on hold till we get a group reaction to the film.

Then we reviewed the material cut since the last time we screened. To my (and I suspect everyone's) surprise, it played flat.

A vigorous assault, excising every dead spot, eliminated two minutes.

Sunday, January 13, 11:00 A.M.: Home

Lunch in—as we finetuned the rest of the reels.

The film to be viewed by Rick, John, and me for the first time in its (rough) entirety tomorrow is ninety-six minutes and several seconds long.

Tuesday, January 15, 8:45 A.M.: Wyndham

All in all, it works!

I've made a list of needed corrections, to be augmented by Rick's and John's notes.

Wednesday, January 16, 8:20 A.M.: Wyndham

We've taken two minutes out of the first two reels.

I gave up things that Rick never thought I'd agree to.

Laura Rogers so busy yesterday that despite our quarters having the dimensions of a midget submarine, I wasn't aware of her.

Thursday, January 17, 8:00 A.M.: Wyndham

We polished from 9:00 A.M. to 8:00 P.M. Snipped, trimmed, and altered. The ninety-six minutes viewed on Monday is now ninety-two.

A cutting dictum (mine): "The less of the audience's time you take, the more they owe you."

Friday, January 18, 9:15 A.M.: Wyndham

Last night's screening went fine despite a no-sound false start and jumping splices.

Sheldon and Margie Harnick hugged me delightedly. Ditto Dennis Smith and his date. They, plus Rochelle (Rick's lady), Hal Levinsohn (sound editor), and Norman and Sarah plus Dan, were the entire audience. The excellence of the screening largely lost on Rick and John, who were fighting for their lives in the rear to keep the single reel on track and dying with each splice jump.

Must not let euphoria blind me to the fact that there is at least two and a half months' work ahead.

Saturday, January 19, 10:00 A.M.: Home

Margie and Sheldon Harnick just phoned to reaffirm the nice things they said the other night. They got on the phone jointly, so the cheering news came double-barrel.

It looks like I'll need $90,000 to complete the picture.

Tuesday, January 22, 8:45 A.M.: Wyndham

We screen for an audience of some forty people tonight. Will do a premix at Magno, involving five scenes, starting at 9:30 A.M. this morning.

Thursday, January 24, 9:30 A.M.: Wyndham

Too hectic yesterday to record anything here.

I felt the film played well Tuesday night. But weak spots surfaced with the pressure of added eyes.

Wayne seemed to like it, but (as learned later) he had been taking notes all during the show, so I wasn't sure what he really saw.

Many people (but not all) lingered after the screening.

Ruth and I went with Jim and Jean McLaughlin to the Plaza Palm Court. The McLaughlins' main criticism (which I share) is that the end needs work.

Via music, I will try to go off on a more upbeat note, short of resurrecting Georgie, whose death Jean and Jim both found offputting. Jim suggested several alternate ending ideas, punctuated by Jean saying, "Jim, stick to bonds."

I breakfasted with Wayne. His notes were in the main helpful.

Jim phoned to report that J. C., on a 1–10 scale, gave *The Gig* a 2.

When I arrived at Tape House, Mark Polycan, who'd been at the screening, stopped me to say it was "the most enjoyable adult film he'd seen in ages." He even quoted a line.

And so it goes.

Met with Tom Distler at 6:00 P.M. to draft a letter to investors outlining plans to raise the needed $90,000.

Friday, January 25, 8:45 A.M.: Wyndham

Bill Goldman, who responded enthusiastically, suggested a small cut after the screening, which has already been executed. Probably the most immediate impact he's ever had on a film.

Sunday, January 27, 9:45 A.M.: Home

The absence of entry yesterday reflects fatigue occasioned by the screening, plus all the odds and ends that fall to me due to Norman's ill-timed departure for Los Angeles.

We have trimmed about a minute and a half while making other adjustments to which that audience (as tough and heterogeneous as any we are apt to face) alerted us.

On Friday we took Laura Rogers to lunch on her last day.

"Wherever you're going, I hope you get there safely," I said to Laura in parting. I meant Los Angeles or Saratoga (she in doubt where to spend the week till classes resumed), but Rick took my words as poetically intended and applauded.

The letter to the investors went out.

Wednesday, January 30, 8:00 A.M.: Wyndham

I like what Rick did to the final scene. Cutting the slow pan lessens the melancholy conclusion.

We screened for Hal Levinsohn and Marshall Grupp (sound editors) and Warren Vaché for music needs. All but two of the new changes work.

Something Hal Levinsohn said alerted me that a particular scene was still too long. We cut twenty seconds, gaining a vital tempo.

Rick talking about a new book detailing the Allies' failure to do anything about the concentration camps prompted my account of viewing Ohrdruf Nord, the first concentration camp overrun in April 1945: 3,200 matchstick corpses that made Patton puke, etc.

Their attention (Marilyn's husband's family killed in the camps) drew me out so that I felt drained at the end.

Friday, February 1, 8:15 A.M.: Wyndham

We locked the film at a shade under ninety minutes, less the end credits, and toasted the event.

Warren in to prepare for the music session next Thursday.

Rick and I interviewing negative cutters—the cleanliness of their work rooms a vital factor.

Like the barber who shaves you, blade at your adam's apple, the negative cutter holds the life of your work in his hands.

Saturday, February 2, 9:00 A.M.: Home

Jim McLaughlin called to assure me of his and J. C.'s financial support, easing my mind no little.

Final length, including end titles, ninety-one minutes and forty seconds.

Wednesday, February 6, 9:30 A.M.: Wyndham

Rick ran the end of the film for Warren and Roger Rhodes, who will be the engineer at tomorrow's music session.

I outlined the goal: to send the audience out as happy as possible (despite Georgie's death) via music.

A call from Wayne explaining that his $9,000 investment toward the $90,000 was just a pump primer. "If you need more, let me know," he said.

"You'll be the first one I call," I assured, which evoked a chuckle.

Friday, February 8, 10:30 A.M.: Wyndham

The recording session, at ERAS Studio on Fifty-fourth Street where we gathered at 2:00 P.M., was joyous.

Warren, Herb Harris, George Masso, Kenny Davern, and two replacements (John Bunch, piano, and the legendary Milt Hinton, seventy-five, on bass) for Dick Wellstood and Reggie Johnson, who are in Europe.

Milt, as he has been doing all his life, photographed the occasion.

I prefaced the session by capsulizing *The Gig* story.

We ran the end of the film on a TV monitor till the musicians were familiar with it.

Then, at Warren's direction, we began.

By 4:00 P.M., we had it.

After drinks at Michael's Pub, Warren, Kenny, and George, in tuxedos, headed for their gig at the Rainbow Room.

Saturday–Thursday, February 9-14: Home

Flu.

Saturday, February 16, 9:00 A.M.: Home

The best news yesterday was Rick's ecstatic report after seeing a sample blowup from 16 to 35 mm.

Tuesday, February 19, 8:30 A.M.: Wyndham

On checking the titles, I found misspellings, misplacements, and wrong-size type. On checking the final scene, I heard a note before the instrument reached the player's lips.

"You came back with an eagle eye," said Rick.

Wednesday, February 20, 8:30 A.M.: Wyndham

I saw the blowup sample from John Allen. It's excellent.

For economy, we will defer making a music and effects track (used in foreign countries for dubbing) until needed.

Thursday, February 21, 8:30 A.M.: Wyndham

Rick and I went over main and end titles with Dick Raugh at the optical house.

After Tony (my eldest son and fledgling screenwriter) told off a fly-by-night producer who had wasted his time, the guy said, "I respect you more now than I ever did because I never respect anyone till they tell me I'm full of shit."

Welcome to the wonderful world of show business.

Tuesday, February 26, 9:00 A.M.: Wyndham

First mixing day.

Running the reel with a dupe of the original production sound track before we began gave Jack Cooley, the mixer, an idea of the overall and reminds me what we have before improvements commence.

We did one reel and were into the second by 6:00 P.M.

Cooley seems to have caught my preference for rough-hewn documentary-like sound.

Bumped into Michael Moriarty, the actor. When he said he and his wife were contemplating an independent movie production, I had dinner with them and offered an overall view of what I'd learned so far.

Wednesday, February 27, 8:10 A.M.: Wyndham

Reel two (of five) completed. A few bird sounds too many when they get to Paradise Manor, which we muted.

To avoid inhibiting the mixer and being distracted from the screen, I sit forward of the console.

Thursday, February 28, 8:05 A.M.: Wyndham

Completed the third reel, which we'll review first thing this morning.

As long as I like what I hear, I am silent.

If I sense too much time spent on a problem that I (the audience's representative) can't detect or feel is trivial, I step in.

Friday, March 1, 7:00 A.M.: Wyndham

Completed reel four.

Cooley, perfect casting for a priest, cleared up the rowboat scene amazingly.

I suspect the more you like your picture, the faster the mix goes. Conversely, when you don't like it, you hide from your assessment by striving for miracles and/or losing yourself in details.

Saturday, March 2, 10:00 A.M.: Home

Ruth and I breakfasted with Dan Petrie.[7] His film *Bay Boy* is out of the Fifty-seventh Street Playhouse before it had a chance to bloom. So much for studio release of small films that need nurturing.

The mix completed on schedule at 6:00 P.M.

Tuesday, March 5, 9:00 A.M.: Wyndham

Bill Goldman and I, en route to the Writers Guild strike-vote meeting, ate at the Carnegie Deli: those mountainous sandwiches that make you choose twixt gluttony and waste.

I left the meeting depressed because those opposing the strike failed to grasp the connection between the benefits now enjoyed (royalties, pension, health) and what it took to achieve them.

Wednesday, March 6, 8:45 A.M.: Wyndham

When I told Wayne I'd lunched with Horton Foote, he quoted a friend of his who said, "Foote has Bobby Duvall, Gilroy has you, and I think Gilroy got the short end of the deal."

We have reserved the Directors Guild Theatre in Los Angeles for a screening on May 2 ($950).

The Writers Guild strike is on.

Zoot Sims, a quintessential jazzman, is seriously ill. One of my treasured jazz memories is he and the pianist Dave McKenna, in duo at Michael's Pub, playing "Jitterbug Waltz."

Thursday, March 7, 9:00 A.M.: Wyndham

Horton Foote briefed me about his dealings with various distributors. In exchange, I unraveled some of the mysteries of super 16. There is a definite fraternity among those who buck the system.

---

7. We met when he directed several scripts of mine in TV's "Golden Age." He directed *Who'll Save the Plowboy?*—my first play produced in New York. His credits in TV and film are many and distinguished. We've shared great success and dismal failure and are still glad to see each other.

Saturday, March 9, 8:30 A.M.: **Home**

The Writers Guild caved in on the cassette issue—probably the most important thing we'll ever strike for.

Monday, March 11, 8:20 A.M.: **Wyndham**

Schedule permitting, I promised Maury Rapf (screen-writer) I'd teach at Dartmouth during the fall semester in the film department, which he heads.

Wednesday, March 13, 8:15 A.M.: **Wyndham**

Norman, Rick, John, and I viewed titles yet again. Front ones fine; the end ones still need work.

We've changed the date of the L.A. screening to Tuesday, April 30.

Saturday, March 16, 8:15 A.M.: **Home**

Got to John Allen's at 8:30 A.M. Some dozen young people bustling about midst cans of film stacked everywhere.

Rick and I, with Mike at the Hazeltine, began color correction.

We found some dirt on the negative in reel three, which hopefully Mike will get rid of via ultrasonic cleaning before the blowup. If not, there are other, more complicated procedures he can employ.

Thursday, March 21, 8:30 A.M.: **Home**

We completed timing.

About the two frames lost in negative cutting: One will be corrected by splice and one on the blowup machine. I'm not clear on the plusses and minuses of the alternatives.

Wayne phoned to ask if our aspect ratio (ratio of length to width on the screen) is 1–66 or 1–85. I learned the blowup will give us 1–66 and the option to show either way. If you are in 1–85, you can't go to 1–66, which gives more top and bottom and a larger picture overall.

Next step: Mike and Rick (or John) will go to the negative cutter to cut the title sequence and montage into the negative. Then Mike will time those areas. And then the blowup can commence. John will deliver the optical track (sound track) to Allen today. Got all that?

Saturday, April 13, 8:30 A.M.: Home

We saw the first answer print.

Colors need work, but the blowup is excellent.

Tuesday, April 16, 5:00 A.M.: Home

Norman's update means I will have to raise another $20,000, bringing the total cost of the film to $610,000.

Thursday, April 18, 8:00 A.M.: Home

John Allen called to cancel viewing of the new print, which he pronounced "unacceptable."

Saturday, April 20, 6:30 A.M.: Home

Norman, Rick, and I viewed the new first reel at John Allen's in Jersey. Colors still not right but better. We then drove to New York where we screened the reel at the MGM screening room to make sure that Allen's projection equipment wasn't misleading us.

What looked good at Allen's looked even better there. Sound similarly improved. We were all encouraged.

Best news: No one could detect, even from the first row, that it is a blowup.

Wednesday, April 24, 8:30 A.M.: Wyndham

We have our first big screening in less than twelve hours, and I won't see a new answer print until this afternoon. Talk about cutting it close.

Thursday, April 25, Noon: Wyndham

Last night's screening went well.

J. C. McLaughlin now loves the film. Apologized for his prior estimate, saying, "Please don't ever ask me to look at another rough cut. I can't handle it."

Abigail McGrath had a reception for cast and crew at her apartment after the screening. A warm mood prevailed. Daniel Nalbach and his dad, who had never seen him act before, beamed.

We screen again tonight.

Friday, April 26, 8:20 A.M.: Wyndham

Last night's screening went even better. Less laughter at the front, but greater impact at the end.

Stanley Jaffe[8] volunteered to help us in any way he can.

Saturday, April 27, 9:00 A.M.: Home

Wayne and I met Julian, who attended the second screening with Meyer, and wanted to discuss the possibility of his company, Castle Hill, distributing the picture in the event we don't make a deal with a major, or minimajor.

Asked what the majors or minimajors could do that he couldn't, Julian said for one thing, because they had a regular flow of product, they could collect more readily since their clout was the next picture.

"You're forgetting," I said, "we have Chuck Wepner."

Rick Shaine reported that Barry Malkin (Coppola's editor) not only liked the picture but said he looked as hard as he could and found no evidence of blowup.

Wayne and I went to see Stanley Jaffe, who advised many word-of-mouth screenings plus a small opening to allow time for the word to circulate.

"Would you like me to call Frank Mancuso [then head of Paramount]?" he asked. When we said yes, the call was placed. Unfortunately, Mancuso wasn't there.

Perhaps the nicest call of the day (peer praise the best) was from the writer David Goodman, who said, "I'm sure I'll be voting for you for best screenplay next year."

Now to prepare for tomorrow's journey to L.A.

Monday, April 29, 8:00 A.M.: Beverly Hills Hotel, L.A.

Sarah drove Norman and me to Kennedy, where Rick joined us for an uneventful flight.

No messages when I checked in; a call from Mancuso was the dream. Rick and Norman are staying with friends.

Tuesday, April 30, 8:00 A.M.: Beverly Hills Hotel

We compete with the Lakers tonight.

8. Partnered with Sherry Lansing, produced *Fatal Attraction*, among other hits. Currently he's the head of Paramount.

I phoned Sam Goldwyn. He can't make the screening but will send his top man.

A calming lunch with Mann Rubin at the Swiss Café.

Wednesday, May 1, 9:30 A.M.: Beverly Hills Hotel

To the DGA screening room at 5:30 P.M. with Norman and Rick.

We ran the first reel. Set sound level; had the projectionist raise his candlepower because the picture looked dark. Triggered the air conditioner to eliminate a stale smell.

To Butterfield's, where Wayne joined us and I had my two pre-screening vodkas.

Back to the DGA. People arriving. Faces out of the past included Norman Panama, who brought me to Hollywood for my first studio job at Paramount.

At ten minutes after eight, 350 people present, but most of the promised biggies absent, I told Rick to signal *go* to the projectionist.

The film played well but differently than in New York. I felt the audience's lack of daily association with blacks gave the black-white friction a more threatening aspect than was intended.

Upon conclusion of Stan Lachow's monologue, several people, as though at a play, applauded.

The one and a half hours sped by.

Undermining the enthusiastic response was the absence of people who could translate praise into distribution offers.

Wayne just phoned word that Greg Bautzer (the well-known Hollywood attorney) called him this morning to say he was so enthused about the film that on his own, he was calling MGM to tell Alan Ladd, Jr., and Jay Cantor that they should see it immediately.

> *11:00 A.M.*

I've been fielding congratulatory phone calls almost continuously since the last entry.

> *11:40 A.M.*

Hal Gaba (Embassy) just called. Would like a screening for the rest of their people.

Wayne called to inform that Howard Koch, Sr., and Al Ruddy volunteered to help in any way they could.

> *3:10 P.M.*

Jay Cantor, second in command to Ladd at MGM/UA, wants to see the film at 4:00 P.M. Norman making arrangements.

5:50 P.M.

Norman just called from MGM. Reported Cantor viewed it with one other, unidentified, person.

Norman quoted the projectionist (who liked it) saying, "Too bad Georgie died." Everybody's a critic.

Thursday, May 2, 8:45 A.M.: Beverly Hills Hotel

Wayne pursuing the possibility of our showing at the Japanese Film Festival.

Wayne said he spoke to Frank Mancuso, who wants me to phone him in New York on Friday, May 10, to set up a screening. Just got off the phone with the McLaughlins (J. C. and Jim), to whom I gave a progress report.

Canby's review of the documentary about George Stevens in the *New York Times* notes the conspicuous omission of his final film, *The Only Game in Town.*

Sam Goldwyn's man likes *The Gig* but sees it as a tough sell.

Noon:

Wayne called to say Greg Bautzer reports that Jay Cantor wants to see the picture again.

Norman reports that CBS Theatrical is interested in foreign rights.

A message that Irving Yablons (Orion) wants to see it before we make a deal with anyone else.

Wayne reports interest from *Playboy.*

12:30 P.M.

Wayne again: Eisner (Disney) wants to see it at 3:00 P.M. Wednesday and hold it over for their other people on Thursday morning.

Hal Gaba setting up a screening for Embassy at 2:00 P.M. on Tuesday.

Cantor's office called. We will screen for him and Ladd at 4:00 P.M.

5:00 P.M.

Tom Sherak, head of theatrical distribution at Twentieth, called. He will see it at 1:30 P.M. on Monday.

It's as though all the ripples from our screening have reached shore simultaneously.

I've postponed departure.

Saturday, May 4, 8:45 A.M.: Beverly Hills Hotel

Rick Shaine said that his uncle, a retired musician, pronounced *The Gig* absolutely accurate. This from a man who played the Catskills and had the band at the Stork Club where Sherman Billingsly, the owner, communicated with him by telegram, even when he merely wanted the music "softer."

Here is our screening schedule for next week:

Monday:	Fox, 1:30 P.M.
	MGM/UA, 4:00 P.M.
Tuesday:	Embassy, 2:00 P.M.
Wednesday:	Disney, 4:00 P.M.
Thursday:	Disney, A.M.

Monday, May 6, 4:00 P.M.: Beverly Hills Hotel

Tom Sherak called. "I liked it personally, but I don't think it's something for Fox to distribute."

Tuesday, May 7, 3:00 A.M.: Beverly Hills Hotel

Ruth's sudden illness alters plans. Taking a noon flight home.

1:00 P.M. (L.A. time): In the Air

Before leaving the hotel, I phoned Wayne, who will lend the company $20,000 needed to complete the picture.

Friday, May 10, 11:00 A.M.: Wyndham

Ruth, at Beth Israel, seems safely over the worst of it.

An AIDS victim across the hall died yesterday. Passing the empty room after the body was removed, I saw a single red rose in a vase.

Norman reports from L.A. that he showed *The Gig* to someone at TriStar who is recommending it for pickup to his superiors.

Disney (Katzenberg) told Wayne he liked it personally, but not to distribute.

The Japanese Film Festival people (the festival somehow connected to a celebrity tennis tournament) want Wayne and me to bring the film to Tokyo for unoffical showing.

Wayne reported having dinner Saturday night at the home of Marvin Davis, who owns Twentieth Century–Fox. When Wayne informed Davis his representative turned us down, Davis asked what *The Gig* was about. Wayne told the story, which Davis appeared to respond to. Howard Koch, Sr., chipped in, "It's a wonderful film."

Tuesday, May 14, 9:00 A.M.: Wyndham

Norman, who delivered the film to Paramount, reports that Mancuso was not one of the four men who viewed it.

Wayne called. He's booked us to Tokyo on May 29 from New York.

Wednesday, May 15, 9:00 A.M.: Home

I bought a Japanese phrase book: *Yes* = HAH-ee EH; *No* = ee-EH; *Thank you* = DOH-moh ah-REE-gah-toh.

Friday, May 17, 5:15 A.M.: Home

I have just about decided not to go to Japan since it is primarily Wayne's playing tennis that interests them and showing *The Gig* would be an improvised affair that we would have to pay for.

Saturday, May 18, 10:00 A.M.: Home

Attended a luncheon at the Plaza (given by the New Dramatists) honoring all Pulitzer-Prize-winning playwrights.

Twenty of us present, including Sidney Kingsley, Jerry Weidman, John Patrick, Paul Zindel, Charles Fuller, Charles Gordone, Sheldon Harnick, Jimmy Kirkwood, Arthur Miller, Frances Hackett, and Marsha Norman, the most recent winner, who made the only speech: an excellent mix of humor and adroit critique of the current theater scene.

I've bowed out of the Tokyo trip.

Sunday, May 19, 4:45 A.M.: Home

Walter Manley trying to get us in the Venice Film Festival and the Deauville Festival.

Abe Burrows died yesterday at seventy-four. A Pulitzer Prize winner, was he aware of the party the day before? I wish I'd saved the antic notes he used to slip me during Dramatists Guild Council meetings.

Sunday, June 2, 6:15 A.M.: Home

David Matelon, TriStar, never showed up to see *The Gig* at the screening he requested.

Saturday, June 15, 8:00 A.M.: Home

We screwed up the rescheduled screening for Matelon, which makes us even. Will try again.

Friday, June 21, 8:30 A.M.: Home

I left for the city at 7:30 A.M. to ensure getting a new print to MGM screening room on time for the 10:30 showing for the Venice Film Festival representative

The audience included several invited guests—the head of Orion Classics acquisitions and a woman representing the Deauville Festival, plus Walter Manley.

At 10:40 A.M. the Italian hadn't arrived. Manley's call woke him. He said he would jump in a cab. Since he was the primary reason for the screening, I apologized to the other guests and waited.

At 11:05 A.M. a scruffy youth dressed in Salvation Army discards arrived with a girl. No, he wasn't the festival representative but an associate who assured me in minimal English the head guy was en route. I said the hell with it and started the film.

Ten minutes into the picture, the representative, as unprepossessing as his aide, arrived.

Manley beseeched me not to pull the plug when I questioned the value of going to Venice.

Wednesday, June 26: 6:30 A.M.: Home

I made a list of the companies that have viewed *The Gig* at least once. It totals thirteen.

Thursday, June 27, 8:40 A.M.: Hanover, New Hampshire

Maury Rapf, head of the Dartmouth film department, recommended *The Gig* to Bill Pence for inclusion in the Telluride Film Festival.

David Matelon called after seeing the picture. He found it "witty and intelligent," but TriStar was not the one to market it. "It needs careful nurturing and would get lost with us."

Wednesday, July 3, 8:30 A.M.: Home

The Venice Festival rejected us.

Tuesday, July 9, 8:30 A.M., Home

Wayne phoned. He said a lawyer who saw *The Gig* and liked it approached him in behalf of a group involved in oil and gas leases that has found a way to apply their tax-shelter formulas to the film business.

Thursday, July 11, 8:00 A.M.: Home

Pat Hart in Walter Manley's office phoned to inform we've been accepted by the Deauville Festival.

Friday, July 12, 8:30 A.M.: Home

Julian Schlossberg wants to distribute *The Gig*. He will draw up two proposals: one if *we* put up the money for prints and ads, another if *he* does it. He sees no advantage in Deauville.

Wayne phoned to report that UA/MGM was screening the picture yet again. He also said the gas and oil people were definitely interested.

Wayne is sending the film to Sid Sheinberg (head of UA) for an at-home screening over the weekend.

Wednesday, July 17, 7:50 A.M.: Home

Norman called to report the picture seen by the Skouras Company. No sale but much praise. The Skouras representative so enthused that she phoned the Toronto Film Festival. And as a consequence, we are sending them a print today.

Wayne reports that MGM/UA, after the latest screening, reiterated "we loved it" but feared it would get lost in their vast machinery.

Thursday, July 18, 5:00 A.M.: Home

We sent *The Gig* via Federal Express to the Toronto Film Festival. Cost one-way: $225.

Saturday, July 20, 7:55 A.M.: Home

Manley called to say he had a letter officially inviting us to

Deauville but only room expenses were on them—all the rest (transportation, food, etc.) was ours.

Saturday, July 27, 8:00 A.M.: Home

Bill Pence informs that despite his high regard for *The Gig*, "Alas, it isn't right for the Telluride Festival."

Wednesday, August 7, 8:30 A.M.: Home

Wayne said Ken Badish (The Movie Store) saw *The Gig* and wants to represent it—will draw up a proposal including that rarest of words in the distributors' lexicon, *advance*.

Friday, August 16, 5:30 A.M.: Home

Wayne called: The gas and oil guys are serious.

Seeking a theater, we screened for Sheldon Gunsberg, head of the Reade chain, who responded enthusiastically.

"It's my picture," he said, alluding to his familiarity with the Catskills.

"Frank grew up with Jews," Julian informed Gunsberg, who rejoined, "So did I."

Wednesday, August 28, 5:00 A.M.: Home

After much back-and-forth, we've made a four-wall deal with Ackerman for the Fifty-seventh Street Playhouse, which is far from idyllic but the best that's available: In addition to paying for all ads, we guarantee $8,500 a week for six weeks and as long thereafter as we pay that, plus 10 percent of anything over $8,500. Opening date contingent on the fortunes of *Colonel Redl*, which precedes us.

We will go to L.A. next week to meet the gas and oil people and Badish.

Friday, September 6, 9:00 A.M.: Los Angeles

We have distribution offers from the gas and oil people and from Badish.

By noon today, we may have a better offer from Hal Gaba, who, surfacing at the eleventh hour, asked us to make no deals till he arranged a screening for Perenchio.

Saturday, September 7, 9:45 A.M.: En Route Home

Gaba phoned to say he was unable to reach Perenchio. "Thanks for the shot."

I informed the gas and oil people and Badish that I would get back to them after presenting their offers to my investors.

Tuesday, September 10, 8:45 A.M.: Wyndham

Frank Weissberg inspected the proposal from the gas and oil people, alerted me to potential problems.

Friday, September 13, 8:15 A.M.: Wyndham

Met Jim and J. C. McLaughlin, Dave Chase, and Mark Piven at 30 Wall Street. Detailed the three alternatives: gas and oil, Movie Store, or open it ourselves. Gave them a typed summary of each, including pros and cons; answered questions.

Led by J. C., all four (investors) opted for doing it ourselves: putting up the money for prints and ads so if we hit, we are unencumbered, free to make any deal.

Dennis Smith, briefed by phone, also favored opening it ourselves.

Since they will have to put up the money, it's a nice vote of confidence.

Sunday, September 21, 8:30 A.M.: Home

I leave for Hanover in a couple of hours (with Ruth to follow in a couple of days) to begin my ten-week residency at Dartmouth.

Wayne phoned to say he visited the Fifty-seventh Street Playhouse and the manager (contradicting Ackerman) said they are not allowed to hang a banner.

Monday, September 23, 10:00 A.M.: Hanover, New Hampshire

Arrived at the home of the artist Varujian Bogosian, which we will be subletting (he in Rome on a Guggenheim).

As happens each time I return to Hanover since graduating in 1950, I was swamped with memories of May 1946 when fresh out of the army, I came here seeking admission, which given my high school record and the number of applicants, seemed quixotic.

Tuesday, September 24, 7:10 A.M.: Hanover

Someone asked me for a syllabus. Seemed nonplussed when I said I didn't know what I was going to teach until I taught it.

Wednesday, October 2, 7:00 A.M.: Hanover

Colonel Redl received a bad review in today's *New York Times*, which could advance our opening date.

Jim McLaughlin called to say he got a Dun & Bradstreet on the gas and oil people that makes us glad we didn't go with them.

Friday, October 4, 7:15 A.M.: Hanover

My "syllabus" has crystallized: I am the head of a movie studio, and they (the class) are my writers. And by term's end we have to turn out a program of short films written, directed, acted, and edited by them on videotape that (unlike 8 mm) permits synchronized sound and (unlike 16 mm) costs next to nothing.

Friday, October 11, 8:30 A.M.: Hanover

After numerous rejections, I've given the go-ahead on two screenplays now in the works. Several other students nearing that stage.

Ruth keeps reminding me mine is not their only class.

Tuesday, October 15, 8:05 A.M.: Hanover

Following *Colonel Redl*'s box-office fortunes to gauge our opening date gives a ghoulish feel.

Friday, October 18, 10:20 A.M.: Hanover

Bill Goldman (whose screen credits include *Butch Cassidy, Marathon Man*, and *All the President's Men*) spoke to the class.

I was surprised that none of the film department faculty showed up despite personal invitation.

Thursday, October 24, 8:30 A.M.: Wyndham

Arrived yesterday with the one-sheet poster Ruth and I designed plus press-kit materials, including all photos and bios.

To Tape House to view the first reel of the new print. Mark Polycan invited several TV commercial directors to view his

(Mark's) appearance in the used-car scene. One of the TV directors said, "I've used Matz and Duncan and never knew they played instruments." "They don't," I said, pleased that we had accomplished the deception so effectively.

Norman and I took the new reel to the Fifty-seventh Street Playhouse, where it looked and sounded fine.

Friday, October 25, 8:15 A.M.: Wyndham

To Renee Furst's to meet Hi Negrin, who will handle brochure, poster, and postcards.

Then to Tape House where Norman and I selected potential scenes for TV clips. Then to Serino, Coyne, and Nappi, who will handle our ads as they did on *Once in Paris*. Then to inspect the screening room (Preview 4 at 1600 Broadway) that will be used for critic screenings. Then to Wayne Weil's (another Dartmouth grad) office to inspect the mechanicals he is doing for the poster. Then back to the Tape House. Gave a stranger bound for Grand Central a lift in our cab. When he offered to pay, Norman told him to see *The Gig* instead.

Tuesday, October 29, 8:00 A.M.: Hanover

Exchanged numerous calls with Renee and Norman about the Thursday screenings, discovered they coincide with Halloween and a Sting movie screening. Ultimately postponed the first screening until next week.

Wednesday, October 30, 8:30 A.M.: Hanover

Renee makes a good point about what day of the week we open: When the big critics note many films opening on one day, they, not wanting multiple credits, will take the top one or two and assign the remainder to underlings. This all but rules out a Friday opening.

Thursday, October 31, 8:10 A.M.: Hanover

We will open on November 27 (the day before Thanksgiving), four weeks from last night.

Friday, November 1, 8:40 A.M.: Hanover

We've switched the opening date from November 27 (when *Santa Claus* and *Rocky IV* premiere) to Tuesday, November 26.

Wednesday, November 6, 8:00 A.M.: Hanover

Our destiny begins to be decided today with the first press screening at 6:00 P.M. in the Penthouse Theatre of Magno at 1540 Broadway.

Thursday, November 7, 7:30 A.M.: Wyndham

Norman phoned at 8:00 P.M. to say the screening went excellently—some thirty-forty people who sat throughout the credits and applauded at the end, which Renee's aide told Norman was all but unheard of at a press screening. I don't think any important critics were present, but it was still good to hear.

Norman and I to Serino, Coyne, and Nappi to plan ads.

Norman went to cover the noon screening while I went to Sardi's. Encountered Ed Kook (Century Lighting). Like all pure theater folk, he dismissed my new film as an embarrassment that a proven playwright should be loath to mention.

Renee arrived. Said there were about ten people at the screening. Norman joined us after the screening. Felt it had gone poorly. Said everyone fled as the first credit appeared. I conclude that noon screenings, when your audience wants to get to lunch, are dumb.

Norman and I went to see Sam Schatz, the man who makes banners, at National Flag, 43 West Twenty-first Street where he's been for forty years. He will do the banner (yellow letters against purple) for $1,200 and will do the strip that hangs from both sides of the theater canopy for another $600.

On to Tape House where Norman and I made final selections of television clips to give TV critics.

Norman handled the 8:00 P.M. screening.

Friday, November 8, 6:45 A.M.: Wyndham

I met Norman at Consolidated Poster to inspect the color key, which is a sample of the completed one-sheet poster.

We ordered 2,500: 1,000 of which will be "wild-posted" (illegally plastered all over town) with *Now playing 57th Street Playhouse* "sniped" on, which means a lettered strip glued to each of the posters.

Tuesday, November 12, 8:30 A.M.: Hanover

We start shooting the first of the student scripts this morning.

Renee Furst just phoned: "I have the headline for your quote ad from Richard Freedman, critic for the Newhouse chain: '*The Gig* is the *Amadeus* of jazz.'"

I don't know what it means, but as first favorable word from any critical source, it made my heart soar.

Wednesday, November 13, 9:10 A.M.: Hanover

The two screenings at 4:00 and 6:00 P.M. today at Preview 4 are almost "sold out." Which I choose to interpret as a good word-of-mouth sign.

Thursday, November 14, 8:40 A.M.: Hanover

One of the student scripts involved a young man in his underwear on Hanover's main street. Anticipating trouble, I advised shooting as discreetly and swiftly as possible. My advice borne out when moments after they got the shot, a cop appeared in response to a complaint.

"We won't have any of that underwear stuff here," he growled.

Norman reported the 4:00 P.M. screening (which Larry Cohen of *Variety* attended) went well.

Friday, November 15, 8:30 A.M.: Hanover

Cynthia, in Renee's office, says all comments she's gotten after screenings are good except for a black friend of hers who found *The Gig* racist. She appended that he found *all* white films racist.

Tuesday, November 19, 8:45 A.M.: Hanover

Asked what the feedback has been. Renee said, "So far, not one negative reaction." The most encouraging sign is the new enthusiasm in her voice.

Tonight's 8:00 P.M. screening "sold out."

Wednesday, November 20, 7:45 A.M.: Hanover

Renee phoned: *People* magazine likes the picture, and Rex Reed requests a special screening tomorrow, which will be accommodated.

The Gig • 239

Renee has booked me for some eight interviews over the next few days.

Thursday, November 21, 5:00 A.M.: Wyndham

On checking in, I was given a note ("urgent") to contact Renee, who informed that the *New York Times* had just called to say that Janet Maslin would review *The Gig*, but *only* if we arranged a special screening for her at 11:00 A.M. on Monday, November 25.

Given my objection to morning screenings and critics seeing films alone, Renee wanted my okay, as if I had any choice.

Norman phoned to say the 6:00 P.M. screening went well but the full house of heavyweights promised by Renee had not materialized.

Friday, November 22, 9:05 A.M.: Wyndham

Larry Cohen, *Variety*, interviewed me. Volunteered no opinion of *The Gig*, which he's seen and is reviewing.

Wayne and I did a Cable News Network interview together in a newly decorated suite John Mados gave us for the occasion.

I did a luncheon interview with Leo Seligson (*Newsday*), who insisted on picking up the tab—a first in my experience.

Rex Reed saw the film alone at 4:30 P.M. yesterday. Norman reports he stayed through the credits and emerged smiling.

Saturday, November 23, 8:10 A.M.: Home

First time home in two months.

Norman informed he'd stopped at the Fifty-seventh Street Playhouse to speak to the manager, who said she had not been told we were hanging a banner and predicted legal problems if we tried to do so.

Did several interviews, some with Wayne.

Sunday, November 24, 8:45 A.M.: Home

D minus 2.

Julian confirmed my version of the theater deal made verbally with Meyer ($8,500 a week, not $8,750, as he now contends) Julian counseled me in future to get a letter of agreement "no matter how close a friend you're dealing with."

D minus 1.

A cold gray day with snow turning to rain forecast for tomorrow, opening day.

That the most important review (the *New York Times*) will be written after Janet Maslin views it, alone on such a morning, gives me a chilly premonition.

Many critics including David Denby (*New York* magazine), who gave *Once in Paris* a glowing review that turned the tide in our direction, will be at either the 4:00 or 6:00 P.M. screening today.

10:00 A.M.

Wayne did well on the "Today" show. Bryant Gumbel asked good questions—the title and theater mentioned several times.

11:15 A.M.

I whirl, I twirl, I worry.

Ackerman still talks $8,750, but not with as much conviction since speaking to Julian, who will consult his notes when he gets to New York.

1:50 P.M.

Norman and I to the Chase branch at Sixth Avenue and Fifty-seventh Street to open *The Gig* account. The night deposit box less than fifty yards from the theater should minimize stickup risk.

Norman reported that the screening for Janet Maslin was moved at the last minute to the ninth-floor screening room (untested by us) *and* the screening preceding Maslin's ran late. Oh joy!

Just did a phone interview with *Boxoffice* magazine in L.A.

4:30 P.M.

The Freedman (Newhouse) review is not as glowing as the *Amadeus* quote would suggest. In fact, he doesn't seem to have liked *Amadeus*.

Right now, the 4:00 P.M. screening is under way.

Did an interview with someone from *Advertising Age* who loves *The Gig* but can do us little good.

8:25 P.M.

David Denby (and other important critics who promised to be there) did not show up at either screening.

Warren Vaché delivered a cassette, selections from his recordings, which we'll play between shows at the theatre.

Tuesday, November 26, 6:10 A.M.: Wyndham

D-Day.

At 9:00 P.M. last night, Norman and I supervised the dressing of the theater front after *Colonel Redl's* last show started.

First the under-the-canopy marquee, then the one above; then (salute) the banner, which looks great if we can legally maintain it; then the ruffle saying *The Gig* in various colors; and finally our poster in three of the available places.

Knowing the *New York Times* comes out at 10:30 P.M., I slipped away to a newsstand opting to face the music before I went to bed. I opened to the film section. Our ad, looking classy, dominates *Rocky IV* and all else (despite diminutive size) on the page.

And on the opposite page, like a twin to the ad, the Maslin review.

I began to read. Knew at once that while not a rave, it was not a pan or a dismissal. She calls it "a nice surprise," making me wonder what she'd expected and why.

The house dressed, Norman and I went to Michael's Pub to check with Gil about the opening-night party.

Arrived back at the hotel where Renee Furst called at midnight to read a fine review from Rex Reed, the New York *Post*, and an equally fine one from Judith Crist, WOR-TV.

Given Gannett, Newhouse, WINS radio, and WOR-TV thumbs-up, we are certainly alive.

Wednesday, November 27, 9:00 A.M.: Wyndham

Rain all day yesterday kept opening business down. At least I hope it was the rain.

Did several interviews.

Of the half-dozen pictures reviewed in *Variety*, ours was the only one reviewed favorably.

John and Suzanne Mados drove Wayne, Ruth, and me to the theater and the party afterwards at Michael's Pub.

Warren Vaché and friends made music.

Among the guests were Bill Devane, Judd Hirsch with Cleavon (who has yet to see the picture), Matt Dillon, and the Bayonne Bleeder himself, Chuck Wepner.

The boys in the band. *Left to right:* Joe Silver, Cleavon Little, Daniel Nalbach, Warren Vaché, Andrew Duncan, Jerry Matz, Wayne Rogers, and me at the drums.

Paradise Manor (Sacks Lodge)—prettier than the brochure. That's Mitgang (Joe Silver) standing in the foreground.

Wayne Rogers. Would you buy a used car from this man?

Left to right: Warren Vaché, Daniel Nalbach, Jerry Matz, Andrew Duncan, and Cleavon Little. Also in this van (but not seen) are Wayne Rogers, driving; Jeri Sopanen, cinematographer; Eric Taylor, sound man; and me on the floor.

Warren Vaché entertaining between takes. Jerry Matz and Andrew Duncan to his right.

Left to right: Nick Romanac (props), Herb Forsberg (assistant cameraman), Jeri Sopanen (cinematographer), and Herr Direktor.

Most of the cast. *Back row, left to right:* Jerry Matz, Andrew Duncan, Daniel Nalbach, Wayne Rogers, Warren Vaché, Georgia Harrell, and Joe Silver. *Front row:* Celia Bressack and Cleavon Little.

1:45 P.M.

Did a photo session with *Newsday*.

8:00 P.M.

Business not good. Rain again, with heavy rain forecast tomorrow and chances of rain throughout the weekend.

Renee informs that Stuart Klein (Channel 5) likes *The Gig* and will say so on the air tonight.

Julian says the good reviews guarantee ancillary sales and ultimately assure profit regardless of theatrical loss.

11:15 P.M.

Stuart Klein found us "irresitibly infectious," or some such usable quote. On that note to sleep—perchance to dream.

Thursday, November 28, 8:45 A.M.: Home

Il pleut buckets.

To my knowledge, we have yet to receive a bad review. No other picture opened in the past two weeks can make this claim.

5:15 P.M.

James Hamilton, photographer for the *Village Voice*, just left after as pleasant a photo session as I've ever experienced. That the *Village Voice* sent him suggests a favorable review.

Saturday, November 30, 7:45 A.M.: Wyndham

Dropped in at the theater during the 5:15 P.M. show. Got caught up in the film via the audience response and watched some twenty minutes. Is there anything nicer than anonymously savoring other people's pleasure in your work?

Sunday, December I, 9:00 A.M.: Home

It rains and rains and rains.

We did $1,988 for the day. Was tempted to tell Norman to buy three tickets to achieve our first $2,000 day, but I refrained lest the gods feel preempted and act accordingly.

Chris Farlekas's interview (how many have we done through the years?) in the Middletown *Times Herald Record*.

Jerry Tallmer (New York *Post*) did a luncheon interview prefaced by his saying, "I liked your movie or I wouldn't be sitting here."

This interpreted as his way of letting me know our Dartmouth connection (he editor in chief of the "oldest college newspaper" several years before me) cut no ice.

Tuesday, December 3, 7:30 A.M.: Hanover

Beware buying ad space at the agency. It's like being in a casino with a liberal credit policy, and then comes the dawn, and your markers are presented.

Wednesday, December 4, 9:25 A.M.: Hanover

All students present for the final session. Most of them (six out of ten) completed their films, and the others were at the brink of production.

Renee called to read a rave review in the *Village Voice* by David Edelstein, which we will display in front of the theater.

Julian said almost everyone's grosses dip the week after Thanksgiving and that next week is traditionally the worst box-office week of the year, with business not reviving till the day after Christmas. He also said that regardless of how one fared in New York, you must play Los Angeles to protect your ancillary rights. To demonstrate his conviction in this regard, he said, "To insure you play Los Angeles, I'll chip in." I asked him to repeat the statement. "I'll chip in for Los Angeles," said Julian, "and you'll notice this time I said it without gulping."

Friday, December 6, 8:25 A.M.: Wyndham

Snow falls, and so do our grosses.

I related to Julian an offer made by a man, who shall be nameless, to secure foreign rights. Julian said, "Frank, as a friend I have to tell you I wouldn't talk to him if he offered a hundred thousand." When I replied that the man had offered more than $100,000, Julian without pause said, "Maybe we should talk to him."

P.S.

We closed in New York after a disappointing six-week run.

The police made us take the banner down. Tom Distler got it flying again. A minimal but pleasing victory.

There were numerous inquiries and meetings about distribution deals that came to naught.

Jeffrey Lyons, CBS radio, raved about *The Gig*, which he urged everyone to see—the day after we closed.

We opened in Los Angeles to fine reviews, and again poor business, which, given the similar fate of *'Round Midnight* and *Bird*, I ascribe to jazz, which many pay lip service to (it would be un-American not to) but few support.

Among treasured souvenirs are Leonard Feather's review and a story in *Downbeat* that says, "There have been many attempts through the years to build a movie around a jazz figure but most have fallen short. . . . Among the few exceptions have been *The Gig*, *'Round Midnight* and now *Bird*."

Also Whitney Balliett (eminent jazz authority) writing in the *New Yorker*: "The best feature film about jazz is the little-known, low-budget *The Gig*."

The most curious trophy of the experience is a cherub-faced ceramic cannister (adorned with numerous vaguely phallic appendages) that arrived without explanation or label. Inquiry discovered it to be from the Polish Jazz Federation honoring *The Gig* as the best jazz film of the year.

The investors have thus far received over 77.8 percent of their money back, with syndication rights still to be sold and cable rentals (we never got a network offer) continuing.

Julian, who eventually got distribution rights, has been in profit almost from the outset. Which, as any distributor will tell you, is as it should be.

One morning I said that unlike many people, I never wake up wondering what to do.

"No wonder," said my wife. "You've always got your windmill."

Review: *The Village Voice*, December 10, 1985

Going for the Biff-Bam-Bang   by David Edelstein

Frank D. Gilroy's low-budget *The Gig* has sneaked into town un-heralded, but I'll be surprised if the movies give us a happier comedy this season. It's a bubbly ensemble piece about six thickening middle- and upper-middle-class men who gather every week to play Dixieland jazz and forget about their ho-hum jobs. (Each in his youth hoped to play profes-sionally, but lacked one or all of the following: talent, money, and courage.) The film is about their first (and probably last) real job at a small Catskills resort, where for two weeks these flabby homebodies try to live the lives of professional, transient musicians; and their dream gig is fraught with panic-attacks, huffiness over their accommodations, attempts to flee, and, finally, their surrender to the music and the weightless joy of a new identity. Much of Gilroy's writing has a rare buoyancy, and his running gag—that most people can find a thousand reasons *not* to Go For It—gives this fantasy a sharply funny edge.

There is also, alas, a lofty side; Gilroy, who won a Pulitzer for *The Subject Was Roses* (not his most interesting play), writes speeches that make you want to blow a trumpet over them. When one departing husband asks his wife why she's not angry, she yells, "Would you prefer tears and hysterics, which, outside of relieving your guilt, would accomplish noth-ing?" (Go ahead: try hollering it.) And the resisters in the group—the ones who don't want to take the plunge—are only persuaded by their bassist, Georgie (Stan Lachow), who announces that he's being operated on next week and that *they* have to go while they've got the shot. Gilroy has a tin ear in these scenes; fortunately, his other ear—the one that picks up banter and casual asides—is in marvelous health. You know you're in good hands in the first five seconds, when Wayne Rogers, as used-car salesman Marty Flynn, delivers a pitch for his autos directly into the camera, and you're struck by Rogers's refusal to condescend to his character. "You come down, you talk to me, *we're gonna make a deal*," he babbles, high on the hog. Even in his gold chains and flowered shirts, Rogers is the first used-car salesman I've seen on-screen that I could imagine buying a car from. (It might be a lemon, but what a great guy.) He's a credible con man, and he spends the movie making spiels to hold his gang together—to keep them from running back to their wives and jobs and sick parents.

For the gig, the group replaces its terminally ill bassist with a professional

(Cleavon Little), who turns out to be distant and black. (His entrance, bass first, elicits a classic exchange: "He's tall." "Looks black." "Is black." "Why a *schwartzer*?") You're prepared for the tight-assed Little to warm up (like Richard Pryor in *Silver Streak* or Eddie Murphy in *48 HRS.*), but that never quite happens; he comes to like these guys, but they're not his brothers in any way. He does, however, help them adapt their Dixieland style to the tastes of the resort owner, Abe Mitgang (Joe Silver), who wants them to skip the "biff-bam-bang" and just "play nice"; and the scenes in which Little murmurs chord changes to the confused musicians (who go with him totally) are *The Gig*'s most transcendent. Although the two crybabies in the group (Andrew Duncan on piano and Daniel Nalbach on drums) can seem a little much, the cornet-player, Warren Vaché (also the film's music director), has an easy, ingratiating presence, and the oil-slick-voiced Joe Silver (the rich Jew in *The Apprenticeship of Duddy Kravitz*) does one of the year's funniest turns. He's both cheap and overflowing—his garrulous patter spins daintily around his chintziness—and the effect is amazingly harmonious.

With the arrival of a has-been crooner (Jay Thomas), his manager (Michael Fischetti), and his bodyguard (Chuck Wepner, the former Bayonne Bleeder and the inspiration for *Rocky*), *The Gig* shifts into a bad, downbeat ending. Killjoy Gilroy brings his characters thudding to earth as a way of trumpeting his integrity—he must think it would be dishonest to leave them with their moment of glory. But he has grounded their triumph so well in who they really are that *The Gig* could end with a flourish and not feel saccharine. (Is it too late to reshoot?) Much of the time, however, this is an honest-to-goodness adventure flick—you feel like you're taking a vacation from American movies and all they've come to mean. It's smart of Gilroy to open the movie with a pitch for used cars; he can relax after that, and give you the soft sell.

McLAUGHLIN, PIVEN, VOGEL INC. PRESENT
a Frank D. Gilroy film

THE LUCKIEST MAN IN THE WORLD

starring

PHILIP BOSCO

co-starring

DORIS BELACK   **JOANNE CAMP**

MATTHEW GOTTLIEB   **ARTHUR FRENCH**

Director of Photography **JERI SOPANEN**   Editor **JOHN GILROY**   Sound **LEE ORLOFF**

Music **WARREN VACHÉ & JACK GALE**

Produced by **Norman I. Cohen**   Written and directed by **Frank D. Gilroy**

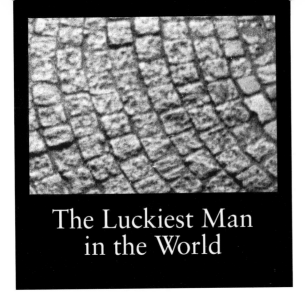

The Luckiest Man in the World

Circa 1974, in Los Angeles sweating out a movie sale of my novel *From Noon till Three* (which I wrote and directed for United Artists, starring Charles Bronson and Jill Ireland), to divert myself from waiting for the phone to ring, I broke ground on an original screenplay.

It involved a wealthy man, a monster in all dealings and relationships, who misses a plane that goes down with no survivors, and the effect on him of this brush with death.

I knew the results should be surprising, comic, and bitter-edged.

I did *not* know how to achieve those ends and gave up after forty pages.

At infrequent intervals I went back to the script and completed it years later under the title *Second Effort*.

Some actors I showed it to said yes. Some said no. Almost all expressed reservations about the ending, which I secretly shared.

A believer that if a script is right to a certain point, there is always a valid next step, I persevered.

Pleased with the new ending, I realized that none of the actors previously seen had won my heart completely.

Enter Phil Bosco.

1987
Friday, June 26, 8:05 A.M.: Home, Upstate New York

My son John took me to the office of a potential money source we'll call Carlos. His money seems to derive from real estate or inheritance. Intrigued by movies, he's financed a couple of bad ones.

I said Phil Bosco was my first choice, which Carlos, who likes Bosco, seemed impressed by.

It occurs to me I better let Bosco read the script.

Tuesday, June 30, 5:30 A.M.: Home

Sent Bosco a copy of *Second Effort*, which he should receive today.

Wednesday, July 1, 8:05 A.M.: Home

I resumed work on story board of *Second Effort*—had forgotten how much energy is required to pick camera angles precisely.

Thursday, July 2, 8:30 A.M.: Home

I drew up a list of location needs. Surprised to find that except for the airport and Bronx exteriors, *Second Effort* can be done in just about any city—Kingston (N.Y.), for instance.

I await Bosco's reaction.

Julian Schlossberg phoned to say his proposal is in the mail. "It's just a first draft," he noted, which suggests his terms will be excessive.

Monday, July 6, 8:30 A.M.: Home

I am seventy-five pages of comic-strip drawings into *Second Effort*—good angles come in a rush like a hot hand in a crap game.

I hear that Phil Bosco, in rehearsal with David Shaber's[1] play, has the flu.

Tuesday, July 7, 8:53 A.M.: Home

Carlos wants to shop the script. I asked if he'd assume part of our risk if he couldn't deal it off. He said no—recalling his heavy losses on prior pictures. I said it was too bad he hadn't come to me sooner.

I received Julian's proposal: A group of lawyers want to put up $1.1 million for 50 percent of profits.

A call from a Henry Sagerman, head of acquisitions at Paramount, who liked *The Gig* and was interested in reading *Second*

1. A successful screenwriter I'd known for years. The play, *Bunker Reveries*, at the Roundabout Theatre, the fulfillment of a dream. Rehearsal reports till Bosco's illness were excellent.

Effort. I said the ship was sailing but if he promised fast reaction, I'd let him see it.

"Is forty-eight hours okay?" he asked. I said yes—so a copy goes to him today.

Wednesday, July 8, 8:30 A.M.: Home

Julian and I are refining his lawyer group's proposal.

Nancy Bosco called to say that Phil is still recovering from the flu, necessitating a postponement of David Shaber's opening. She said Phil had read the script and was interested.

Thursday, July 9, 8:20 A.M.: Home

Julian drafting another version of his proposal.

Bill Goldman gave me a thought that could improve the ending.

Saturday, July 11, 8:30 A.M.: Home

Should complete story board today. Have Carlos's proposal, which I'll study.

Sunday, July 12, 9:00 A.M.: Home

The camera angles I pick now provide a safety net. I may improve them the day I shoot, but no matter how fatigued or uncreative I feel, I have those angles to fall back on. No wondering what to do next.

Tuesday, July 14, 8:25 A.M.: Home

Julian and Meyer Ackerman want 5 percent of all money they bring in and 5 percent of gross sale price if they sell the picture.

Wednesday, July 15, 8:25 A.M.: Home

I understand Phil Bosco has suffered a relapse and David Shaber's play is in jeopardy.

Friday, July 17, 8:45 A.M.: Home

Jim McLaughlin called to say that a man named Roger Holmes wants to be a part of *Second Effort* and offers his sixty-five-foot yacht for any movie purpose.

Saturday, July 18, 9:00 A.M.: Home

Engines revved by myriad calls and activities, I was poised for takeoff with no place to go.

Received Carlos's letter. Basically I have trouble grasping the advantage (which he assures is there) of doing a film for $2 million that I can make for $1 million.

Monday, July 20, 8:30 A.M.: Home

I hear Phil Bosco is in the hospital.

Tuesday, July 21, 8:40 A.M.: Home

The key provision of Carlos's proposal is that while I will make the film for $1 million, Carlos will tell whoever the distributor is that it cost $2 million, requiring an inflated budget. When I said I didn't like that notion, Carlos said, "Distributors screw you all the time. Now it's your turn to do it to them."

The rationale is that the distributor will give you only 70 percent of the cost of the film for all domestic rights because statistics say 70 percent of return on a film comes from domestic and 30 percent from foreign.

I asked Carlos for his bank statement and bank reference. He refused to supply a financial statement, said he'd give a bank reference when appropriate; made it clear that if I wouldn't say the budget was $2 million, there would be no deal.

Saturday, July 25, 11:30 A.M.: Home

Warren Vaché just called to inform that Dick Wellstood died on the West Coast of a heart attack.

Warren said of Dick, "He had a great deal to tell you if you asked the right questions."

Tuesday, July 28, 9:00 A.M.: Boothbay Harbor, Maine

Just learned that Phil Bosco's illness has forced him to withdraw from David Shaber's play—is home convalescing.

Since I had not planned to go into production until David's play concluded its run, this could force my hand.

Friday, July 31, 7:40 A.M.: Home

While visiting the Gays last week in Boothbay Harbor, Maine, I noted the multicolored script of John Gay's adaptation of Sidney Sheldon's *Windmills of the Gods*, now shooting. Opening the script, I found a color code of successive rewrites.

With John's permission, I recorded them.

       One—Blue
       Two—Pink
       Three—Green
       Four—Yellow
       Five—Lavender
       Six—Goldenrod
       Seven—Grey
       Eight—Tan
       Nine—Cherry
       Ten—Buff

I've tacked a list of these ten colors (not including John's original) on my wall to remind me why I make independent films on days when I wonder if it's worth it.

Saturday, August 1, 8:45 A.M.: Home

Nancy Bosco called to inform me that Phil has an offer of a Broadway play in October. She said he would rather do my movie but if I want him, I will have to move immediately.

Sunday, August 2, 8:30 A.M.: Home

I drove to Phil Bosco's home in Teaneck, New Jersey, where he is convalescing from something akin to Legionnaire's disease.

Phil asked what made me think of him for the part. I said it was largely intuition. Confessed I didn't know what he would do and suspected he didn't know either, which he confirmed.

"We'll explore in rehearsal," I said. "I don't want to read you, which might force you to premature results."

Bottom line: I said I wanted him to do it, and he accepted.

I said I would need him for six weeks starting October 5 with a seventh week optional. Nancy said that Phil's agent (Alan Willig) must give the play people an answer by tomorrow night and expressed fears that despite my solid credentials, this picture, like so many independent movie ventures, might fail to happen. I said I was prepared to make a "pay or play" offer guaranteeing Phil full compensation even if the film isn't made.

It was left to Phil's agent to read the script and call me tomorrow.

Tuesday, August 4, 7:40 A.M.: Home

Jim McLaughlin called as I was about to leave for my appointment with Bosco's agent. He thought the $800,000 required to make the film was Canadian dollars. I told him it was $800,000 American. He asked where I was going to get the rest. I said I didn't know and would make up my mind en route to the city whether to abort.

As I drove to New York, I sought decision in my gut.

By the time I reached the George Washington Bridge, I knew I would sign Bosco to a pay-or-play contract that I would personally guarantee.

To Willig's office where the deal was consummated. So I'm working without a net again.

I have eight weeks before rehearsal and not a penny in hand. Think goldenrod, baby.

Wednesday, August 5, 8:30 A.M.: Home

Son John bridled at my hasty signing of Bosco—fails to grasp that opportunity rarely beckons at our convenience.

The McLaughlins guarantee me enough to get the picture "in the can," which means shot but unedited. At that point, to cover postproduction, I will have to raise the rest.

Bad news: Norman (Cohen) sees no way to get the picture in the can in Montreal for less than $650,000. Consequently he is making calls to the Florida crew we used on *The Gig* and will scout the Kingston area for interior locations that might pass for New York.

Having signed Bosco and announced the start date, I feel things begin to move in spite of themselves.

Saturday, August 8, 6:15 A.M.: Home

I resist a dawn urge to surrender after scouting locations in Kingston and Albany yesterday. The prospect of makeshift on a budget that wouldn't cover most movies' petty cash is all but overwhelming. In bed it seems worse. With coffee, the problem reduces.

I met Norman at the Ramada Inn in Kingston. We drove to Rondout, a restored section by the river. I love those slice-of-life glimpses you get when scouting locations. The hungover guy in his underwear, smoking and bleary-eyed as he admitted us to his apartment. Was the child his daughter that he had custody of?

To the apartment of George James—actor, cowboy, musician, and composer. His apartment would do nicely. Norman assures we can find the other two apartments we need in that immediate area.

We found the bar around the corner. We found a handbag factory that would be fine for Posner's dress plant. We found a hospital that will work. All these interiors to be matched with New York exteriors.

We drove to Albany to check the airport. Would any airport let us do a scene about a plane crash? Such practical considerations don't hit you until you really start looking. Present plan is to shoot the Rolls Royce pulling up to La Guardia Airport and steal a shot of Posner entering the terminal. The interior scene will probably be shot in Kingston at an "airline counter" we'll have to build. I'm not fully sold on this concept.

Back to Kingston to see the flea market where Norman suggests building the airline counter. Then to a health club, seeking the steam-room location.

Norman assures he can find the men's room with five stalls and the tenement interior we need. If so, we can shoot seventy-six pages of the script's ninety-six pages in Kingston and get exteriors in New York.

Location scouting is a creative and crucial part of moviemaking from which (I say yet again) the writer should never be excluded.

Tuesday, August 11: 6:15 A.M.: Home

Norman found a steam room in Kingston. Suggested Newark Airport instead of La Guardia.

Wednesday, August 12, 7:45 A.M.: Home

Carlos can't make the deal he proposed, wants to come in with us "nakedly," which means cash at risk with no distributor set. He's checking with his bank and will have a final yes or no on Monday.

Monday, August 17, 8:30 A.M.: Home

Over 150 people killed in a plane crash in Detroit last night. If such a crash took place just before *Second Effort* opened, I think I'd be in trouble.

Thursday, August 20, 8:05 A.M.: Home

I began to go through the script with the hard eye invoked when the prospect of actors actually saying the lines is imminent.

I scouted Stewart Airport. Encountered six security guards, coffee in hand, outside the terminal being constructed. I asked one of the guards when the terminal would be completed. He said he didn't know and less than graciously informed me that I was interrupting a meeting.

Friday, August 21, 4:35 A.M.: Home

Carlos has crapped out: "My bank won't give me the money on an unsecured loan."

Saturday, August 22, 8:00 A.M.: Home

Is it an incipient cold, some interior breakdown, or Norman's new budget (escalating the cost of getting the picture in the can) that threatens me—suggests the picture may not be done after all.

I met Norman at the Ramada Inn in Kingston at 9:00 A.M.

We started well: Nailed Sheldon's and Laura's apartments in the same building. We inspected the men's room in a Catholic school—no good. We viewed a men's room in a public high school—no good.

We drove to a public school in Saugerties. Found a three-stall john that could work minimally. We went to the YMCA in Kingston to see a steam room. Before the director would show it to us, I had to recite the story of *Second Effort* to ensure no possible embarrassment to the Y. The steam room could work, but curiously, real steam defeats us because standing in that heat, I realized that the camera would instantly fog as my glasses did.

We visited the Lynches, whose home we used as a penthouse in *The Gig*. It could do as the penthouse in *Second Effort*, but I hope for something more lavish.

We entered a home where, Norman said, we were expected, but no one appeared. There was a dead bird on the stairs by the partially open back door. Norman calling "Anyone home?" we advanced into the house where we tripped a burglar alarm. Norman repeatedly reassuring me we were expected, we toured the house, which I vetoed as a location, and departed before the cops arrived. As we toured, the alarm wailing, I half expected to find a body—a good movie opening.

To Norman's home, where we went over the schedule. Found ourselves in perfect harmony on how the eighteen shooting days would be spent. All fine till he presented me with the new budget, which was not what he'd led me to expect.

Once again an honorable reason for abandoning the project beckoned. That I would have to pay Bosco in any case prevented a stampede in that direction.

Sunday, August 23, 9:00 A.M.: Home

Norman and I went to work on the budget (he in Woodstock, I here) with numerous phone calls back and forth through the day. By evening, with my deferring everything and other cuts, we had the $730,000 figure down to $592,000 and the picture still in 35 mm. But we'll have to get it lower.

Tuesday, August 25, 9:10 A.M.: Home

Met Norman in Kingston. We drove to two steam-bath sites. The second one, at a golf club, will do nicely. Then to Norman's house to crunch the numbers yet again.

The goal was to get the picture in the can for $500,000. I was less than sanguine by the time we got through and about to say that we would have to do the picture in some other fashion or abandon it when Norman said, "I want very much to do this picture with you" and volunteered deferment of his salary.

With both of us deferring, a new spirit prevailed, and the picture now seemed doable.

Norman will check John Allen for blowup prices. If we go to super 16, as I think we will, then Jeri Sopanen is first choice as cinematographer since he's proven himself.

Thursday, August 27, 8:45 A.M.: Home

The meeting with Roger Holmes went well—looks like he'll be an investor.

To the Colton office where I met with Marsha Brooks, Tom Distler, and the fifth and newest legal cub I shall raise—Gil Karson.

Friday, August 28, 5:00 A.M.: Home

I have been in my workroom since 4:00 A.M. polishing the script, aware that the rest of the day will belong to money-raising and logistics.

Dennis Smith is in for a point.

Marsha Brooks volunteered how much she enjoyed my visits to the Colton office—the refreshing "let's make a show" spirit.

Saturday, August 29, 9:15 A.M.: Home

John Huston dead at eighty-one. His films, as a body, strike me as the greatest overall achievement of any American director.

Sunday, August 30, 9:00 A.M.: Home

Added a new moment to the script derived from Joe Beruh's[2] long ago recounting how a derelict asked him for a dollar to get a drink and Joe, in a burst of generosity, gave him $10, which the man refused to take, saying, "What are you trying to do, kill me?"

It's fun rewriting with Phil Bosco's talent to presume upon. Recalls writing that "Studio One" play as a vehicle for Jackie Gleason.

I notified Bosco that all proceeds on schedule without mentioning the money I still needed. He volunteered his services to assist in casting, said that after *Second Effort* he will do a bit in a Woody Allen film.

Tuesday, September 1, 5:10 A.M.: Home

Nerves registering everything excessively, I walked from the bus terminal to the Colton office to gain composure. Which is vital since everyone, lawyers included, key on my confidence and energy. Columbus did the same when the others doubted they'd make land. And if I remember correctly, he too had trouble with financing.

2. General manager and company manager of *Roses*, he was a vital contributor to the success of that dream. Partnered with Edgar Lansbury, he coproduced *Godspell*, *American Buffalo*, *The Magic Show*. Speaking at his memorial service last year, I realized how deeply and irrevocably the *Roses* adventure had bound Joe, Edgar, Ulu, Paul Leaf, and Max Eisen, who were there from the beginning.

Marsha and Gil Karson attended me at the Colton office.

As we went through the legal papers, Gil volunteered he'd read the script of *Second Effort* and liked it so much that he told the story to his wife, which cheered me inordinately.

The papers will be ready to file by Tuesday. The crucial item is that I have assumed, in writing, the personal obligation to raise the remaining $280,000 in nine months with potentially dire consequences if I don't.

Alan Willig called to say that Woody Allen had so taken to Phil Bosco that he wanted to give him a bigger part in his film, provided Phil could shoot in the middle of November. I said my schedule couldn't accommodate this.

To Julie Gottfried's at 3:30 P.M. Informed of what I'm again risking to make a movie, Julie said wondrously, "How does Ruth cope?"

Thursday, September 3, 8:50 A.M.: Home

Alan Willig called to relay great pressure from Woody Allen's people to spring Phil Bosco for a few days in the middle of my shooting schedule. I repeated I would like to accommodate them but couldn't. He asked if Bobby Greenhut, Woody's producer, could call me. I said sure.

Later in the day Bobby phoned. He said Woody was smitten with Bosco. I said that demonstrated Woody's good taste. Their problem is Mia's impending delivery of Woody's heir, and Bosco's scenes would be with her. I was sympathetic but said I simply couldn't alter my schedule since Bosco is in every scene.

Friday, September 4, 8:45 A.M.: Home

Finished the shooting script, which will be Xeroxed today.

Saturday, September 5, 8:00 A.M.: Home

Scouted locations with Norman yesterday from 10:00 A.M. till 4:00 P.M. Nailed the hospital, factory, men's room at the flea market where we will also build the airline ticket counter.

Saw the Holiday Inn where we'll live. They have a sauna we might use for the steam-room scene.

I've decided to shoot in super 16.

Monday, September 7, 8:15 A.M.: Home

Bob and Lila Ehrenbard have invested in the movie. I appreciate their well-wishes and the spirit in which the investment was made as much as or more than the money itself.

Am making a list of insert shots, which, unless noted, one is apt to overlook in the heat of shooting.

Wednesday, September 9, 8:15 A.M.: Home

Still haven't received Bosco's signed-deal memo from his agent.

Patricia Elliot called to see if she could read. I said if she hadn't called, I was going to call her, having seen her excellent work in *Bunker Reveries*, David Shaber's play.

On the phone several times with Gil Karson about offering circulars and private-worth questionnaires, all of which I should have ready to send to investors tomorrow.

Sent shooting scripts to Norman, Jeri Sopanen, and Abigail McGrath.

Norman met with Julie Gottfried and Ashoka Daibee; appears to have worked out accounting procedures.

Thursday, September 10, 8:00 A.M.: Home

Received Bosco's signed agreement.

The pope arrives in Florida today, and who can doubt his powers given how all the homeless and derelicts have vanished from the streets he'll travel?

Friday, September 11, 5:15 A.M.: Home

Ann Sacks disappointed we won't be residing at Sack's Lodge. A film company invited to stay at a place where they stayed before may be a first.

I told Norman he must guard against his reluctance to bring me bad news because we have little margin for error, which dictates no surprises.

Arriving home, I dealt with the documents requiring immediate attention. Sent shooting scripts to Bosco and a Fred Stewart, who will see what if any commercial tie-up opportunities the picture offers.

Saturday, September 12, 8:00 A.M.: Home

The needed $260,000 looms large this morning.

Monday, September 14, 8:45 A.M.: Home

Abigail arrived at noon. Norman arrived. What was anticipated as a short preliminary casting session turned into a full all-out exercise from noon till 6:30 P.M.

Abby was thoroughly prepared, enthused, and quick to read my preferences and intentions. John and Ruth were intermittently part of the process. Everyone chipping in names and expressing opinions. An enjoyable and productive day.

At day's end, Norman introduced bad news: We can't get insurance in the five boroughs of New York if we don't get shooting permits from the city. And if we proceed without permits, meaning no insurance, then I am personally liable for any accidents, etc.

The upshot appears to be that we'll shoot in Newark instead of the Bronx and use Newark Airport instead of La Guardia.

Wednesday, September 16, 8:25 A.M.: Home

October 19 scheduled as the first day of shooting, and I have $500,000 pledged—none of it received yet—plus $40,000 more pledged for delivery December 1.

Thursday, September 17, 8:15 A.M.: Home

Norman and I to Newark Airport where we met John, with his video camera, at 11:00 A.M.

We found a fairly deserted terminal and took Polaroids of various ticket counters in addition to video.

Satisfied we can "steal" what we need, we drove into Newark seeking devastation and found it galore.

I pointed out the sort of house whose interior we will match in Kingston.

None of the pledged money has arrived yet.

Friday, September 18, 5:50 A.M.: Home

After a fine productive and pleasureful day of casting during which we interviewed some twenty-five actors, I arrived home to find Jim McLaughlin's check, *but* the crucial page, allowing me to use his money before the full amount is raised, was not signed because the offering circular warns that by so doing, the signer exposes himself to "unlimited liability."

I called Jim, who very rightly wants to know why such a phrase is in there. I forwarded my dilemma to the lawyers who are working on it—everyone aware that if I can't use the money until all the money is in, the picture must be canceled.

Jim doesn't want me to close down, said, "Use my money. I won't sue you if you lose it." I thanked him but explained I can't use it without that page signed or I'm breaking the law. We agreed to wait and see what the lawyers advise.

Today we start to read actors. I will hear the script from Phil Bosco's lips for the first time. I was looking forward to it, but now a part of me hopes Bosco will be atrocious so that I'll want to call it off.

Saturday, September 19, 9:45 A.M.: Home

The lawyers found a solution that involves closing the partnership at the present level so there is no unlimited liability for the investors.

Jim called to say I shouldn't be distracted from my creative work by such matters.

The closer I get to shooting (like a pregnant woman nearing delivery), the more deferential and considerate everyone about me becomes. Is it any wonder many directors run from picture to picture so they can live continuously in this pampered atmosphere?

Among the actors seen was Rebecca Darke. How could twenty-five years have passed since her brilliant performance in *Who'll Save the Plowboy?* (my first New York play) for which she won a Clarence Derwent Award?

Norman and I lunched at Moran's—a dark wood bar that invites you to tarry and drink away your cares.

Back to the Off-Center Theatre at 2:00 P.M. for the crucial moment when Phil Bosco would first speak the words as he assisted in casting the other roles. You remind everyone (especially yourself) that nothing should be expected. But you and everyone else present know that no matter how rough and premature the effort, some spark of life should be perceived.

Patricia Elliot and Doris Belack read excellently for the wife's role, and we found two prime contenders for the son.

Phil, reading with each of these and other actors, got better and better. As John said later, it was incredible to see Bosco don the character and go to work so effortlessly.

Sunday, September 20, 8:30 A.M.: Home

Beseiged by money problems, I curse Bosco for being so fine on Friday that he prevents me from abandoning the whole thing.

Norman, a new spring in his step due to Friday's sample of the merchandise, has located the "Bronx" apartment in Kingston and is meeting the mayor of Kingston tomorrow, seeking the city's support via police and permits, etc.

Monday, September 21, 9:15 A.M.: Home

Marsha Brooks phoned, her Sunday call reflecting her genuine concern that I am too much at risk. She suggested postponement while more money is sought. I thanked her but said it was now or never.

Spoke to Bosco to be sure he'd be free to read with other actors on Thursday. He shares my joyful anticipation based on Friday's sample.

Tuesday, September 22, 8:40 A.M.: Home

Jeri Sopanen called to say he liked the script and looked forward to doing it.

Scrambled dreams, related to money fears.

Wednesday, September 23, 8:15 A.M.: Home

Never was the temptation to quit this project greater than at this moment. None of my phone calls struck gold—some calls not even returned. I leave for New York shortly to see actors. Since everyone plugs into my demeanor, the day looms excruciating.

Thursday, September 24, 8:30 A.M.: Home

Bob Fosse died last night. I will miss our infrequent but always amiable chance encounters.

We saw actors from 11:00 A.M. to 5:30 P.M. yesterday. Will start to read the finalists with Phil today.

Susan, my daughter-in-law, will read against four actresses. The role calls for someone Jewish, making Susan a very long shot, which she understands.

"Of course, if you cast me, you get to see your grandson," she reminded.

Friday, September 25, 9:00 A.M.: Home

Read actors with Phil from 11:30 to 5:30 P.M. with a lunch break. The high point was Joanne Camp reading for the part of the mistress.

There was a striking actress, Bergmanesque, who made mouths water, but she's too young to make the relationship with Phil credible. Phil volunteered to darken his hair.

Saturday, September 26, 8:30 A.M.: Home

We appear to be at $560,000 pledged.

Norman seeing to insurance, will make sure Boyar covers us on scouting trips.

Notified Doris Belack that she had the part. "You made my happy New Year," she said. She'll wear the burgundy suede suit that she wore to the reading.

Decided on Joanne Camp for Laura; Arthur French for Cleveland. Am tending toward Matthew Gottlieb for Sheldon but still not sure.

Bosco so unerringly credible that anyone less so who acts with him registers especially false.

Norman suggested Stan Lachow, who did the excellent monologue in *The Gig*, to play the union leader. Of course, Stan Lachow! He will get an offer.

I worked on the script—adjusting things gleaned from readings.

Sunday, September 27, 9:45 A.M.: Home

Norman found a dilapidated apartment in a run-down section of Kingston that will pass for a Newark slum. Had to satisfy the owner he wasn't a narc to gain admittance.

As Norman and I descended the stairs, a suspicious belligerent woman asked what we were about. When I said we were making a movie, she said, "You'll have to do better than that."

With the requisite brashness of the gifted location finder, Norman got the door to a gutted factory open despite a sign prohibiting entry. It is just what we need when the hoods spot Posner.

The script calls for a rooftop, but I have no trouble converting to a street-level location. Once again, the advantage of taking the writer along when you scout demonstrated.

A kid looking out a window wondered what we were doing. On the chance the kid's apartment might be better than the one we found earlier, Norman asked him to fetch his mother or father. The mother appeared. Norman called our credentials up.

The woman admitted us. Two rooms—squalid, airless. The most weathered deck of cards I've ever seen spread on the kitchen table where we'd interrupted a game of solitaire. The game resumed as we viewed the place, which proved too small and too depressing for our purpose.

Then to Woodstock, ten miles (but light years) away. Met the minister of the church that borders Sack's Lodge. I'll read him and his wife for small parts. Made it clear I wouldn't give them the roles (if they weren't right) in order to use the church. They said they understood.

I told Tony (my son), who is worried for me, that I can see my life beyond failure of this project but not beyond abandoning it. He said he understood.

Monday, September 28, 8:30 A.M.: Home

I told Norman what a good job I thought he'd done on Saturday.

If I look ahead, what must be done looms insurmountable. One day at a time is mandatory.

Tuesday, September 29, 8:00 A.M.: Home

Incipient cold—I dosed with vitamin C.

Reworked my miniature stick-figure story board. Ten copies Xeroxed for Norman, Jeri, etc.

Bank account opened—will contain $450,000 by end of today. One $50,000 pledge yet to be fulfilled.

Several calls to and from Abigail about casting.

We'll read Matthew Gottlieb once more and then decide.

Phil Bosco so used to accommodating other actors that I must guard against it. He is the star this time.

I called Martin Sheen[3] in Dublin where he's shooting *Da*. I offered his company a coproduction deal or invited personal investment. A script, offering circular, and letter en route to him via Federal Express.

Phil volunteers his grandson as Mrs. Gonzalez's kid. A good idea.

Thursday, October 1, 5:15 A.M.: Home

Started to worry (in bed) about all that must be done in the eighteen days that remain till we start to shoot. Thought it wiser to get up and face the demons.

John (who will edit the film) drove me to Kingston yesterday.

Norman picked us up in a rented van with Pepper Sinkler and Lois Hartwig, who will cover production for Norman in the office while he works the set as first AD. We drove to the train station in Rhinecliff to meet Jeri and his gaffer Ned Hallick. The train was one and a half hours late.

It was raining. This, plus the train delay and people waiting at locations we were to inspect, produced anxiety. As they grew tense, I experienced that absolute calm that is my automatic response to emergency.

With me depicting each scene and shooting plans, we toured Laura's apartment, Sheldon's apartment, the slum exterior, the hospital, the slum interior, and the bar.

We also viewed the highway selected for the traffic snarl and accident; the steam bath; the flea market where we'll construct the airport ticket counter and use the men's room as the airport men's room; the church; and the penthouse apartment.

I answered questions as we drove.

I felt Ned, who was new to me, start to sour a bit as the pace fatigued. I asked his background. He began as a theater-lighting designer. When I said I'd worked with Jo Mielziner, Jules Fisher, Tharon Musser, and George Jenkins, he warmed considerably.

We finished at 6:00 P.M. with a sense of achievement and hope.

One location I forgot to mention was the factory office, where I encountered a man who identified himself as having attended P.S. 82 with me in the Bronx when we were kids. Instinctively, my hand went to his cheek with affection as we chatted.

3. He opened in *Roses* on Broadway with Jack Albertson and Irene Dailey. Played the role for two years, the second year in a national tour. Made his movie debut in the film version.

Arrived home to find no check or the signed papers I await on one investment.

Friday, October 20, 8:45 A.M.: Home

Read actors from 11:00 A.M. to 6:00 P.M. with Phil.

Broke from 1:00 to 2:00 P.M., during which I dashed to the lawyer's. In my absence, I told Jeri to shoot some close footage of Phil's face outdoors to check his complexion.

Jeri, who'd watched me audition four black women for the nurse's role, said he liked them all, asked how I'd decide between them. I said that in close calls I went always with my gut.

Phil a workhorse and never less than amiable. Without exception, you feel him trying to make the other actor look good. I rarely regard him during the readings—keep my eyes on the applicant.

Norman had a good meeting at SAG, aided by the fact that Herb Ratner, the SAG official he dealt with, loves *The Gig*.

Still some items to be worked out, including their request for a $50,000 bond, which we can't afford.

We've nailed every role except the reporter and the union guy, who will be Stan Lachow if he can rearrange his schedule. Daniel Nalbach, who was the drummer in *The Gig*, will play the priest. Tony McGrath, Abigail's husband, will play the derelict.

The actress who got the nurse's role (Teodorina Bella) shrewdly had the dialogue translated into Morse code, which is vital to the scene.

Matthew Gottlieb called back for the son's role, gave the pressure reading of the day and was so fine that I told him on the spot, "The role is yours." All present concurred, including Phil, who had championed another candidate.

Norman says he's getting the crew for less than was budgeted so far. Good news since we're setting sail with only $350,000 in hand and me responsible to return that if we don't get enough to complete the picture.

Saturday, October 3, 5:30 A.M.: Home

I brought Jim McLaughlin up to date. Let him know money was being spent despite the iffy status of one pledge. I said if he wanted to call it off, he should speak now.

"Keep punching," he said.

The Luckiest Man in the World • 273

Sunday, October 4, 6:30 A.M.: Home

Worked very well on the script, which reassures and diverts me from financial concerns.

I called Phil to tell him he's off on Monday. He volunteered he liked *The Gig*, viewed on cassette. Seemed greatly relieved that he was unable to tell that it had been shot in super 16.

Right now it's snowing. The earliest snow date in our experience!

Monday, October 5, 6:15 A.M.: Home

Phil Bosco on salary today.

I will feel a good deal better if the papers arrive authorizing me to use the other $100,000. That would give me a total of $450,000 to spend while shooting.

Tuesday, October 6, 7:30 A.M.: Home

Finished rewrite of shooting script—affecting sixty-five out of ninety-nine pages, so we Xeroxed entire script anew.

I went to the Holiday Inn in Kingston where Norman opened a production office: rooms 322 and 324.

I signed DGA and SAG agreements.

Met a local accountant who will handle things while we're shooting.

If the pledged money and the signed papers don't arrive by tomorrow, I shall become seriously concerned.

Wednesday, October 7, 9:00 A.M.: Wyndham Hotel, New York City

Checked in at 10:00 A.M. To barber for last shearing before we shoot. Read actors all morning with Phil's assistance.

Lunched with Phil—a long script talk. He questioned things, opened up. I answered in a way calculated to encourage his probing.

I (with Linda Benedict, wardrobe; Pat Coll, leadman; Norman; and John) viewed the footage Jeri shot. His new lenses make for sharper definition. Phil's complexion fine, might need a bit of light for his cavernous eyes. Met with Norman, Linda, Pat about costumes and sets at the Wyndham bar.

Norman, John, and I toured Tape House's new facilities: Mixing room looked fine, but editing space, now crammed with junk, needs work. We decided to synch the dailies there but deferred decision on transferring, editing, and mixing.

Learned I will not be able to rehearse as many people as I'd like because of cost.

To the Off-Center Theatre where I found Phil entertaining the two actors competing for the reporter's role. It was not our intention to have them there at the same time, but one arrived early. Knowing each other, they handled it well. J. D. Clarke got the role.

At lunch, Phil and I discussed the script. As he questioned me, I realized how much I assumed (from performance) he understood that he is totally ignorant of.

Doris Belack and Phil went through the new material. Two fine players gracefully batting the ball back and forth. We were fine-tuning before we knew it. Linda came by to discuss clothes with Doris, who, graciously and shrewdly, will wear her own.

Harmony and hope reigned. Ah, if they but knew that during the day Ruth called to report needed investment papers and a vital check still not arrived.

Norman reports SAG (given our $30,000 bond) will sort of let us read through the script next Tuesday.

Abigail got a bit overloaded yesterday. She's doing a fine job. Might be trying to do too much, like the rest of us.

Friday, October 9, 8:45 A.M.: Home

Phil and I to Moe Ginsburg Clothiers to meet Linda and inspect suits for him. Phil has no concern or feeling for clothes. Said anything is fine with him.

We settled on a gray plaid.

Linda walked back with us. In three blocks, all wardrobe matters were settled.

Ruth called: Still no check or papers.

I was about to give the part of the anonymous resonant voice in the john to another actor when Moses Gunn[4] appeared. Perfect

---

4. We'd last met in 1965 when he appeared in a television play of mine (*Far Rockaway*, directed by Ulu Grosbard). Also adapted as a ballet and an opera celebrating Lincoln Center on Channel 13.

from first to last, Moses won it hands down.

All sorts of scraps and bits of people's lives stay with you after interviews and readings. One black actor told us—apropos of what, I can't remember—that he threw two prominent white men out of his house because they started criticizing Jews. "I figured blacks were next, so I asked them to leave," he said.

When Phil's first check failed to arrive as promised, I blew my top. Learned it was due to a messenger foul-up. Had a new check delivered immediately because in low-budget enterprises, immediacy of payment is critical.

Saturday, October 10, 8:30 A.M.: Home

Phil arrived at 11:30 A.M., and with time out for lunch, we read the script, probing line by line (aloud, with me playing all other parts) till 6:30 P.M.—a most exhausting but rewarding session. Any line he didn't grasp the reason for was explained, and if I couldn't justify it, I altered it. He is a bear for logic. Several times he challenged mine and was right.

Frankness begetting frankness, he voiced concern (no news to me) that he feared playing the role seriously would rob the movie of comedy by making him detestable. I said the risk was a calculated one in the hope of achieving something that wouldn't be possible if we went for comedy alone.

Sensing my willingness to risk all, he responded in kind. He mentioned Scrooge at some point. "That's a wonderful analogy," I said as the similarities of *Second Effort* and *Christmas Carol* struck me. Told him to "lock up" the script except for minor changes I've yet to make.

The sum total of our day was excellent.

Sunday, October 11, 6:00 A.M.: Home

The days gain momentum; more activity and detail than I have time to record.

SAG won't give waivers, so the gospel group must be Guild members.

We drove to Woodstock where I read people for bit parts. The best find was Virginia Downing, who appeared in *The Gig*. I did not give the reverend and his wife speaking parts, but they will be extras in the airport scene.

Scott Hancock arrived. He and Barbara Knaust, who met at Sack's Lodge while we were shooting *The Gig*, will be married on December 12 at Sack's Lodge. This, plus that they'll be working on *Second Effort*, seems the fairest of auguries.

Drove back to the Holiday Inn to see people (Hispanic and black, for the Newark scenes) Abigail had assembled.

Norman confident $500,000 will see the picture in the can *if* I can make the schedule.

It doesn't seem remotely possible that four weeks from now the movie will be completely shot. . . . Perhaps it isn't.

Monday, October 12, 9:00 A.M.: Home

Best sleep in ages. Rewrote (and Ruth retyped) fourteen pages yesterday. Changes suggested by my session with Phil on Friday.

A call from an associate of Martin Sheen's to inform me no investment possible.

Wednesday, October 14, 9:00 A.M.: Wyndham

As I checked in yesterday, I received a panicked call from Abigail: "Come boss us," she said, regarding how chairs, etc., were to be grouped for the reading.

Arrived at the theater at 10:45 A.M. The insurance doctor, like all doctors I've met who do such work, communicated a less than dedicated air.

He was more thorough than previous ones, said new forms dictated it. Questions about any fever sores in the past five years, doubtless occasioned by AIDS.

The actors arrived from their SAG meeting. Filled out forms and mingled while the five most prominent (to be insured) had physicals.

I asked Phil what the doctor made of his recent bout of Legionnaires' Disease. He said the doctor's response was a description of his own multiple-bypass operation.

I took the stage with Phil; Abby to read women not present; Joel Rooks to do absent men. I summarized stage directions and parts too complex to be acted. Actors read from where they sat, except Doris, Joanne Camp, and Matthew Gottlieb, who came on stage for their scenes.

Despite roughness, there were enough moments of life to cast a favorable glow over the proceedings.

It was the only time that most of them would meet in the course of the picture, which (to give everyone a grasp of the overall) was my intention.

In fine spirits, we (the company) lunched at Moran's. After which I took Phil to Pepe's (my barber) for a haircut and manicure.

John gave me a store-bought birthday card listing people born on October 13, which included my name, along with Margaret Thatcher and Lenny Bruce.

Thursday, October 15, 8:30 A.M.: Wyndham

Excellent rehearsals yesterday. We found some fine moments, and I saw camera angles not thought of previously.

Stock market dropped a record ninety-five-plus points. The recent rumblings of a turnabout in the economy increases my anxiety about where and how I'll get the money to complete the film.

Friday, October 16, 4:00 A.M.: Wyndham

Awake since 2:30 A.M. Eager to be off to Sandy Hook to shoot the poster scene. A fine warm day forecast.

One investor, whose money is pledged but not in, appears shaky.

Rehearsals yesterday went well. Joanne Camp is perfection as the mistress. I have no script person until Sunday, which compels us to make notes as we go, the actors recording their moves.

Just before lunch a disconcerting note by way of a phone call for Phil. When he returned from taking it, I sensed he was uneasy. I asked what was wrong. Phil said, "They [Woody Allen's people] want me to shoot tomorrow." "Impossible," I said. "Of course," said Phil, "and I told them that before." Something tells me I haven't heard the last of this.

I auditioned gospel groups that Abigail brought in. The five young men who composed the first group (14 Karat Soul) were so moving that Abigail wept.

Saturday, October 17, 9:00 A.M.: Home

Yesterday could not have gone better. Merry Traum drove Yamil Borges (Mrs Gonzalez), Linda, and me to the beach at Sandy Hook where we rendezvoused at 11:30 A.M. with Norman, Scott, Jim Robinson (set propman), Jeri, and his assistant, Peter Hawkins.

Pepper Sinkler, location manager, arrived with a lunch she'd prepared. Phil drove down on his own.

Jeri and Peter just back from Africa and France, where they filmed Jane Goodall and the chimps and then the caves with petroglyphs.

We were all done (including stills that might prove to be the poster) by 1:00 P.M.

Bad dreams triggered by the stock market's greatest one-day drop (108 points) in history.

Sunday, October 18, 8:00 A.M.: Holiday Inn, Kingston

D minus 1.

Experienced a minor panic attack as I packed and prepared to leave home for the duration yesterday morning.

Arrived here a little after 11:00 A.M. and scouted locations.

The first stop was a possible alternative to the "penthouse" we were going to use, which Lois stumbled on at the eleventh hour.

Norman feared repercussions if we damaged the marble floors or any of the expensive furnishings. Normally I adjust to any approximate location, but I wanted this one.

By day's end, Mr. Clemente, the owner, agreed to $1,500 for two days—only $500 more than the other place. If we get it, the crew will work shoeless in deference to new carpets.

On to the flea market to see the airline ticket counter Nick Romanac, production designer, is building. It looks most promising. Glanced at the flea market men's room where, simulating a men's room at Newark Airport, I'll shoot tomorrow.

Came back here to meet with Ashoka Daibee and Abby Sheckley, the local accountant who will do the day-to-day work, to be reviewed by Ashoka when he visits us each Friday.

After lunch, I resumed scouting. Picked the highway spot for the traffic jam, for which Lois must now obtain state permission and cooperation. Back here to inspect wardrobe with Linda, then props with Patrick and Jimmy.

I interviewed the former boxing champ Billy Costello, who Norman brought in to audition for the tough-guy role on the highway. My affection for boxers derives from my father (a good amateur fighter), who introduced me to the likes of Abe Attel, Benny Leonard, Mickey Walker, etc.

I've decided to hire the 14 Karat Soul group.

A disconcerting note: Peter Hawkins, the assistant cameraman who was with us on Friday, has come down with a flu-type illness picked up in Africa or France. I pray Jeri and Lee Orloff, the sound man who was on that shoot with Jeri, don't suffer the same fate. Herb Forsberg, who was Jeri's assistant on *The Gig*, will fill in for Hawkins temporarily.

I to sleep at midnight . . . awake at 4:00 A.M. . . . read P. D. James till 5:00 A.M. . . . slept till 7:30 A.M.

My room five yards from our production office.

John arrives today. He will videotape me every night (our secret project) to record how things progress.

Now to prepare for tomorrow, the opening salvo.

Monday, October 19, 7:10 A.M.: Kingston

D-Day.

Norman and Sara hosted the company at their home last night. Phil and Nancy, son, daughter, grandchildren, and mother-in-law present.

When John taped me last night, I did not confess to a slight feeling of staleness. I'm sure it was nerves and that once we roll, I'll be my usual self.

Someone trying to break into the room next door at midnight, occasioning screams and tumult, didn't ease me to sleep. My gut churns a mite—a good sign. Avanti!

Tuesday, October 20, 6:00 A.M.: Kingston

Yesterday will go down in history with Pearl Harbor and JFK's assassination, et al., because the stock market plunged *over five hundred* points. All day long, as I was shooting in the men's room at the flea market, I could hear off-stage reports: "The market down two hundred, three hundred, four hundred, [etc.]."

Since the money for this picture derives in good measure from Wall Street, I knew I was in serious trouble before I got back to the Holiday Inn where a message awaited informing that one pledge for a considerable sum had been withdrawn. Oh boy!

Despite the crash, I shot almost all that was scheduled.

Phil made bold choices. Moses Gunn never let us down.

We finished shooting at 7:30 P.M.

Wednesday, October 21, 7:00 A.M.: Kingston

Yesterday was great. The most difficult and pivotal scene (the airport counter) licked, if I judge correctly. Bless Jerry Matz, Hazel Medina, Virginia Downing, Fanny Bakst, and Gordon Cook, who delivered all the crowd dialogue.

We even got the men's-room entrance and exit shots missed the previous day.

Stock market up one hundred points.

Thursday, October 22, 6:45 A.M.: Kingston

Another fine day's work despite crisis when the aged Cadillac scene, a night shot, began to unravel.

I felt ominous vibes about doing lines with the car, not in the best shape, moving on the highway. On a sudden intuition, I wrote new lines on the spot and shot it in the parked car before it leaves for the airport.

Everyone's nerves frazzled, but we ended up, hopefully, with a better scene than originally planned.

Norman doesn't think we can get the picture in the can for less than $500,000. And we have but $450,000.

Dailies at 10:00 P.M.—no supper.

Market up again. I know little else of world events—or care.

Friday, October 23, 7:40 A.M.: Kingston

We shot from 9:00 A.M. to 9:00 P.M. with one hour for lunch. I think (hope) I got everything needed to make the slum party scene work. I feel what I did get is excellent, thanks to Phil (who gets better and better) and the greatest group of extras—twelve of them—I've ever worked with. All nonpros, eager, willing, and friendly. My telling them the entire story of the movie, so they knew how their roles fit in, helped.

Have seen no dailies since Tuesday because of messenger breakdowns, etc.

John is now taking over the responsibility of the dailies. He went to New York this morning to get the projector fixed and shape up synching procedures.

Money pressures mount.

John and I too spent to record our daily video report last night.

Stock market down again.

For the second night in a row, John and I failed to do our video journal—an indication of how hectic things are.

I shot the Sheldon scene, some eight pages, yesterday. After one take, the crew broke into applause.

Some two and a half hours' worth of dailies last night because with super 16, you're compelled to see everything you shot instead of selected takes.

To avoid the rock band in the lounge, we viewed dailies in the executive offices of the Holiday Inn.

John now the official projectionist in addition to his other duties.

Jeri taking penicillin against a leg-wound infection suffered in Africa. Did I note Peter Hawkins's illness is serious? Malaria and hepatitis.

Since one and all will be reading me for reaction to dailies, I'll wear a better jacket.

Ashoka paid his weekly visit. Says we're on budget or better so far.

Sunday, October 25, 9:00 A.M.: Home

Barbara drove me to the location at 8:00 A.M. Twelve hours later she drove me back to the Holiday Inn.

In the interim, I shot ten-plus pages—the mistress scene plus other bits and pieces.

Joanne Camp was all I hoped for. Phil excellent.

We were able to get the entire scene only because we'd rehearsed and the writer was present to make last-minute changes.

One virtue of a highly compressed shooting schedule is that the actors are too exhausted by day's end to make trouble, even if so inclined.

Coming home for a day in the midst of shooting is akin to a combat soldier getting a brief respite at headquarters that he can't fully enjoy because he knows in hours he'll be on the line again.

We end the first week *on schedule.*

Monday, October 26, 5:30 A.M.: Kingston

To New York and the Off-Center Theatre yesterday, where we had the exciting pleasure of hearing 14 Karat Soul led by Glenny T. They did "Can't Get to Heaven on Roller Skates" with Ruth's additional lyrics, which occasioned a frisson up the spine. I gave Abby the check that will get them into SAG.

Tuesday, October 27, 6:00 A.M.: Kingston

Shot the bedroom and bathroom scenes of the Posner penthouse.

All in fine fettle until we viewed the dailies of the Sheldon scene. Not one laugh during the fifty-five-minute screening of what will be a five–six-minute sequence. It has a biting, sad edge for sure, but I don't want the humor lost completely. I trust when it's cut, the laughs (a couple for seasoning) will surface.

Market down big again.

Wednesday, October 28, 6:15 A.M.: Kingston

Rain.

Shot till 9:00 P.M. last night to finish everything in the Clementes' home. While we were shooting, a large group of their neighbors and friends arrived, which stimulated Phil and Doris — theater pros. At one point, I said "cut" in the middle of a speech that Phil was making, which he insisted on completing for the sake of the audience.

I had a drink with Roger and Maureen Holmes and their guests, then a shower; a sandwich and two brews while viewing two hours of dailies. Good spirits restored. Slept from 12:30 A.M. to 5:00 A.M. Now to prepare.

Oh yes, a bleak note: The guy who made the $50,000 pledge has definitely crapped out.

Thursday, October 29, 6:50 A.M.: Kingston

The wedding scene, some eighty to a hundred guests, went excellently. The 14 Karat Soul group lived up to expectations.

Shooting the church scene, I put Jim and Jean McLaughlin and Roger and Maureen Holmes in aisle seats where the camera would be sure to pick them up. It's the least you can do for investors.

I nailed Lee Sarokin[5] clapping on the offbeat in the gospel scene.

---

5. A classmate of mine (1950) at Dartmouth who had become a distinguished federal judge in New Jersey. It was he who freed Reuben Carter and made other controversial rulings that have caught the public eye. He was a genuinely talented big-band drummer at college.

Lunch for all hands at Sack's Lodge, then back to the flea-market men's room. Got the dream sequence plus two pickups.

Dailies looked fine.

Friday, October 30, 7:00 A.M.: Kingston

Phil questioned the steam-room scene before we shot it—felt the humor was exaggerated.

I cough and cough after some nine hours in artificial steam-room smoke, which everyone assures us is the nontoxic kind.

Saturday, October 31, 6:00 A.M.: Kingston

Shot ten pages at the Kingston Hospital.

High spirits till I saw the dailies of the steam room. Phil was right about the comic exaggeration. It's just not credible. To make it work, we will have to edit the scene drastically.

This, plus money worries, makes it my low point to date.

Sunday, November 1, 9:00 P.M.: Home

Got all the factory scenes yesterday. Shot till 8:00 P.M.

All went well except for a moment when I felt overloaded by Norman and Jeri, who were suggesting more than I could assimilate in orderly fashion. I called a break. Told them not to do that again. After a few moments alone, I was even keel, and we progressed to day's end in harmony.

The company was having a Halloween party.

The director's presence inhibiting to any social occasion, and needing time alone, I came home.

Jim McLaughlin says that he will make good on the pledge of the guy who reneged. Amen.

I told Norman to make the editing-mixing-investment deal with Mark Polycan and Tape House.

I added dialogue to the Whitley phone call, which will give us an escape hatch from the steam-room scene if we choose to abort it.

Must prepare now for tomorrow's Rolls Royce shots and the appearance of Jerry Cooney,[6] who got the tough-guy role.

6. The unbeaten "white hope" heavyweight contender till he met Larry Holmes and subsequently retired (twice). This would be his acting debut.

Monday, November 2, 7:00 A.M.: Kingston

The weather looks fair for outside work.

Ned Hallick, the gaffer, breakfasts early. He and I the only ones in the dining room, as usual. As always, his eyes appraise me for an estimate as to how we're doing. Everyone greets me thus first thing every morning. Can Jerry Cooney act? Can Arthur French[7] drive and act simultaneously? Stay tuned.

Tuesday, November 3, 6:00 A.M.: Kingston

For the first time, we didn't get all the work scheduled.

We did get the traffic jam, accident, and Cooney bit. Flu invades the company. Lunched with Cooney, who made a favorable impression. Blinking-scene dailies at the hospital look fine.

John and Bobby Gay to my rescue via investment.

Wednesday, November 4, 6:15 A.M.: Kingston

A monster shoot yesterday — caught up to schedule.

Seventy-two minutes of tight master time logged by Cindy[8] so far.

John and I ate late. Again no time for our video diary. Every day brutal for a different reason. Awake since 4:30 A.M. preparing. Must run.

Thursday, November 5, 6:05 A.M.: Kingston

We have completed shooting in Kingston and leave for New York at 7:30 A.M. The crash scene went better than anyone could hope, thanks to J. D. Clarke's driving: He hit the plastic garbage cans, which sent the metal ones flying.

In the midst of shooting, Phil was phoned by Woody Allen's people in another attempt to spring him prematurely. I again explained why our schedule didn't permit it. This pressure from Woody's office is disconcerting. I wonder how he'd react if the situation was reversed.

7. That he'd been driving *Miss Daisy* (as an understudy and replacement since the play opened) should have assured me I was in excellent hands, which proved the case.

8. Cynthia Streit, script supervisor. Like the very best at her craft, she imposes logic and order on the most chaotic days, gives the director heart wordlessly.

Friday, November 6, 7:30 A.M.: Wyndham

Arrived New York at 10:00 A.M., checked in.

Norman, Jeri, and I to Thirty-fifth between Seventh and Eighth avenues where we found the building to simulate entrance to Posner's factory. We put our van in a parking place to hold it till the Rolls arrived. A white 1959 antique, it drew attention, but not enough to disrupt.

Turned Jeri loose on the garment area for the title sequence. We did all the Rolls stuff. Rendezvoused at the Off-Center Theatre. Ate on the street. Got a bit of Phil against a true graffitied wall.

In caravan to Newark Airport. Stole our shots inside and out. Cops approached, but we always moved before contact was made.

We even got a moon shot of the airport for the dream sequence.

Back here by 6:30 P.M. Viewed accumulated dailies (three and a half hours) at Tape House.

Saturday, November 7, 6:45 A.M.: Wyndham

Day 18 (hopefully the last).

We fell apart in Newark slums yesterday.

Atmospheric shots (when we should have shot essential dialogue) cost us the cloud cover we had rigged for. God knows what we got—if anything.

I called off the rest of the day when we got back to New York at 3:00 P.M. Spent the afternoon scouting establishing shots—the connective tissue that will give what we shot in Kingston a New York feel.

Dailies a mess. Besides no passing shots of the Rolls in New Jersey, there were other goofs. A reshoot seems mandatory.

John and I wrestled with these problems as we ate.

At 4:00 A.M. this morning, a possible solution occurred to me. We'll see.

The weather seems to hold.

Sunday, November 8, 8:30 A.M.: Home

As bad as Friday went, yesterday was a dream.

First to Central Park—Phil walking midst joggers. As always, shooting in 16 mm attracts no more attention than a video camera. Then a pan up to a luxury Fifth Avenue penthouse to establish the Posners' residence. We found Sheldon's building on Sixty-second Street and shot Phil arriving by cab. Then, shooting in the other direction, we got Phil coming out of the mistress's building. Then to Sixty-seventh Street and the phone booth. Then to Seventy-ninth where several people (including three young men with yarmulkes) recognized Phil by face but not by name.

Now down Eighth Avenue, where we shot Phil entering the Barking Fish restaurant.

Finally to Broadway for a couple of shots, and that was it. All the establishing shots in New York I could think of, accomplished in less than three hours. The movie suddenly endowed with a cast of thousands, who in quintessential New Yorker spirit not only did not look at the camera but actively spurned it.

Wrap party at Sack's Lodge.

Cindy and Nick at our table. This was her twenty-fifth film. She had been a stockbroker in Canada and sold yachts in Florida before becoming a script supervisor.

During the party, Nick let me know that he and others in the crew would like to invest in my subsequent films by way of encouraging me to do more of them. I was more touched and pleased than I possibly expressed.

Monday, November 9, 8:00 A.M.: Home

I gulped sleep as camels do water after long deprivation.

Post partum blues and fatigue spawn doubts, of course.

In sleep I pursued the phantom shot, as usual. Dreamed I was about to fall out a window. Called for help to Bobby Duvall, only to have him push me nearer the edge. I shouted and gratefully awoke.

Tuesday, November 10 , 6:45 A.M.: Wyndham

Met John at Tape House at 1:30 P.M. to review all the Rolls footage. Decided we don't need to reshoot dialogue scenes but must get pass-bys in New York and Jersey, including airport.

We will reshoot with Rolls and actors tomorrow or Thursday. How I loathe the necessity. My sleep again riddled with pursuit of the phantom shot without which the story can't be told. Last night worse than ever, exacerbated no doubt by the need of a reshoot.

The dailies of Newark and New York look fine.

Thursday, November 12, 6:30 A.M.: Wyndham

Called off today's Rolls reshoot because of snow and icy conditions.

Friday, November 13, 8:40 A.M.: Home

Think I found a sublet a ten-minute walk from the editing room, which would be ideal. Figure to begin work next Thursday, which will allow John and his crew several days to settle in.

The owner of the sublet refers to it as "the most discreet sort of rental."

Pursuit of the phantom shot still punctuates sleep. Waking up is the only relief, and even then I must convince myself that such a shot is not needed.

Saturday, November 14, 8:40 A.M.: Home

Great news from Ashoka: We appear to have the movie in the can (everyone paid except Norman and me) for $415,000.

Our second bank loan on the house has been approved.

Sunday, November 15, 8:30 A.M.: Home

No phantom shot last night. Ruth told me I awakened the previous night and asked her if the crew had arrived.

Monday, November 16, 8:30 A.M.: Home

The phantom shot reduced to a bit of undertitle footage, but still it nags my sleep.

A plane crash on takeoff in Denver yesterday. Relatives and friends clustered silently in front of the ticket counter awaiting word, just as I'd staged it.

Dan reported a story several days ago about the lone survivor (because he missed the plane) of a basketball team wiped out in a crash—and how greatly it affected his life.

Tuesday, November 17, 8:30 A.M.: Home

The phantom shot again last night, but not so acutely.

John has converted what was a storage room into a most livable editing chamber. Sam Adelman, his assistant, displays a heartening enthusiasm.

Thursday, November 19, 8:30 A.M., Home

The sublet appears to have gone to a higher bidder. When I complained, the owner said, "Doing business in New York is so complicated."

Until I do the Rolls reshoot, the phantom shot will pursue me as it did last night, albeit daintily.

Friday, November 20, 8:30 A.M.: Home

How did I occupy my time before my quest for a sublet?

Saturday, November 21, 9:00 A.M.: Home

Once again I think I have a sublet. Kingdoms have changed hands with less ado.

Tuesday, November 24, 7:10 A.M.: The Sublet, New York

I've got a sublet that requires masquerading as a cousin of the owner.

We started editing scenes involving the Rolls so I will know precisely what's needed when we reshoot on Friday.

John has created a climate that allows Sam to feel free about making suggestions. Jeff Kushner, the apprentice, seems bright and industrious. If we prevail in this Rolls sequence, we should be able to lick any other part of the picture.

Thursday, November 26, 9:00 A.M.: Home

It was unrealistic to think I could write a new movie while editing this one. I forgot how much creative energy it takes to wrest the best from the meager amount of film I shoot. John, by the first hurdle, is working well. Like me, he shows signs of becoming consumed by it to the exclusion of all other concerns.

SAG is holding up return of our $30,000 bond because two actors complained that the group read-through (and lunch later) constituted a rehearsal for which they weren't paid. This despite the fact that we told the actors they didn't have to attend the read-through, which was designed as a social get-together—an occasion to let them meet each other, see where their role fit in the overall, and break bread at our expense.

Saturday, November 28, 9:00 A.M.: Home

John and I left for city at 7:15 yesterday. Rendezvoused with Scott, Herb Forsberg (substituting for Jeri), Arthur French, Phil Bosco, and the driver who comes with the Rolls.

A gray, raw day. Snow did not seem far away. I had a list of needed shots. Regretted not bringing a sun gun for more light.

We rigged on Eighteenth Street, had the camera mounted to shoot out the rear station-wagon window.

John and I in the Rolls (with Phil, Arthur, and a walkie-talkie), we preceded the van down Ninth Avenue and through the Holland Tunnel. Got pass-bys en route to the Newark Airport. Shot Phil's arrival and departure at two terminals.

Phil, John, Herb, and I entered the terminal.

Herb positioned with the camera (16 mm attracting no attention as usual). Phil, at my signal, entered the terminal and sprinted to his plane. Then we shot him fleeing in the opposite direction, which we'll cut in with the crowd shouting after him "You're the luckiest man in the world." (Is that possibly a better title?)

We also picked up other bits and pieces that should help to blend the ticket counter (shot in Kingston) and Newark Airport.

By 1:30 P.M., we were at Moran's basking in the glow of a difficult job well done. That we'd "stolen" it spiced the achievement.

Phil, asked about working with Woody Allen since we'd last seen him, having signed a waiver which swore him to secrecy, said that he wasn't at liberty to tell us anything.

Monday, November 30, 8:25 A.M.: Home

Must run to make a bus to the city—bearing the negative of Friday's shoot.

Tuesday, December 1, 9:00 A.M.: New York Sublet

John showed me his version of the office-factory scene. I had that gut response attending fine work; saw no need for any further exploration or change.

We tried to get some of the elevator improvisation in. No dice—the picture wouldn't hear of it.

Friday, December 4, 9:10 A.M.: New York

Another good editing day. We are up to the ticket counter; reviewed the footage that John will take a crack at in my absence this morning.

Saturday, December 5, 9:00 A.M.: Home

I went to see Ashoka. The production-cost figures are outstanding. We are under budget in almost every category. Norman deserves praise.

Sunday, December 6, 9:30 A.M.: Home

A disturbing dream toward morning: I encountered Bob Fosse on Fifty-eighth Street looking better than he ever did in life, heavier and better dressed, bearing a briefcase. I asked what he was working on. He said a film titled *You Need a Warning* or *Take This as Your Warning*. The *warning* clearly aimed at me. Then I was in an editing room being shown what I took to be a rave review of my latest film. But as I read it, I noted photos of me in various phases of my career. An obituary? I recall one photo of Jack Albertson.

In today's *Times*, Woody Allen is accorded praise for making his new film for $10 million. Why am I not impressed?

Monday, December 7, 8:30 A.M.: Home

John reports the Steenbeck editing machine on the blink, so I'll get a later bus.

Tuesday, December 8, 9:00 A.M.: New York

Arrived at the editing room raring to go after so many hours away from my obsession.

We spent the day roughing up the ticket-counter scene—giving it a jumble and tumult that hopefully will prove as exciting this morning as it seemed when we finished at 8:00 P.M.

Wednesday, December 9, 7:40 A.M.: New York

The ticket-counter scene passed morning inspection.

Phil looking better and better. One goes to his takes with absolute confidence.

We have ten minutes and forty seconds of film at page 14.

Friday, December 11, 9:00 A.M.: New York

We reviewed the material of the drive back to the airport. I discussed it with John and then absented myself while he assembled.

John summoned me in late afternoon to see what he had so far.

My eye stuck on an early flaw that (as always) rendered me insensitive to all that followed till it was corrected.

Ruth and I with the Sarokins to see Warren Vaché in the band playing the Benny Goodman charts at Michael's Pub.

Warren impressive, as always, as was Butch Miles, who might be the best big-band drummer in the world.

How about Warren doing the music for the film?

Saturday, December 12, 7:50 A.M.: New York

I did not go to the cutting room (good name for a jazz club) until almost 4:00 P.M. when John notified me he'd finished the first of the drive-back dialogue scenes.

From 4:00 P.M. to 7:00 P.M. we finetuned.

In my concern about the length of the film, I envision the longest credits in the world—the slowest, anyway.

The week concludes on an upbeat note.

Sunday, December 13, 9:30 A.M.: Home

John said they'd underestimated the time, and (to my great relief) we now have fifteen minutes of cut film from the first eighteen pages.

Given financial problems (both personal and film-related), I would be in a most depressed state if the film weren't going well.

Ruth and I went to Sack's Lodge for Scott and Barbara's wedding. A location romance with a happy ending that will last, if I'm any judge.

Monday, December 14, 9:05 A.M.: Home

John called from the cutting room to say it had been broken into but nothing was missing. Also, Sam Adelman (whose presence is a continuous joy) will be out for a couple of days with a bad back.

Will have to phone an investor about pledged money that hasn't arrived. And of course I'm still far shy of the money needed to complete postproduction.

Onward, in any case, since no other direction offers possibility of relief.

Tuesday, December 15, 8:05 A.M.: New York

About the break-in: They got into our place by breaking through a wall. We lost a couple of cheap speakers but, amen, they didn't trash our footage.

Most of the day was lost.

Wednesday, December 16, 8:30 A.M.: New York

We attacked the resistant bedroom scene, John and I shoulder to shoulder, starting at 9:30 A.M. Ate in—the hard rain all day lent itself to remaining in the bunker and pressing relentlessly.

I fell asleep for twenty minutes in midafternoon while John worked, with Jeff, in Sam's absence, assisting as best he could.

Things began to take shape. We realized we didn't want to cut as often as we thought initially. Jeff made a suggestion that worked—a thrill for him to be a creative contributor.

By 7:00 P.M. we had it!

Thursday, December 17, 9:30 A.M.: New York

John and I reviewed all the living-room material, which took three hours. We went back and forth deciding (unanimously in every case) on selected takes and bits of potential benefit in other takes.

One negative registered: The moment when Mr. and Mrs. Posner swap love terms ("poogy-poo," etc.) registers as exaggerated comedy, violates the credible line we have so scrupulously adhered to.

Reassuring news: Woody's new film is *eighty-two* minutes, and Huston's *The Dead* is only *eighty-three*.

Friday, December 18, 8:35 A.M.: New York

John worked all day on the "poogy-poo" scene, which was near completion when I viewed it at 7:00 P.M. As we anticipated, there are problems.

Norman paid himself the rest of the money he's due, says he will lend it to the company if needed.

SAG still holding out $5,000 while they explore the read-through lunch.

Saturday, December 19, 7:30 A.M.: New York

We worked all day on the living-room scene. Improved it significantly, but we're still not through. John's amiable diligence unwavering.

Wish I could avoid the emotional highs and lows of my varying appraisals of the movie.

Sunday, December 20, 10:15 A.M.: Home

I joined John in the editing room (he'd been working there for an hour) at 9:00 A.M.

We worked on the living-room section until 4:15 P.M.

We licked it!

Tuesday, December 22, 9:30 A.M.: New York

We reviewed footage of the father-son scene, which looked better than remembered.

The takes now preferred are often not those selected while shooting because current choices are dictated by the edited footage so far. Plus selections (made at dailies after shooting) reflect extreme fatigue and distraction.

Wednesday, December 23, 8:30 A.M.: New York

Viewed a rough assemblage of the father-son scene.

Speeded up Phil's arrival in the taxi via a jump cut, eliminating three dead seconds occasioned by Phil (in his scrupulous attention to detail) paying the driver, which no one could see.

Thursday, December 24, 10:00 A.M.: Home

We licked the father-son scene, engendering a celebratory mood that sent John and me to Michael's Pub where Warren Vaché again triumphed over the minimal use of his talent by playing in a subdued, controlled way that like the tip of an iceberg, spoke to bountiful reserves; invested his brief solos with unmistakable mastery and class.

Tuesday, December 29, 8:15 A.M.: New York

Arrived at the cutting room at 5:30 P.M. John just finishing the hospital scene. Fine work. Especially cheering after the Christmas hiatus.

Wednesday, December 30, 9:30 A.M.: New York

John having a go at the blinking scene.

We know if you let the semaphore eyeblinks go on for as long as they would in real time, the scene would be interminable. Conversely, if you rush the blinks so they are patently fake, you also fail.

I was derelict that day as director. Made a note in future to beware those scenes you are so confident of in script that you lower your guard when shooting.

While John worked, I walked up Third Avenue to the movie district, not sure what to see. Decided on *The Dead*.

What exquisite work. Must reread the Joyce story to see how it was done. The sort of acting by *all* hands that transcended acting. So graceful the camera angles and moves in that restricted setting, you forgot the film was directed. My heart soars at such excellence. That Huston did it at age seventy-nine is especially heartening.

Back to the editing room. Viewed the beginning of the blinking scene. John has caught the rhythm, near perfect.

Thursday, December 31, 8:00 A.M.: New York

Viewed the blinking scene at 7:15 P.M. A few touches to be made this morning, but it's excellent. Runs over four minutes, giving us forty minutes of film at the halfway point (fifty of ninety-nine pages) in the script.

1988
Friday, January 1, 9:30 A.M.: Home

Must not think about the money crunch down the road when we get into sound, music, mix, and blowup. To have that on my head made viewing *Ishtar* (on which $60 million or so was squandered) especially repugnant.

Wednesday, January 6, 7:25 A.M.: New York

John showed me what he's done so far on the mistress scene.

Sam Adelman, viewing with us, expressed my upbeat reaction: "More, more."

Friday, January 8, 7:30 A.M.: New York

The mistress scene runs six minutes and twenty seconds, giving us a total of forty-seven and a half minutes. A moment or two when my eye stuck, occasioned by a shot I'd failed to get. But when a scene works as well as this one, polishing is a pleasure.

We'll review the steam-bath material today and decide whether to ignore the anticipated problem (comic excess undermining credibility) and cut the scene as written *or* acknowledge the problem and try to solve it as we cut, instead of corrective surgery later.

Saturday, January 9, 9:30 A.M.: New York

We will meet the steam-bath problem head-on with drastic dialogue cuts.

Sunday, January 10, 9:30 A.M.: Home

We are licking the steam-room scene in fine fashion.

A misunderstanding between John and me because when I told him I had enough money to complete the picture cut, he thought I meant I had enough money to complete postproduction.

How difficult it must be for him to go from working for Coppola to my bare-bones operation.[9]

Monday, January 11, 7:20 A.M.: Home

Everyone fearful of the stock market after Friday's 140-point drop. Another and possibly blacker Monday? And me with money yet to raise.

Tuesday, January 12, 8:50 A.M.: New York

John gave me his list of postproduction procedures — succinct and neatly done.

We viewed his cut of the steam room. Excellent. We changed one line reading and a shot at the end. Excellent, I say again.

Viewing the shots of Phil walking around New York, John, Sam, and I pounced on the Shubert Alley shot as wrong. It's a favorable sign when a film refuses to accept anything, no matter how small, that rings false or excessive.

Wednesday, January 13, 8:45 A.M.: New York

While John assembled the bar scene, I went to the accountant to review finances. We are definitely in need.

9. One day John said, "You know, Pop, I made more in per diem working for Coppola than you're paying me." "That's true," I conceded, "but there's one difference: You don't owe Coppola. You owe me."

Thursday, January 14, 10:50 A.M.: New York

John came to see me. Much heat, basically stemming from his concern for me. I laid out the financial situation in detail. We agreed the best way he can help is to continue editing as fast as possible so I can evaluate what we have before I go out and try to raise the money needed to complete the picture.

Viewed Newark slum arrival—the "devastation" montage. We nailed it by 5:30 P.M. Now have fifty-eight minutes of film.

Dined with Bill Goldman, who pressed me for a progress report on the film. When I concluded, he said the two things I hear most often: "You love to live dangerously" and "How does Ruth stand it?"

Friday, January 15, 10:15 A.M.: New York

I went to Jim McLaughlin's office at 30 Wall Street. Met Al Vogel (the Vogel of McLaughlin, Piven, Vogel whose name appears above my films) for the first time.

Jim said he was aware of the financial bind I'm in with the film and let me know that he'd bail me out in the absence of alternative.

Had a cabdriver whose father owned a barber shop on Burnside Avenue in the Bronx, a couple of blocks from where I grew up. Like me, he went to P.S. 26, P.S. 82, and DeWitt Clinton High School; learned to shoot pool at Lou and Macy Kay's room and was in Patton's Third Army.

Sunday, January 17, 10:00 A.M.: Home

Yesterday, Saturday: I brought coffee and Danish to the editing room where John and Sam were already working at 9:00 A.M.

Tomorrow will be three months from the day (Black Monday) when I began shooting.

Tuesday, January 19, 8:30 A.M.: New York

Reviewed the Gonzalez arrival scene. No picture changes needed—sound suggestions made.

Liked the party dailies much more than expected from my one late-night glimpse after a hard day's shoot.

Wednesday, January 20, 8:45 A.M.: New York

Midway through page 86, and we have sixty-seven minutes and

The Luckiest Man in the World • 297

forty-five seconds of film. Given the physical activity in the remaining thirteen pages, I estimate eighty minutes without titles.

Thursday, January 21, 8:30 A.M.: New York

I phoned John in the afternoon, learned the dream sequence was proving more complicated than envisioned.

The scene still not ready at 4:00 P.M. I voiced impatience.

Phoned at 5:00 P.M. to apologize and suggest I not come in until this morning. John insisted I see it last night, which I did at 6:30 P.M. Was pleased to find he'd accomplished my intention better than I'd envisioned it.

Saturday, January 23, 9:15 A.M.: New York

To the accountant, then to the editing room.

Reviewed the fantasy section. Didn't like it as well as before, which puzzled until John informed he'd made some changes on his own. I requested he put it back the way it was, which occasioned a slight ruffling of feathers.

We worked out a tentative schedule that envisions completing this cut by next Wednesday, premixing the following Wednesday, and screening for ourselves at MovieLab (our first larger-screen view) a day or so later, with other screenings (before locking the picture) to follow.

Sunday, January 24, 9:20 A.M.: Home

John had the morning-after-the-party scene ready at 2:00 P.M. Convinced me the only change I suggested was wrong. We now have seventy-four minutes of film.

Monday, January 25, 9:30 A.M.: Home

Feel derelict because I am not going to the city today, even though John has more than enough work to keep him busy through tomorrow.

Wednesday, January 27, 7:30 A.M.: Home

Heavy snow.

Could use another day to lick this cold, but John has two scenes ready.

Thursday, January 28, 8:40 A.M.: New York

John showed me his cut of the rescue scene. I felt there was more excitement to be obtained from the admittedly limited material. When I suggested a different approach, he said, "We tried that." A reminder that directors not in constant contact with the editing process lose touch with their pictures.

Friday, January 29, 8:30 A.M.: New York

We keep looking for a better title. Sam Adelman suggested *Dear Sam*.

Saturday, January 30, 10:20 A.M.: New York

We licked the penultimate scene.

Marty Donovan[10] came by to pick me up for lunch. I noted ours was the largest cutting room he'd probably ever seen. He said ours was the *first* cutting room he'd ever seen.

Sunday, January 31, 8:30 A.M.: New York

John Gay dropped in. Another reminder how divorced most screenwriters are from the nuts and bolts of their profession when he (like Bill Goldman and Marty) said his acquaintance with editing rooms was limited to visiting me.

Tuesday, February 2, 9:15 A.M.: Home

John, working on the final scene, disputed a cut I suggested a priori. I insisted he make it. While he did so, I made a sign that I taped to the wall: *ALL TIES GO TO THE DIRECTOR.* Sam and Jeff laughed. John gave a grudging smile, which broadened when upon viewing my requested change, I agreed it was awful.

We completed the first cut of the picture at 7:30 P.M.!

Wednesday, February 3, 7:35 A.M.: New York

At 10:00 A.M. yesterday, we turned off all lights, suspended in-

10. TV and movie writer. We met as messengers at Young & Rubicam in 1951 when he, head messenger, handed me a package and said, "Take this to Hoboken." He, as story editor for the "Kate Smith Show," called me on a rainy winter day in 1952 when I was trying to rent beach cabanas on Long Island and said, "Can you use three hundred and fifty bucks?" by way of announcing I'd just made my first TV sale of a sketch to the "Kate Smith Show." It starred Robert Sterling and Rita Gam, and to her dying day, my mother-in-law maintained it was the best thing I'd ever done.

coming calls, held all work, and ran the first reel—some twenty minutes of film.

Would like to attribute my reaction to all the sound things that got screwed up or are lacking. But for the first time in a long time, I sensed the picture might not work.

We made corrections until 8:00 P.M. Deleted over a minute.

Realize a lot of premixing is required before we show it to anyone.

Over all hovers the $80,000 needed to complete the film.

Thursday, February 4, 8:50 A.M.: New York

We had the Warren Vaché recordings I selected as temporary music transferred and inserted.

The danger, as always with temporary music, is that we will become so wedded to it that Warren will be hard-pressed to equal it when he composes the score.

Optimism as the day progressed.

Friday, February 5, 7:45 A.M.: New York

Reviewing and reworking (we're on reel three) nonstop to 7:00 P.M.

The picture rejected music for the reporter-bar scene. A good sign when crutches are spurned—the movie insisting it can walk on its own.

We will not premix until a week from Tuesday. In the interim, all needed sounds will be gathered; a black-and-white dupe made of our work print to spare the work-print damage during the premix process.

Saturday, February 6, 9:00 A.M.: New York

At 2:30 P.M., the first draft of the film completed, I took the crew to lunch.

Sunday, February 7, 9:30 A.M.: Home

John and I, alone in the cutting room, ran the entire picture nonstop for the first time. *It works!* This despite much sound work and a bit of picture work left to do.

It came to a bit over seventy-nine minutes, which will bring us in at about eighty-three with titles.

John wants to give Sam Adelman a music editor as well as assistant picture editor credit, I said fine—can't fathom why people are stingy about credits, which don't cost a dime.

Wednesday, February 10, 9:25 A.M.: New York

Feeling subpar, I decided not to accompany Lee Orloff on his "ambient sound" trek.

Jeff took my place.

John and Sam doing myriad things required for the premix.

Friday, February 12, 8:30 A.M.: New York

I met with Frank Military and Maxine Lang at Chappell Music. They generously educated me about music rights to facilitate an equitable contract with Warren Vaché. An arresting bust of Frank Sinatra in Military's office. Not Sinatra young or old, but poised between, which lends a tension.

Saturday, February 13, 9:30 A.M.: Home

My feelings about the movie fluctuate. When I regard it overall, I'm sanguine. But as we focus on sound flaws—on *any* flaws—I'm depressed.

Sunday, February 14, 6:00 A.M.: Home

Up and about, I can cope with anxieties that loom insurmountable in bed.

Tuesday, February 16, 8:15 A.M.: New York

If the rough cut disappoints, how and where will I get the money to finish? This little picture should not be burdened so.

Warren Vaché just informed me he goes to France March 5 for a one-month tour. Oh boy, oh boy.

Wednesday, February 17, 8:30 A.M.: New York

The premix with Dom Tavella at Photomag went well. We worked from 9:15 A.M. to 2:00 P.M. Dom (twenty-five or so) proficient and not so long in the job to assume the autocratic manner of some mixers.

We brought only the sections to be mixed, which gave him a

patchwork sense of the story. Our first audience, he seemed intrigued, several times voiced curiosity about what happened next.

Thursday, February 18, 8:20 A.M.: New York

To MovieLab at 3:00 P.M. for the first viewing on a full-size screen.

John, Sam, Jeff, Ruth, and I, plus Warren and his collaborator, Jack Gale, the audience.

I felt caught up in it almost continuously.

The "audience" was most enthusiastic in their comments. The projectionist, George (known for his cruel candor and Yogi Berra-type reviews), volunteered how funny he felt it was.

We will have a real screening on February 23 at 5:00 P.M. I've already invited Jim and J. C. McLaughlin.

With all bills paid through this week, we have only $15,000 left. If the Tuesday screening doesn't succeed, money problems will be compounded.

Friday, February 19, 8:40 A.M.: New York

A good aftertaste from the screening reflected in the upbeat spirit of all hands. Sam Adelman pronounced the film "a steak ready to be served."

Warren, Jack, and I went over the film on the Steenbeck. Made a few music extensions and added a cue or two. They share my feeling that music should be a delicate seasoning rather than a heavy gravy ladled indiscriminately, as is the norm.

The conditions Norman now attaches to his loan are unacceptable, so there will be no relief from that quarter.

Saturday, February 20, 9:10 A.M.: Home

John did a nice job shortening the end (in the absence of credits) for next Tuesday's screening.

Something Happened (a line in the film) would be a fine title, but Joe Heller used it too notably and recently.

Monday, February 22, 8:20 A.M.: New York

Second Effort still the title despite everyone seeking something better.

Tuesday, February 23, 9:00 A.M.: New York

My fortunes will rise or fall precipitously at tonight's 5:00 P.M. screening for some thirty-five people, including Jim and Jean McLaughlin, Roger and Maureen Holmes, Lila and Bob Ehrenbard (investors all), plus a man I've never met who loved *The Gig* and might be a source of money to complete this picture. That most of these people have never seen a rough cut is an obstacle.

J. C. McLaughlin ("I can't bear rough cuts") has bowed out.

3:30 P.M.

This morning I asked for, and Pepe assured me I received, one of his extra-lucky beard trims.

I am about to seek a bar near Movielab for my ritual vodka before a screening.

Wednesday, February 24 , 9:20 A.M.: New York

The screening was a success.

The audience somewhat inhibited by the mix of comic and tragic elements. It was the serious side of the film that carried the evening.

Jim and Jean McLaughlin took a group of us, including the Holmeses and a potential new investor, to the Oak Room for dinner. A celebratory mood prevailed.

I am drained.

Thursday, February 25, 7:40 A.M.: New York

J. C. called to say he heard how well it went.

We are making some picture changes.

Warren and Jack Gale have composed a nice theme, but it doesn't accomplish the new objective (born of the screening), which is to signal the audience at the top that it's all right to laugh when you feel the impulse, despite serious moments cheek by jowl with funny ones.

Warren called last night to ask if Vic Dickinson, the late great jazz trombonist who combined humor and serious purpose in his playing, was an example of what I wanted. "Bull's-eye," I said.

Friday, February 26, 8:15 A.M.: New York

I spent two and a half hours yesterday morning with the new investor, who will supply the $80,000 needed to complete the picture.

After our agreeable and extended conversation (his life, my life), I gave him the offering papers.

To the cutting room, feeling good.

Quest for a better title continues.

Saturday, February 27, 8:45 A.M.: Home

Warren and Jack Gale came by with several new themes I didn't respond to.

I hear a muted cornet talking to a muted trombone. Something at once comic and poignant. Warren said they'd be back on Monday with new approaches.

Our music needs total about fifteen minutes. Sam said the average music minutes in pictures today is thirty–fifty.

I lunched with Bob Ehrenbard. Lila Ehrenbard, whom I'd spoken to earlier on the phone, said, "We don't just like your picture, we *love* it." And then, cryptically, "Bob will tell you more."

What Bob told me at lunch was one of the most pleasant surprises I've ever experienced. "Lila and I want to increase our investment in the picture," he announced. I thanked him for the vote of confidence as well as the money.

I phoned Dennis Smith, another investor who was at the screening, for suggested changes before we lock the picture. He felt the party montage was a shade too long. On reexam, we clipped it by a few seconds.

I will focus on a new title for the movie this weekend.

Sunday, February 28, 8:20 A.M.: Home

Favorable reaction to the screening continued. Roger Holmes increasing his investment.

Tuesday, March 1, 9:45 A.M.: New York

Warren and I met at Michael's Pub. He had two themes for me to check out. One heard the other day, which Warren felt I'd underappreciated.

On reexam, he's right!

Wednesday, March 2, 9:15 A.M.: New York

End-money pledged, we embarked on a full-court press.

Negative cutter (Ron Vitello, who did *The Gig*) hired.

John, Sam, and I to the optical house to discuss titles.

Friday, March 4, 8:40 A.M.: New York

Jess and Doris Soraci (sound editors) viewed reels one and two with John, Sam, and me to establish needs.

Warren drove John and me to Jack Gale's house in New Jersey where we arrived at a definitive version of the theme and finalized cues.

Warren takes his picture cassette to Paris while Jack works here.

Saturday, March 5, 8:30 A.M.: Home

Reviewed the last two reels with Jess and Doris. Like all sound editors (as he himself said), Jess could use more time but concludes he will have the picture ready to mix by Monday, April 11.

Sunday, March 6, 9:00 A.M.: Home

I am all but positive that the title will be a line from the picture.

At one point, early on, it was suggested but discarded as too on-the-nose, and probably used before.

"The envelope please . . . and the probable winner is—*The Luckiest Man in the World*."

When it hit me, I went to the Maltin TV book (17,500 films), which lists numerous titles with *luck* or *lucky* but nothing close to ours. Warren's theme circulates endlessly in my head.

Monday, March 7, 9:00 A.M.: Home

The Writers Guild of America on strike as of today at noon. It affects Dan and Tony directly.

The new title enthusiastically and unanimously embraced by everyone I've tried it on.

Saturday, March 12, 9:30 A.M.: Home

My presence in the editing room not required as they ready for the mix.

The new investor has still not made good on his pledge.

Tuesday, March 15, 8:00 A.M.: New York

I am becalmed while the sound editors work. Will review some of their material today.

Walked the picket line at ABC.

Wednesday, March 16, 9:00 A.M.: New York

A session with Jess, checking sound effects, making choices. At one point I found myself auditioning toilet flushes—industrial versus home.

Wednesday, March 23, 9:20 A.M.: New York

Big turnout to picket at the Twentieth Century–Fox office. Someone said, "We should picket the Russian Tea Room—hit them where they work."

Warren says that Connie Kay and Major Holley will be included in the recording session for *The Luckiest Man*.

I'm still not comfortable saying that title after years of the other.

Sunday, March 27, 8:15 A.M.: Home

A letter from the new investor reconfirming his pledge of $80,000, but the money will not be forthcoming until some other deal is consummated.

Friday, April 1, 8:15 A.M.: New York

The recording session at Astoria Studios went excellently.

We began at 3:00 P.M. The Latin party music matches the Tito Puente material we used as a temporary track. Paquito D'Rivera contributes a wild solo. Warren added over-dub.

Friday, April 8, 4:00 A.M.: New York

Here are the things that prevent sleep: indications that the new investor will not make good on his pledge; mix scheduled for next week and my energy down; once finished, how do I sell it?

Sunday, April 10, 9:45 A.M.: Home

I have a full-fledged cold, and we start to mix in less than twenty-four hours.

Who said it should be easy? But must it be this heart? I meant to say *hard*. Fathom that one.

Monday, April 11, 8:10 A.M.: New York

If I get through today (the first mix day), I think I'll be all right.

Now to don my armor (two sweaters), mindful they keep mixing rooms on the cool side in deference to the machinery.

Tuesday, April 12, 7:45 A.M.: New York

We completed reel one at 6:15 P.M.

Wednesday, April 13, 8:20 A.M.: New York

There is good news and bad news and bad news.
On the plus side, we completed reel two and were well into number three by 5:45 P.M.
On the down side, money woes. Short-term and far-reaching.

Thursday, April 14, 8:05 A.M.: New York

As we mixed, financial matters made repeated intrusions.
Working through lunch, we completed reel three by 5:15 P.M.
J. C. McLaughlin to my immediate rescue with an added investment.

Friday, April 15, 7:30 A.M.: New York

We completed reel four (the final reel) by 2:30 P.M.
Warren Vaché joined Jess, Doris, Sam, John, Dom (the mixer), and me at Magno, where we reviewed the mix at 4:00 P.M.
After each reel, I dictated notes to Jess. Other notes from those present will be assembled this morning.
We parted in fine spirits.

Saturday, April 16, 8:20 A.M.: Home

What loomed as a few easy hours of polishing proved otherwise due to an equipment failure.
We worked beyond the point of diminishing returns. Suspect major overhaul and revision might be necessary.
In addition to sound problems, there is the possibility of grain in the end-credit sequence.

Wednesday, April 20, 8:30 A.M.: Home

It's six months since the first day of shooting, but I suspect I've aged more than that.
Am pressing to get promised checks to satisfy immediate creditors.

Thursday, April 21, 8:15 A.M.: Home

The blowup sample by John Allen looks fine—not a hint that it is a blowup.

Comparing reel one (mixed) with the unmixed version the audience heard at the screening, we all three (John, Sam, and I) realized that in attempting to improve what we had, we'd lost many elements that infused the track with excitement: raucous sounds smoothed out or eliminated to accommodate specific and logical effects at the expense of the overall.

Saturday, April 23, 8:45 A.M.: Home

We remixed reel one.

Friday, April 29, 8:15 A.M.: Home

To John Allen's at 11:00 A.M.

Reviewed the work print on the Hazeltine with Mike, who will make color corrections on the 35-mm negative. Each camera angle recorded in film feet. Then red, blue, and yellow assigned a number according to how much of each is wanted in a scene. The numbers recorded on a computer so all prints will look the same.

Monday, May 2, 8:40 A.M.: Home

I briefed Jim McLaughlin on the current game plan: Screen in New York in May to see what we have, then to L.A. in June (the "world" returned from Cannes) to seek distribution.

Friday, May 6, 8:30 A.M.: Home

John Allen saw the first answer print (the completed film in 35 mm with sound track) on "the bench" last night. He said the colors are good, but "some density needed, for which we want your input." I'm meeting him to view it this morning.

Thursday, May 12, 8:00 A.M.: Home

John Allen says the new sample is "much improved, with greater density and saturation resulting in a richer print."

I love dealing with people who take such obvious pride in their work.

Saturday, May 14, 8:15 A.M.: Home

John and I to John Allen's to view color correction test. It's better but still needs work. They will make a new answer print for us to see next week.

Wednesday, May 18, 8:15 A.M.: Home

Norman painted a bleak picture of prospects for independent films: The cassette market shot, he said 37 percent of independents don't get released, etc. No wonder I dream of money and windfalls.

Tuesday, May 24, 7:30 A.M.: Home

John and I to John Allen's to view the new print. A huge improvement but still some color corrections to be made.

Pleased by what we'd seen (the blowup so fine, we never once thought of grain), I had John book Magno for a screening on Thursday, June 9.

John Gay called from Los Angeles to say the two sides were still meeting several hours after the strike negotiation session began. He said the strike story in the *New York Times*, West Coast edition, carried my picture. The story itself (printed here as well) is shallow and misleading. Once again, as almost always, I am dismayed by the shabbiness of the reportage in a story I have first-hand knowledge of.

Tuesday, June 7, 5:10 A.M.: Home

John and I screened the new print alone at Magno at 4:00 P.M. It's fine. A sense of mutual accomplishment at the end, we shook hands.

Saturday, June 11, 9:00 A.M.: Home

We met the McLaughlins and guests of theirs for a prescreen feed at the Sea Grill at Rockefeller Center.

The last time I was in that area, it was to film Anne Baxter, ice-skating, in the Nero Wolfe I wrote and directed.

Had my usual prescreening vodkas.

Departed to make sure all was in readiness at the screening room: sound level and focus checked.

The picture held every inch, got stronger and to my surprise had a bigger emotional effect on many people than I'd hoped to achieve.

The audience lingered till I initiated a move to the elevator.

Negative reactions included Phil Bosco's vague disappointment.

Not unprecedented in my experience when actors see their work for the first time.

"Well, as long as you're pleased," he said when I reiterated how delighted I was with his performance.

Sunday, June 12, 9:00 A.M.: Home

I began inviting people to the L.A. screenings.

Wednesday, June 15, 8:45 A.M.: Home

My weight down to 183½. I intend 180 (fighting trim) by the time I leave for L.A. on Monday.

Thursday, June 16 (Bloomsday), 8:15 A.M.: Home

I drove to John Allen's—saw and approved a new print that is being shipped to Scott Hancock in L.A.

Friday, June 17, 5:30 A.M.: Home

To Pepe's for a tight beard trim that should make me look presentable for a week.

The prospect of raising money to open the film in the absence of a sale is too appalling to contemplate.

Monday, June 20, 5:45 A.M.: Home

About to depart for El Dorado yet again. A can of film in each hand.

Tuesday, June 21, 8:30 A.M.: Los Angeles

Ruth drove me to Newark at 6:00 A.M. yesterday. Walking through the airport where I'd shot so recently, I felt I was in my own movie.

A woman, midthirties, overly made up, rose from the aisle seat to let me take the window seat. She exuded a nervous air that coupled with vaguely Arabic looks made me think fleetingly of hijack.

When she began to write a note (contents shielded from me) as the plane waited clearance for takeoff, I again thought hijack.

Moments after we took off, I felt a tapping on my arm. Turned to the woman, who proffered the note she had written. Opening it, I read, *The man seated in front of you is my boyfriend. We have had a fight and are not speaking. Do you think I should ask the man in front of me to change seats with me?*

I said, "Yes." The seat switch was made. She and her "boy-friend" didn't speak until we landed. Strange.

John Gay met me at the plane.

Jerry Perenchio called to say he and Margie would be at Thursday's screening. Invited me to the Tyson-Spinks fight party he's giving at Chasen's on Monday.

Wednesday, June 22, 8:10 A.M.: Los Angeles

Double D-Day. The first L.A. screening and the Writers Guild vote on the Alliance's latest offer. Management in a full-court press via dissidents to urge acceptance.

I drove to the Academy on Wilshire to inspect the screening room. Closed, but an accommodating guard showed me the room, which is less than ideal: too long, too narrow.

Sam Goldwyn's office called. They can't make it Thursday but would like a private screening at their place.

Today's newspapers, TV, and radio in L.A. boil with writers' strike vote stories and the horrible consequences if the latest offer is rejected. Finally it dawns on them that nothing happens in Hollywood till someone puts words on paper.

Thursday, June 23, 9:00 A.M.: Los Angeles

I had my usual prescreening vodkas.

Went to the second floor of the Academy to be alone before the screening. Viewed the posters of all the movies that won Best Film through the years. Noted how the writer's credit went from nonexistent to miniscule mention and slowly evolved to what it is now. Thanks to the Guild.

The screening went excellently.

Only two people came from Cineplex Odeon instead of the team promised since we were giving them first view. Peter Elson, one of the two, was enthused about foreign rights.

Norman gave an impromptu party after the screening, which is some reflection of how well things went.

I am eager for tonight's screening, which will include many writer friends who couldn't make it last night because of the strike vote.

Friday, June 24, 8:40 A.M.: Los Angeles

Last night's screening did not go nearly as well as the night before. A definite setback to our hopes, especially measured against the enthusiastic response on Wednesday, which heightened expectations.

Only two of the five companies who promised to show attended.

The Guild rejected management's offer by a 3–1 vote, evoking coverage worthy of an earthquake.

Saturday, June 25, 6:10 A.M.: Los Angeles

Perenchio phoned to apologize for missing the screening. Invited me for dinner tonight. When I accepted, he asked me to bring the film and show it at his home. Despite a gut feel that Malibu was not the ideal venue for a film whose basic theme is "you can't get to heaven on roller skates," I agreed.

After doing a "guest" picket at ABC in Burbank (over two thousand writers in fine spirits) I lunched with Mann Rubin. Invited his candid appraisal of the movie, saying I knew it hadn't played well at the screening he attended.

Mann said he felt the audience, composed largely of friends, did not expect such a fanciful script from me, was thrown by it.

That would account for the better screening on Wednesday when the audience, strangers to me and my work, was not hampered by preconceptions.

Sunday, June 26, 9:15 A.M.: Los Angeles

The guard at the Malibu Colony entrance checked my name against his list, gave me a visitor's pass.

Present at the Perenchio's (to my surprise) were Lee Rich (movie producer and studio head), David Geffen (record and movie producer), and Irwin Winkler (movie producer) and his wife.

I complimented Winkler on producing 'Round Midnight, which seemed to embarrass him. Probably because the picture lost money and he preferred not to have his association with it reprised in that company.

After dinner, Jerry announced they were going to see my film instead of Red Heat, the new Schwartzenegger movie they expected.

Asked to say a few words about *Luckiest Man*, I quoted a slogan Norman suggested: "A comedy that sticks in your throat."

"If we don't like it, can we turn it off?" Jerry asked, half joking—but only half.

I said once they started, they were in for the full experience.

Given the palpable disappointment that it wasn't *Red Heat*, the picture played about as well as it could, which wasn't very.

Monday, June 27, 8:20 A.M.: Los Angeles

Called Jim McLaughlin. Reported it looked increasingly (a la *Once in Paris* and *The Gig*) as if we'd have to open the film ourselves.

Tuesday, June 28, 9:40 A.M.: Los Angeles

Pulling up to Chasen's, I was acutely aware of my Toyota (dirty to boot) midst all the limos and Mercedes.

The whole place (fifteen TV sets scattered about) reserved for Perenchio's party. A number-one table evolved. But then it wasn't number one because Frank Mancuso (Paramount head) and Kerkorian (MGM boss) sat elsewhere.

Excellent buffet.

Tyson, no robe or socks heightening his brutal aura, entered the ring where Spinks, with the fixed smile of the totally intimidated, awaited.

Down . . . up . . . down . . . and it was over.

In the exodus, I encountered David Gerber, for whom I'd written and directed *Gibbsville*, based on John O'Hara's stories.

"I know they don't gross much," he said, "but keep making those wonderful pictures you make because quality is what it's all about."

Egad.

Wednesday, June 29, 9:00 A.M.: Los Angeles

Just opened the current issue of *Los Angeles* magazine listing the forty richest people in L.A. Perenchio is listed nineteenth. Actually he's in a tie with Merv Griffin.

Scott screens for Goldwyn at 4:00 P.M.

Thursday, June 30, 6:15 A.M.: Los Angeles

I console myself that no one bought *Desperate Characters,* *Once in Paris,* or *The Gig* until I opened them—not a nibble prior to reviews.

Scott reported delivering and picking up the film at Goldwyn's. He has no idea who saw it.

Saturday, July 2, 10:00 A.M.: Home

Arrived home Thursday.

A message awaited that Ann Templeton, head of acquisitions at Goldwyn, had called, leaving her home number because she wouldn't be in the office until Tuesday.

Since they never thank you for letting them see your picture, her call suggests a favorable reaction.

Wednesday, July 6, 10:00 A.M.: Home

"Your movie is fabulous," said Ann Templeton. "We all thought so. We almost never get to see a picture that good." I said that was nice to hear. "But it's so special," she went on. "I don't see anyone under fifty coming to see it. So how will we get our money back?"

A pause while I wondered if I'd called her. And then she appended, "Of course, Sam doesn't agree with me and will be calling you separately."

Wednesday, July 27, 8:00 A.M.: Home

Not having heard from Sam Goldwyn, I wrote to him:

Dear Sam,

I write to insure no missed communication between us via third parties.

The facts as known to me are these:

I was invited to screen my new film (*The Luckiest Man in the World*) for your company.

I said I would be glad to do so on assurance you would view the film personally.

That assurance given, the film was delivered to your office on June 29.

Ann Templeton called me subsequently: pronounced the film "fabulous" (a judgment in which she said you concurred) appending other accolades modesty forbids repeating.

And then the *but.*

She said the film's special nature restricted its commercial potential to the point that "I don't see how we'll get our money back." To which she appended, "But Sam doesn't agree with me on this and will call you separately."

Expecting to pursue the matter with you, I did not ask her what sort of money she had in mind and what rights she attached to them.

I would still like your thoughts.

With every good wish,

Friday, July 29, 7:00 A.M.: Home

Sam Goldwyn called. Said he liked all my work, but pronounced *Luckiest Man* "the best movie you've done."

Bottom line: He'd been sorely tempted to distribute it but concluded the upside potential wasn't large enough.

Sunday, July 31, 8:45 A.M.: Home

Strike talks collapsed again.

Mike Eisner (Disney) made $63 million in 1987, which is $6 million more than the residuals earned by all nine thousand members of the Writers Guild collectively.

Thursday, August 4, 9:45 A.M.: Wyndham

Last night's screening was the best we've had.

Renee Furst (publicist on *Once in Paris* and *The Gig*) truly enthused. A good tongue to have wagging in your behalf.

Walter Manley (who handled the foreign rights of *Once in Paris* so admirably) said, "If you want me, I'm yours."

Tony was delighted and relieved. My suspicion he hadn't liked the rough cut confirmed when he said, "Don't ever invite me to a rough cut again."

Roger Holmes (as gracious an investor as I've ever had) repeated his invitation to seek his aid if I have to open the film myself.

J. C. McLaughlin said, "That's a lot better than I was led to believe." From him, that's a rave.

Monday, August 8, 5:30 A.M.: Home

The strike is over.

Scott Hancock delivered *The Luckiest Man* to Sherry Lansing's home on Friday night.

Tuesday, August 9, 8:25 A.M.: Home

Sherry Lansing called to say she "loved" *Luckiest Man*. I said worldwide rights were available. She is going to set up a screening for Paramount.

Manley has set up a Friday-morning screening for the three heads of Orion Classics, which necessitates changing the date for Cinecom.

Friday, August 12, 8:30 A.M.: Home

Barry London (Paramount) just called: "Interesting concept, but appeal too limited for us."

Friday, August 19, 8:45 A.M.: Home

When John picked up the film after a screening for the executives of Forum Films, the projectionist volunteered that the Forum people asked him what he thought of it. He told them he found it "very funny." They said, "So did we."

Monday, September 5, 8:30 A.M.: Home

Just learned the lead character in *Crossing Delancey* is also named Sam Posner.

The best account of the strike that I've seen is by Joan Didion in the *New Yorker*.

Friday, September 9, 8:45 A.M.: Home

Norman reports that MCEG (Manson) wants to buy *only* foreign rights. Splitting up the package at this point is not to our advantage.

Thursday, September 15, 5:30 A.M.: Home

Just learned that *The Luckiest Man in the World* was not the title of Arthur Miller's first play, as I'd recently been told.

Saturday, September 17, 5:30 A.M.: Home

Hoping to get the Sixty-eighth Street Playhouse, I've made repeated attempts to contact Ralph Donnelly (City Cinema booker) without success.

Wednesday, September 21, 8:20 A.M.: Home

I placed another call to Ralph Donnelly, which hasn't been returned.

Thursday, September 22, 8:10 A.M.: Home

Figuring on a high Jewish holy day only the goyim would be in the office, I took another crack at Ralph Donnelly, who answered the phone, apologized for not getting back to me, said he'd attend next Tuesday's screening.

Wednesday, September 28, 8:45 A.M.: Wyndham

I took Renee Furst to lunch. Critiqued her work as publicist on *The Gig*, saying I felt she'd undervalued the picture until the night we opened when she saw it for the second time with her husband, Peter, who loved it. At which point her own enthusiasm increased, *but* too late to help me.

With appealing candor, she confirmed my assessment.

En route to the afternoon screening, I stopped for my usual vodka.

Some thirty-five people, minus Ralph Donnelly, who sent a surrogate.

To my delight, Jim McLaughlin made a surprise appearance.

A fine screening. The mixture of serious and comic did not throw this group a bit.

Abigail McGrath, seeing the film for the third time, said, "It's as though the actors were getting better and better."

Jim and I repaired to Sardi's: two boys from modest means (he, Brooklyn; me, The Bronx) who got into an Ivy League school via World War II, we toasted our good fortune repeatedly.

Friday, September 30, 5:50 A.M.: Home

Norman reports difficulty in getting definitive word from Cineplex Odeon. All this, mind you, just to get a theater.

Wednesday October 5, 6:20 A.M.: Home

I viewed the daily video sessions John did of me while shooting *Luckiest Man*. They are sufficiently interesting to make me regret that fatigue compelled us to abandon the project.

Friday, October 7, 8:30 A.M.: Home

Norman called to say that the assistant to the assistant theater booker at Cineplex Odeon said his superior, who saw *Luckiest Man,* was away and they'd get back to us next week.

Wednesday, October 12, 8:45 A.M.: Home

Cineplex Odeon won't give us a theater.

Thursday, October 13, 9:15 A.M.: Home

Inquired about getting one of Dan Talbot's movie screens. Found out they are booked solid until March 1989.

Thursday, October 20, 8:15 A.M.: Home

Yesterday, the one-year anniversary of our first day of shooting and the stock market crash.

Weekly *Variety* front-page headline announces only half of the independent films made will get theatrical release and for those (like us) with no preproduction distribution deal, the odds are even worse.

Wednesday, October 26, 8:45 A.M.: Home

Every so often today I must repeat "The destinies of Dukakis and my movie are *not* intertwined."

Tuesday, November 1, 5:10 A.M.: Home

I delivered the poster ingredients to Wayne Weil, who did *The Gig* poster. He made suggestions that improved on our concept— will have a layout to inspect next week.

Norman (in L.A.) reports that Mel Maron, representing Julian Schlossberg (Castle Hill), expressed interest in distributing *Luckiest Man.* It's almost mystical how Julian has been involved in all three of my previous independent films and is now a candidate for the fourth.

Thursday, November 10, 8:30 A.M.: Home

Met Jackie Reynal, owner of the Carnegie Screening Room, who will see the film.

Saturday, November 12, 8:50 A.M.: Home

I contacted Charlie Moss (of UA/Moss theater chain). He will view the film next week.

Monday, November 14, 8:20 A.M.: Home

Two photos of Phil Bosco in yesterday's *Times* and his name headlined in today's review of *Devil's Disciple*, which (glowing for him) can't hurt us.

Thursday, November 17, 8:30 A.M.: Home

Not having heard from Mme. Reynal, I called her. She wanted to postpone screening *Luckiest Man* till after Thanksgiving. I explained I was screening for someone else on Monday and would like to know how she felt so I didn't lose out on the possibility of another theater.

John delivered the film to her Bleecker Street Theatre last night.

Friday, November 18, 7:45 A.M.: Home

Mme. Reynal phoned. She liked it because it was "so different—not like an American film."

Tuesday, November 22, 9:00 A.M.: Home

Charles Moss liked the film. Asked what it cost. When I said under $2 million (the party line), he was enormously impressed.

Wednesday, November 23, 9:00 A.M.: Home

Julian (Castle Hill) will put up no money to open the film.

They propose trying to sell the home-video rights prior to opening. If a sale is made, they will use the money (exclusive of their commission) to open in New York, L.A., and wherever else is required by the terms of the cassette deal.

Hank Lightstone (UA) called. Moss must have given us a good sendoff because Lightstone wants to see the picture as a potential distributor as well as theater booker.

Wednesday, November 30, 9:00 A.M.: Home

Several copies of the *Luckiest Man* poster arrived. Look less vivid and glossy than I recall from the sample—will investigate.

Thursday, December 1, 8:00 A.M.: Home

Does Mme. Reynal's failure to return my calls reflect a change of heart?

Renee Furst, matter-of-factly, said, "She probably got a better offer—is dangling you till it's confirmed."

Saturday, December 3, 5:30 A.M.: Home

Variety headline about distributors forced to postpone openings till next year because of product glut is not encouraging.

I said, "You have to be crazy to make an independent movie."

"And even crazier to marry someone who makes them," Ruth rejoined.

Wednesday, December 7, 8:15 A.M.: Home

Sam Adelman graciously taking the film to Hempstead for the United Artists screening today.

Thursday, December 8, 9:00 A.M.: Home

Went to Mme. Reynal's office. We seem to have made a deal.

Saturday, December 10, 5:00 A.M.: Home

Mme. Reynal wants to advance the agreed-upon opening date (February 15). I said it wasn't possible. She bowed to that. Says her lawyer is drawing up the contract.

Saturday, December 17, 8:30 A.M.: Home

Wrote to the investors informing them of the opening and seeking the wherewithal to do it.

Wednesday, December 21, 5:10 A.M.: Home

Renee Furst just told me she'll be at the Berlin Film Festival from February 8 to 23, suggested I change the opening date. I told her I couldn't.

Thursday, December 29, 7:00 A.M.: Wyndham

En route to meeting a money guy that someone had recommended, Norman and I stopped at Mme. Reynal's office. Received an unsigned contract that in addition to other changes to what we'd agreed on, states that our opening date (February 15) can be changed by her with two week's notice. She wasn't there, so we couldn't discuss it.

On to the office of the "money man," who presented himself as "cash rich" and wanting "safe action."

He'd seen *Luckiest Man* and liked it. Said he'd put up some print and ad money but only if it was totally secured by being first money paid back, plus points, etc.

A familiar sort, he longs to be a part of the creative side but will go to his grave unfulfilled because it entails *risk*.

He said the market for small art films like ours was all but gone.

1989
Wednesday, January 4, 9:20 A.M.: Home

Press-kit literature ready: photo stills narrowed down; film clips for TV ready to be made.

We've moved the opening date to either March 1 or March 8 so Renee can handle it personally, which Madame insists on.

Friday, January 13, 9:00 A.M.: Home

In the theater contract that just arrived, Madame has switched the opening to February 17 or 24, which precludes Renee's personal involvement. Go figure.

Monday, January 16, 6:10 A.M.: Home

February 22 is the new "firm" date, which Madame says she'll verify in a new contract to reach me tomorrow.

Thursday, January 19, 5:15 A.M.: Home

Madame would prefer I open on a Friday instead of Wednesday. I explained that for a small film to open the same day as five or six other pictures is unwise since I can't compete with their huge ads and any chance of getting the top reviewer is diminished.

Sunday, January 22, 9:00 A.M.: Home

Seeking money to open the film, I have been shot down repeatedly.

Just about decided I would have to cancel the opening, I phoned Roger Holmes, who pledged enough to keep me plugging.

Thursday, January 26, 5:05 A.M.: Home

Assembled *Luckiest Man* material (posters, artwork, slides, etc.) and drove to the city.

Ordered three thousand postcards announcing the opening.

Then to Renee Furst's office. Met Bruce Glynn, who will cover for Renee while she's in Berlin.

They will be on salary for four weeks, three prior to the opening and one after.

To the Colton office where I gave Gil Karson a *Luckiest Man* poster to commemorate his first movie deal. He read the intensely small print of the theater contract, pronounced it acceptable with one needed clarification.

Wednesday, February 1, 8:45 A.M.: Home

The theater contract signed—money changed hands!

Finances so limited, we are dispensing with a trailer, which would cost about $10,000; "wild posting" (posters slapped on construction sites, etc.), which costs another $3,500; and no opening-night party, another $5,000.

Friday, February 3, 8:00 A.M.: Home

Renee and I went to Stringfellow's for the annual *Village Voice* film luncheon. Introduced to Merchant, of Merchant & Ivory, I noted, "We work the same side of the street," which he acknowledged with a smile appropriate to members of a secret society.

Renee says, as of now, no one else is opening February 22.

Saturday, February 4, 8:15 A.M.: Home

John Cassavetes died yesterday, age fifty-nine. I wish I knew his wife well enough to call.

Renee reports that Van Gelder, who writes a movie column in the *Times*, and Howard Feinstein, head of the film department at the *Voice*, decline invitation to our four scheduled press screenings and insist on viewing a cassette of the film before they will grant me an interview.

Renee told them she knew I wouldn't like having my work first seen in this way, but they wouldn't budge.

It was right after this call that I heard of Cassavetes' death and could picture him saying, "You see, Frank, it's like I told you—they hate us."

Tuesday, February 7, 6:00 A.M.: Home

Our first critics' screening at 6:00 P.M. today.

Bruce wrote a good "pitch letter" seeking to interest editors in Phil Bosco and me.

Tony will cover the screening. I like to have someone there who will report how it went, warts and all.

I noted the absence of a running time in the press kit, which creates anxiety, especially at a predinner screening. It will be typed in.

I loaded the car with posters, etc., which I took to the Off-Center Theatre where Abigail will forward them to the actors for dispersal. Though casting directors aren't usually listed on posters, I regretted not having done so because of Abby's unflagging enthusiasm and contribution.

I called Matty Serino (Serino, Coyne, Nappi), who did the ads for *Once in Paris* and *The Gig*. Told him the theater contract locked me into ARC (Diener-Hauser).

He said a full page movie ad in the *Times* now costs about $42,000. He tipped me to ask for "the contract rate," which involves a 5 percent to 8 percent reduction the theater enjoys. He said that rate includes the agency fee. As for mechanical cost (the charge for setting up the ad), he said a good rule of thumb is 10 percent of the ad price.

Wednesday, February 8, 8:05 A.M.: Home

Tony reports the first press screening went well—some thirty people. He said the picture played the best for him it ever has. Renee, who was there, called later to confirm this. Distressingly, she told me she has lost partial vision in one eye, is having tests run.

Thursday, February 9, 8:40 A.M.: Home

Pepe said from now to the opening he'll give my beard the extra-luck trims reserved for similar occasions through the years.

Renee, despite eye trouble that may cause her to skip Berlin, works with her usual verve.

She and I met Larry Cohen of *Variety* for an interview at the

Russian Tea Room. En route, we reminded each other not to look for or try to coax Larry's critical response to the picture, which he saw last night.

During the interview, I thought I caught intimations that he liked the movie, but as experience has cruelly taught, I don't presume.

4:00 P.M.

Dan just called. Reports two-thirds of a house. Laughs where I wanted, starting early. Half the audience stayed through the credits. Print looks fine. No changeovers missed. My reading from Dan's report is that the screening was not as upbeat as the first one.

Friday, February 10, 8:00 A.M.: Home

An excited call from Bruce to say the *New York Times* wants to interview me for a Sunday "Arts and Leisure" piece.

The writer they've assigned will see the cassette in Renee's office this morning and interview me immediately after.

With ringing phones, people coming and going, it is a less than ideal way to view a picture, but we need the publicity.

Saturday, February 11, 9:00 A.M.: Home

Stopped at the Carnegie Screening Room. The postcards and posters, sent by overnight mail, had not arrived. Learned I'll need colored stills to go with the poster to fill their display case.

To Renee's. Had a croissant and tea while the *Times* writer, a young freelancer, concluded his viewing in the other room. Since this was a piece for the Sunday *Times* (the sort of advertising we could never afford), I gave it my best shot for two hours.

Renee definitely not going to Berlin. She said it is uncertain whether the *Times* interview will run before we open.

Tuesday, February 14, 10:00 A.M.: Wyndham

Went to ARC, the ad agency, to meet Ernie Shapiro, who will be handling our account. We settled on an ad in the *Village Voice* and the *New York Times* on opening day.

The *Times* charges $318.94 for a one-column inch. The *Voice* charges $4.00 a line. The *Voice* ad will cost $800.00 plus the agency's charge for mechanicals. The *Times* ad, five inches (two and a half inches by two columns) will cost $1,600.00 plus mechanicals.

Of course, Ernie opted for larger ads. Of course, I vetoed the thought.

To Renee's to do two interviews. The first with Fern Segal of the New York *Tribune*, who predicted it would be a sleeper gem.

As often when people are genuinely enthused, she recited the plot to me.

The next interviewer, Louise Tanner, National Board of Review, was equally encouraging.

None of the major reviewers have signed in to see the picture at the scheduled screenings.

Kathleen Carroll, the *Daily News*, wants a private screening on Friday morning. There goes another $300.

Wednesday, February 15, 9:00 A.M.: Home

D minus 7.

To the Surrey Hotel to do Casper Citron's radio program. Sophie, Renee's assistant, there despite my saying I didn't need anyone to baby-sit my interviews.

Renee called to say it looked like the *Times* interview would appear this Sunday. They might want to shoot a head shot of me at their office, so I should remain available.

A call from Elizabeth (in charge while Madame is in Berlin) asking the show times of *Luckiest Man*. I told her 12:00, 1:30, 3:00, 4:30, 6:00, 7:30, 9:00, 10:30. She was dismayed because Cineplex Odeon, from whom Madame sublets, likes fifteen minutes between shows, whereas my schedule allowed but seven. I told her those were the times previously agreed on and already placed in ads.

To Renee's for an interview with Charles Ryweck of *Hollywood Reporter*. A most ingratiating man, who has interviewed me previously.

Edelstein, of the *Post*, will see the picture at the private screening arranged for Kathleen Carroll. I question the wisdom of this. Suspect it's better to have one critic see it alone rather than two—each sensitive to the other's reaction in an otherwise empty room.

Thursday, February 16, 5:15 A.M.: Home

D minus 6.

Renee, via Bruce, reported yesterday's screening was "sold out."

Tony, who covered it, pronounced it half filled—the audience less responsive than the other screening he covered. Walter Goodman (the *New York Times*) present. If he's the reviewer, it means opening on Wednesday in the hope of getting the first team failed.

John will deliver two prints (one a backup for emergency) to the theater on Monday.

Renee called with the best news to date: She had an advance copy of this Sunday *Times* "Arts and Leisure" section with my interview.

Friday, February 17, 6:30 A.M.: Home

D minus 5.

Did a lunch interview with Richard Freedman (the Newhouse chain), who suggested Gay Lib might take exception to the father-son scene. I said that would surprise me since the aim was reconciliation.

To Renee's office, where I read the *Times* interview. I found it flat but to our advantage nevertheless.

To the ad agency—proofs satisfactory.

Stopped at the theater. Our poster in the lobby looked every bit as good as those flanking it that cost many times more.

10:30 P.M.

John called with a disconcerting report on the screening he'd just covered:

David Denby (*New York* magazine), whose favorable review was so vital to *Once in Paris*, was present. Since he was the pièce de résistance, Bruce, in deference, began the film shortly after his arrival, which proved premature: people arriving well after the film began.

This gave the screening a ragged quality from the start, compounded by the early exit of a spacey trio, which impressed John as a deliberate and perverse disruption.

What about Denby?

John said he sat through the end credits, which, given his recent pan of a film he'd seen only forty minutes of, gives some comfort.

Saturday, February 18, 8:30 A.M.: Home

D minus 4.

We know Carroll and Edelstein saw the picture yesterday morning.

We also know that students from someone's film class attended the screening without Renee's or my knowledge. *What a mix!*

Tuesday, February 21, 5:15 A.M.: Home

D minus 1.

How do I feel less than twenty-four hours before I open the *New York Times* to the first, and most important, critical salvo? Gut scared. Forecast of rain doesn't help.

I have less than $15,000, of which $10,000 goes for theater rental for weeks three and four.

1:45 P.M.: Wyndham

Just came from the theater, where I answered questions following a screening by the National Review Board.

7:00 P.M.

Just finished three interviews for National Public Radio, WBAI, and the *Film Journal*.

One interviewer noted echoes of *The Christmas Carol*. One tried to get me to say something critical about the *New York Times*.

10:00 P.M.

Opting not to inflict my anxious self on anyone, I ate alone. Browsed Doubleday's, carefully avoiding collections of movie reviews lest I read one damning past work that might deepen my foreboding.

Walked to the newsstand at Sixth and Fifty-seventh. They said the *New York Times* came in at 10:30 P.M.

If it's a favorable review, someone will call me within the next forty minutes. In the absence of a call, I'll go to sleep suspecting the worst but still hoping.

10:25 P.M.

No calls.

10:40 P.M.

Still no calls.

10:45 P.M.

I begin to fear the worst and console myself that *Desperate Characters* and *Once in Paris* succeeded without *New York Times* endorsement.

11:20 P.M.

No news is, I suspect, bad news. And now a sleeping pill, perchance to dream.

11:45 P.M.

Tony just called (sure I'd read the *Times*) to console me. It's a bad notice. Worst of all, Tony feels awful for breaking the news.

It's a long cold day that awaits me tomorrow and tomorrow.

Wednesday, February 22, 7:15 A.M.: Wyndham

Up since 5:30.

Went out and got the *Times, News, Post* and *Village Voice*, which I read in that order of diminishing expectations.

The *Times* not quite as bad as perceived on hearing. The reviewer's being third string helps.

The *News* and the *Post*: two stars.

Braced for the coup de grace from the *Village Voice*, I turned to a review headlined "King of the Schmattes" by Renee Tajima. Lo and behold, it's a rave!

Now to set sail for five scheduled interviews, starting with "Good Morning America."

Later:

The *Variety* review is excellent. *Newsday*, two stars—familiar blah-blah about a playwright who should have stuck to his last.

Thursday, February 23, 9:40 A.M.: Wyndham

Did an interview with Chris Chase for the *Daily News*.

Told Ernie Shapiro I wanted to run the entire *Voice* review in the *New York Times*. All we can afford is two columns by five inches, which will cost $3,400.

Bruce took me to Center Street, where I did the Leonard Lopate show for WNYC. From there to Trinity Place, where I did two TV tape interviews for some cable religious outfit.

To the ad agency, to the theater, and then to Renee's for another WBAI interview.

11:00 A.M.

We did $1,064 yesterday, which seems to please Madame. Of course, the weekend will be critical.

Friday, February 24, 8:00 A.M.: Wyndham

The cashier at the theater (servicing the Carnegie Screening Room and the Carnegie Hall Cinema jointly) says the blowup of the *Village Voice* review, mounted on an A-frame beside the box office, stops people, who read it and sometimes buy tickets as a result.

Our box-office numbers in the Diener-Hauser daily sheet, which reports every theater's business the previous day, are encouraging. Our opening-day figure doubled what the film *Paper House* did in the Carnegie Hall Cinema (owned by Cineplex Odeon).

I understand WNEW radio gave us a fine review.

> *1:00 P.M.*

Renee called to say that Jeffrey Lyons went to the theater to see the movie and "liked it," or did she say "loved it"?

Renee says that David Denby will definitely review us a week from Monday, swears she has no clue as to his sentiments. Come on, Denby, make my year.

Saturday, February 25, 5:15 A.M.: Home

The big snow forecast with such dire certainty never happened. As usual, the false prediction cost theaters, restaurants, etc. a fortune as people altered plans.

We did $829 yesterday. Not great, but a pulse.

Sunday, February 26, 4:10 P.M.: Home

I just learned that the sound system at the theater broke down yesterday (Saturday) and they had to cancel the 4:30, 6:00, and 7:30 shows!

No explanation why I wasn't alerted or why repair took so long. Blow winds; crack your cheeks, and bugger off.

Tuesday, February 28, 6:15 A.M.: Home

Advertising reduced to starvation rations: a one-inch ad in tomorrow's *Times* ($318 and mechanicals) and a "biggie" in the *Voice* ($850 and mechanicals).

Wednesday, March 1, 5:45 A.M.: Home

I called the theater yesterday morning to get the previous day's figures. Madame got on the phone somewhat agitated, said she didn't have the gross for Monday because the head of Cineplex Odeon, Garth Drabinsky, showed up at the theater Monday night, and "everyone was running around, and there was confusion."

I had a sudden intuition that in the wake of Drabinsky's visit, Madame had been ordered to remove the A-frame blowup of our *Village Voice* review. I kept this thought to myself because it smacks of paranoia.

When Madame failed to get back to me by 4:00 P.M., I called Tony and asked him (realizing I sounded like a cuckoo) to go to the theater and verify that the blowup (so helpful to our walk-in business) was still in place.

He called back shortly to report the blowup was gone.

Unable to reach Madame, I contacted the theater manager, who said the blowup had been removed because it was a fire hazard.

Thursday, March 2, 5:15 A.M.: Home

Renee still has no word when and if Denby's review will appear. I voiced displeasure that not one TV critic has been to see us after we prepared all those clips.

Our *Voice* blowup now fixed to the back wall in the entryway, where no one is apt to see it. When I complained, Madame took me to the theater manager, who started in about fire hazards. Having checked, I told the manager, a woman, there was no such law prohibiting A-frame displays. She said she'd see what she could do.

Apropos the daily gross list, which shows our numbers to some, if meager, advantage, Ernie Shapiro said, "You're still in the game."

The flyer looks good. Splurged on a two-inch ad tomorrow. Settled my tab to date, which totals, including flyers, about $8,000. If this isn't a record low expenditure for a New York opening, it's close.

Back to the theater, where the A-frame is still not displayed as desired. The manager said the district supervisor for Cineplex Odeon "insisted" on this. I asked Madame if their opposition derived from the fact we were doing better than the film in *their* house. "You're probably right," she admitted. "They always want to be on top."

Note that the Carnegie Hall Cinema (Cineplex Odeon) has a weekly nut of $12,500, while the Screening Room's is under

$5,000, and you see the possible cause of this tempest.

Saturday, March 4. 6:00 A.M.: Home

Chris Chase's interview in the *Daily News* captures my speech rhythm with accuracy and a fresh slant.

For what it's worth, box-office decline began the day the blow-up was removed.

Renee says Denby's review has been postponed another week.

Sunday, March 5, 8:30 A.M.: Home

We did $781 on Friday, which is encouraging since it's only a shade down from what we did the first Friday.

Madame called to inform that the display case had been broken into and the still of the girl in our poster stolen.

We got a great review in the New York *Tribune*, a paper whose existence is unfortunately a well-kept secret.

Had no idea how far-reaching National Public Radio was until people in six far-flung states reported hearing my interview.

Monday, March 6, 6:00 A.M.: Home

I see no point in advertising the last two weeks. Better to husband what we can and seek a theater in Los Angeles for a last go at the brass ring.

Wednesday, March 8, 4:10 A.M.: Home.

Met Barry Cunningham (Channel 11) at the theater, where he did a story on me. Barry's crew consisted of one man, Tony, who did camera, sound, and lights with remarkable efficiency.

Thursday, March 9, 6:00 A.M.: Home

Stopped at the ad agency. Relieved to see everyone's grosses down precipitously due to the cold.

I did the Joan Hamburg–Arlene Francis radio show from Sardi's. Following the Taffetas, I shared the mike with Phil Bosco and Tovah Feldshuh, who were plugging *Lend Me a Tenor*.

I stopped at the theater and in a burst of frustration, moved the *Village Voice* blowup to its original position beside the box office. Told the cashier if anyone asked, say I did it.

Shades of Ensign Pulver.

Monday, March 13, 7:45 A.M.: Home

We did $759 on Saturday. Since we haven't advertised in the *Times* for over a week, it's encouraging. I still feel we might have a crowd-pleaser *if* we had a crowd.

Tuesday, March 14, 4:55 A.M.: Home

An investor known not to like the picture phoned all excited because Jeffrey Lyons (CBS) gave us a favorable review. That he heard it on the radio endows the picture with a validity it (for him) lacked before.

The bottom line on David Denby, via Renee, is no review.

Wednesday, March 15, 7:45 A.M.: Home

How do you account for the $288 we grossed on Monday, which is almost double last Monday's figure? What an irony if we start to build after I canceled the fifth and sixth weeks.

Saturday, March 18, 5:15 A.M.: Home

We went up again on Thursday over the previous Thursday. That's the fourth day in a row we've climbed over the previous week.

Sunday, March 19, 6:45 A.M.: Home

Up again on Friday a bit—five days in a row.

Monday, March 20, 8:00 A.M.: Home

We dropped precipitously Saturday and Sunday. Especially disappointing after the continuous weekday rise.

Wednesday, March 22, 7:40 A.M.: Home

Met Mel Maron and Julius Schlossberg at the latter's office (Castle Hill) to discuss their distributing *Luckiest Man* domestically.

I said it bordered on the magical that I've done four independent films and no matter where I start from, I in every case wind up talking to Julian.

If we go with Castle Hill, Mel will try to get a theater in Los Angeles. I will pay all ad costs. Mel will seek a 25 percent floor, meaning we get one-quarter of whatever the gross is, less Castle Hill's commission.

I related Castle Hill's terms to Jim and J. C., saying they were far from desirable. But in the absence of other offers and unable to go any further on my own, I recommended acceptance. They agreed.

Called for Monday's gross, expecting the lower depths after the sharp drop on the weekend. To my surprise and puzzlement, we did $324, continuing our weekday climb—up for the third Monday in a row.

At 10:30 P.M. last night, I was poignantly aware that our last show of the run was starting.

Thursday, March 22, 7:45 A.M.: Home

Neither Ernie nor Renee have ever encountered a gross pattern like ours—up three weeks in a row on weekdays, and down on the weekends, with virtually no senior-citizen business to account for it.

Friday, March 23, 6:00 A.M.: Home

Received a bill from Madame for a screening I knew nothing about. It turns out Bruce had booked a screening for the "Today" show people, none of whom appeared.

Friday, March 30, 8:30 A.M.: Home

Mel Maron (in L.A.) has gotten us a 150-seat house at the AMC fourteen-theater complex in Century City. We open Friday, May 5.

Why does Bill Moyers want a clip from *Luckiest Man* in which "Amazing Grace" is sung?

Wednesday, April 12, 7:30 A.M.: Home

Hired Melody Korenbrot, a publicist from L.A., to represent us there.

She warned me AMC will boot us if we don't do business instantly.

Saturday, April 15, 9:00 A.M.: Home

Mel Maron liked the idea of showing John's film, *Big Moose* (which he directed, fresh from the AFI Film Festival) as short subject with *Luckiest Man*. AMC gave approval. So Gilroy and Gilroy will share the bill.

Walter Manley will handle foreign rights to *Luckiest Man*. He's advancing a few quid toward the L.A. opening.

Wednesday, April 19, 8:00 A.M.: Los Angeles

Still trying to get what's due from Madame. When I said that if I didn't get it, I'd turn the matter over to my lawyer, she said, "But the lawyer will cost you more than the *money* involved."

Friday, April 28, 7:45 A.M.: Los Angeles

Uneventful flight yesterday.

The trunk of the car I rented at the airport contained a movie script, part of a candy bar, one sock, and several copies of *Variety* and the *Reporter*, suggesting someone left town in a hurry.

Saturday, April 29, 8:10 A.M.: Los Angeles

Melody said the screening went well. Kevin Thomas, the *Los Angeles Times* critic, was there, but she had no clue to his reaction.

Feeling a need to turn my back on the world for a day, I phoned Marty Donovan and suggested a trip to Hollywood Park.

He said, "But I won't have time to handicap." I said, "That could be the break we need."

John Gay, going off to speak to film students at AFI, took *Luckiest Man* flyers to distribute. Bobby Gay took some for her friends at the Nine O'Clock Players. Investing in my movies entails more than financial risk.

Back from the track (a petit winner), I was met by Bobby Gay, who said, "I have wonderful news for you."

She led me to the answering machine and Melody's breathless message that Kevin Thomas loves *Luckiest Man*.

In addition to reviewing us, he is going to tell Chuck Champlin they have to do something to help this film, which is so underfinanced that they can't afford an ad in the Sunday "Calendar" section.

My heart soared, and I was about to broadcast the news when I recalled how prone press agents are to exaggerate. Will say nothing till it's in print.

Philip Bosco and Yamil Borges.
We're looking for the poster shot.

Still looking.

And *still* looking.

Mrs. Posner (Doris Bellack) and Mr. Posner (Philip Bosco). She seems to be buying it.

Producer Norman Cohen's expression (*far right*) suggests we're on schedule.

Posner (Philip Bosco) rehearsing his proposal to Laura (Joanne Camp), his mistress of many years.

The Posners (Philip Bosco and Doris Bellack) the second time around. Friends and investors are among the extras.

Sunday, April 30, 8:20 A.M.: Los Angeles

En route with the Gays to Dan Petrie's screening of his Hall-mark show at Disney's, we stopped at Century 14.

I wanted to make sure our display was up and that the flyers were being distributed.

The display up, but no flyers.

The theater manager, most obliging, found the flyers and positioned them immediately.

John Gay, witnessing the lowly details the independent film-maker must attend to, felt demeaned on my behalf.

On to the screening at the Disney Studio in Burbank. My first time there since the fall of 1958 when I quit Disney (where I was doing television scripts—"Texas John Slaughter") to write a feature for Dick Powell at Twentieth.

Nearing the Disney lot, I remembered that last day: Encountering Walt (first names de rigeur) late in the afternoon as I walked down a shadowed corridor.

"I understand you're leaving," he said.

Incapable of calling someone that much older by his first name and forbidden to say "Mr. Disney," I said, "Yes, sir."

I knew he liked my work, that I could have stayed indefinitely, but my goals were elsewhere.

Mutually inarticulate, we stood there a moment (awkward, melancholy) and then parted.

Harry Keller reported I no sooner left than Walt announced I was never to be allowed on the lot again.

And so last night (Walt's influence undiminished) I half expected the guard to forbid me entry.

The "Calendar" section in today's *Los Angeles Times* lists *eight* films, including *Luckiest Man*, to open on Friday. We are conspicuous by the absence of any ad.

Wednesday, May 3, 8:00 A.M.: Los Angeles

A call from Melody informing that Gary Franklin, the CBS TV critic, is going to give us a 10 (his highest rating) and pronounced *The Luckiest Man* "memorable"!

Friday, May 5, 8:00 A.M.: Los Angeles

The *Los Angeles Times* review (Kevin Thomas) that greeted my eye at 6:00 A.M. this morning is headlined "Luckiest Man: Alive with Fine Acting, Humor."

It begins: "Only a born story teller as sincere and inventive as Frank Gilroy and an actor's actor like Phil Bosco could get away with *The Luckiest Man in the World*. Making its twists seem fresh, funny and poignant instead of a gimmick."

To top it off, Thomas concludes with a nice word about *Desperate Characters, From Noon till Three, Once in Paris,* and *The Gig.*

Saturday, May 6, 8:30 A.M.: Los Angeles

Phone calls, phone calls, and more phone calls apropos the *Los Angeles Times* review.

Met Norman and Sarah at the theater at 7:00 P.M. The house manager said we were doing nicely.

To help the cause, we *bought* tickets.

Sunday, May 7, 8:30 A.M.: Los Angeles

We did $1,231 on Friday (opening day), which was the fourth-highest gross of the fourteen films playing.

The Gays and I went to the 5:30 P.M. show.

Conspicuous in the sold-out audience was a group (some fifteen people, men and women) in white gowns and robes from head to foot, identified as members of a Sikh sect who were ardent movie-goers.

After the show, I was introduced to the leader of the Sikh group, who pronounced the picture "delightful."

I flashed an ad: "The Sikh-est picture in town."

Monday, May 8, 9:40 A.M.: Los Angeles

The *Los Angeles Times* "Calendar" capsule on the film says, "Wise, rueful, beguiling. . . . Bosco is wonderful."

We did $4,991 for the weekend despite senior discount tickets (sold at all times here), which cost us over a grand.

Best news: We made the cut, are being held for a second week.

P.S.

With no money to advertise, we didn't make the cut the second week, and our Los Angeles run ended.

The making of *Luckiest Man* coincided with the bottom dropping out of the independent film business. Failure to make a cassette sale, from which independents derive print and ad money, sealed our fate.

Leonard Maltin (*TV Movies and Video Guide*, 1990) accords us three stars. An irony since we've yet to make a video deal.

But as long as you own the negative (which we do), anything is possible. Who knows?

Review: *The Village Voice*, February 28, 1989

King of the Schmattes   by Renee Tajima

It's a typical day for Sam Posner, irascible king of the rag trade with John Gotti's fashion sense and a similar regard for humankind. Using the phone as a weapon and lethal wit as ammunition, Sam puts the screws on everyone: a smart wife, a dumb mistress, the union, and business associates alike. All this earns him a wealth of disposable income and even more animosity. Posted on the factory wall is a tribute from his employees: "Happiness is seeing your boss's picture on a milk carton."

Frank D. Gilroy's *The Luckiest Man in the World* is a delightful, Capra-esque tale of a Seventh Avenue Scrooge who, even when sudden tragedy moves him to redeem his evil ways, continues to reap what he's sown. Sam's reckoning comes when he arrives late at the airport. (He reminds his chauffeur to wait a few minutes, so he can fire him in case he's missed the plane.) It seems Sam has been spared by crosstown traffic: Flight 6 crashed on take-off. Stunned by his fate, Sam hightails it to the john, where he ponders the inevitable question, "Why spare me?" The answer emanates from a pair of two-toned wingtips in the next stall. It's a second chance, the other-worldly voice tells him. Thus enlightened, Sam sets out to make amends.

Philip Bosco as Sam is the consummate character actor—a lovable villain who discovers there are no Tiny Tims in the world. This is New York City, 1989, baby, and nobody wants to be Christmas turkey. When Sam promises to love and cherish his much-abused wife, she eyes him warily, "What's the angle?" His son, Sheldon the queen, is furious at his father's new leaf: "The one thing that keeps me going is my hate for you. Would you deprive me of that?" At points, the story treads in predictable territory. Sam's woes become belabored—even a drunk in Central Park gives him grief—but Gilroy manages to take a few left turns toward a fresher narrative course.

Gilroy, who won the Pulitzer for *The Subject Was Roses*, writes his women characters fuller and with even more complexity than he does the men. As Mrs. Posner, Doris Belack is absolutely brittle—a woman vulnerable to her husband's romancing, but whose protective armor rises on automatic. Joanne Camp's Laura, the sweet-tempered mistress, is no bimbo, but a thirtyish romantic who realizes that she never wanted to marry Sam after all; she just wanted to be asked. There are no visual pyrotechnics or profound moral sketches in this movie. *Luckiest Man* is simple and fun. It's a writer's film with minimal production values and a pace set by dialogue and wit. The only thing keeping it out of a larger venue is a budget that deprives it of bigger stars and slicker looks.

Review: *Los Angeles Times*, May 5, 1989

Luckiest Man: Alive with Fine Acting, Humor
by Kevin Thomas

Only a born storyteller as sincere and inventive as Frank Gilroy and an actor's actor like Philip Bosco could get away with *The Luckiest Man in the World*, making its twist seem fresh, funny, and poignant instead of a gimmick.

This fine little film is roughly a reverse take on *It's a Wonderful Life*. In the beloved Capra classic an angel shows a despairing James Stewart all the bad things that would have happened to his family and his friends had he never been born. In writer-director Gilroy's film almost everybody wishes apoplectic, ruthless New York garment manufacturer Sam Posner (Bosco) were dead. They almost get their wish; Sam barely misses a plane for Miami which crashes on takeoff, killing all aboard. Nudged by a sepulchral voice (Moses Gunn), Sam is confronted with what a monster he is and becomes eager to make amends.

The challenge, of course, is in sustaining Sam's odyssey, which is where Gilroy and Bosco shine. (Bosco is best know to moviegoers as the financier in *Working Girl*.) The responses of Sam's family, employees, and colleagues are consistently imaginative, as full of humor as they are of pain, and Bosco is as convincing as the newly warm Sam as he is as the cold jerk of the past. Some encounters are a little more persuasive than others, and there are a few moments of hesitancy on Gilroy's part as to how to wrap everything up. However, it's quite easy to be beguiled by this wise and rueful fable.

This is a very New York film, with its emphasis on characterization rather than style, with its cast composed of actors rather than movie stars. The wonderful Bosco, stocky, open-faced, and expansive, is well supported by Doris Belack as his understandably cynical wife; Joanne Camp as his perplexed mistress; Matthew Gottlieb as his confounded transvestite son; and Yamil Borges as the beautiful young widow of the man who took Sam's plane on standby. They and many others, including Joel Friedman as Sam's paralyzed ex-business partner, are a constant pleasure. *The Luckiest Man in the World* is the kind of film that many people would enjoy; it has more substance than chic, and its sensibility and perspective are comfortably middle-aged. Gilroy still remains best-known for his 1964 Pulitzer prize-winning play *The Subject Was Roses* and for its 1968 adaptation to the screen. He also wrote and directed such satisfying and intimate films as *Desperate Characters*, *From Noon Till Three*, *Once in Paris*, and *The Gig*.

—— *Epilogue*

I've made a solemn vow to my family that I will never again raise money for an independent film. My wife vows something to the same effect, which includes the phrase "my dead body."

The fact is that if I hadn't made these pictures (deprived of people and experiences I would never otherwise have known), I'd be infinitely poorer.

John Huston, after an especially difficult production, said, "The important thing is, we made the picture." So it is, and always will be, long after the grosses are forgotten.

Any regrets?

That some of the people I worked with (Urs Furrer, cinematographer; Renee Furst, publicist; Joe Silver, actor; Dick Wellstood, pianist; Dick Vorisek, mixer) passed away, depriving me of the chance to work with them again.

Anything else?

I've written a new script, which Julian Schlossberg (once again) says he can get the financing for.

Stay tuned.

Filmography Index

—— *Filmography* ——

The Fastest Gun Alive

Released by MGM in 1956. Shot in black and white. Has been computer-colorized.

Director: Russell Rouse

Screenplay: Frank D. Gilroy and Russell Rouse (from the teleplay *The Last Notch* by Frank D. Gilroy, produced by "U.S. Steel Hour").

Cast: Glenn Ford, Jeanne Crain, Broderick Crawford, Russ Tamblyn

Running time: 92 minutes

The Gallant Hours

Released by United Artists in 1960. Shot in black and white.

Director: Robert Montgomery

Screenplay: Bierne Lay, Jr., and Frank D. Gilroy

Cast: James Cagney, Dennis Weaver, Ward Costello, Richard Jaeckel

Running time: 111 minutes

The Subject Was Roses

Released by MGM in 1968. Shot in color.

Director: Ulu Grosbard

Screenplay: Frank D. Gilroy (from his play)

Cast: Patricia Neal, Jack Albertson, Martin Sheen

Running time: 107 minutes

The Only Game in Town

Released by Twentieth Century–Fox in 1970. Shot in color.

Director: George Stevens

Screenplay: Frank D. Gilroy (from his play)

Cast: Elizabeth Taylor, Warren Beatty, Charles Braswell, Hank Henry

Running time: 113 minutes

Desperate Characters

Initially released by ITC in 1971 and subsequently distributed domestically by Paramount Pictures. Shot in color.

Director: Frank D. Gilroy

Screenplay: Frank D. Gilroy (from the novel by Paula Fox)

Cast: Shirley MacLaine, Kenneth Mars, Gerald O'Loughlin, Sada Thompson, Jack Somack, Rose Gregorio

Running time: 88 minutes

Gibbsville: The Turning Point of Jim Malloy

TV movie produced by Paramount/ABC in 1975. Shot in color.

Director: Frank D. Gilroy

Screenplay: Frank D. Gilroy from stories by John O'Hara

Cast: John Savage, Biff McGuire, Peggy McKay, Gig Young, Kathleen Quinlan, Janis Paige

Running time: 78 minutes

From Noon till Three

Released by United Artists 1976 (a Mike Frankovich production). Shot in color.

Director: Frank D. Gilroy

Screenplay: Frank D. Gilroy (from his novel)

Cast: Charles Bronson, Jill Ireland, Douglas Fowley, Stan Haze, Damon Douglas, Anne Ramsey

Running time: 99 minutes

Nero Wolfe: The Doorbell Rang

TV movie produced by Columbia Pictures Television in 1977. Shot in color.

Director: Frank D. Gilroy

Screenplay: Frank D. Gilroy from the novel *The Doorbell Rang* by Rex Stout

Cast: Thayer David, Anne Baxter, Tom Mason, Brooke Adams, John Randolph

Running time: 97 minutes

Once in Paris

Initially released by the Once in Paris Company in 1978. Shot in color. Subsequently distributed domestically by Atlantic Releasing Company and now by Castle Hill Productions.

Director: Frank D. Gilroy

Screenplay: Frank D. Gilroy

Cast: Wayne Rogers, Gayle Hunnicutt, Jack Lenoir, Clement Harari, Tanya Lopert, Doris Roberts, Phillipe de Marche

Running time: 100 minutes

The Gig

Initially released by The Gig Company in 1985. Subsequently distributed domestically by Castle Hill Productions. Shot in color.

Director: Frank D. Gilroy

Screenplay: Frank D. Gilroy

Cast: Wayne Rogers, Cleavon Little, Andrew Duncan, Jerry Matz, Daniel Nalbach, Warren Vaché, Stan Lachow, Joe Silver, Jay Thomas

Running time: 92 minutes

The Luckiest Man in the World

Initially released by The Second Effort Company in 1989. Subsequently distributed domestically by Castle Hill Productions. Shot in color.

Director: Frank D. Gilroy

Screenplay: Frank D. Gilroy

Cast: Philip Bosco, Doris Belack, Joanne Camp, Arthur French, Stan Lachow, Moses Gunn

Running time: 82 minutes

Index

Frank D. Gilroy is a playwright, novelist, television writer, screenwriter and director, and independent filmmaker. He graduated from Dartmouth after army service in World War II and attended Yale Drama School. He has taught screenwriting at Dartmouth and at Yale. His awards include a Pulitzer Prize (for *The Subject Was Roses*), an Obie (for *Who'll Save the Plowboy?*), and a Silver Bear (for *Desperate Characters*) from the Berlin Film Festival. A member of both the Writers Guild and Directors Guild of America, he is past president of the Dramatists Guild, of which he is a lifetime council member.